UNGLOVED

UNGLOVED

MEMORIES FROM THE RING

BENJAMIN CALDER-SMITH
FOREWORD BY RICHARD CLARK

First published by Pitch Publishing, 2015

Pitch Publishing
A2 Yeoman Gate
Yeoman Way
Durrington
BN13 3QZ
www.pitchpublishing.co.uk

A CIP catalogue record is available for this book
from the British Library.

ISBN 978-178531-030-0

Typesetting and origination by Pitch Publishing

Printed in Malta by Melita Press

Contents

Acknowledgements. 8

Foreword by Richard Clark 12

Introduction. 15

  1 Rod Douglas .19

  2 David O'Callaghan. 31

  3 Tony Conquest 44

  4 Steve Goodwin 50

  5 James Cook 61

  6 Herol Graham. 80

  7 Billy Schwer. 117

  8 Wayne Alexander 131

  9 Colin McMillan 151

10 Sammy Reeson 176

11 Derek Williams. 184

12 Jim McDonnell 203

13 Horace Notice. 226

14 Mark Prince. 239

'Now, whoever has courage,
and a strong and collected
spirit in his breast, let him
come forward, lace on the
gloves and put up his hands.'

Virgil (Aeneid 5.363–364)
19 BC

Acknowledgements

THIS part of the book was always going to prove very challenging. It was like locking the front door to your house and starting the journey to your holiday destination while wondering if you had turned everything off. The following people have played pivotal roles in helping me see this project through and turning a long-lasting vision of mine into something real and tangible. Looking back, I just hope I've turned everything off and not left anyone out.

The time, enthusiasm and energy given by the 14 principals featured have made this book what it is. Rod Douglas, David O'Callaghan, Steve Goodwin, Tony Conquest, James Cook, Herol Graham, Billy Schwer, Wayne Alexander, Colin McMillan, Sammy Reeson, Derek Williams, Jim McDonnell, Horace Notice and Mark Prince; my appreciation for what you have all contributed to make this happen is boundless. I just hope the words in these pages do you and your careers justice. Fourteen stories. Fourteen men. Fourteen champions.

My eldest brother, Anthony, for giving me my first taste of 'The Noble Art' with a trip to the old ABC cinema on Chelsea's Kings Road in 1982 to watch *Rocky III*. It was around my eighth birthday and my blurring hand speed, missing a lamppost by inches while waiting for a bus back home, and using Ant's hands as pads marked the peak of my pugilistic ability. I deteriorated massively from that moment on.

My other brother, Dominic, for being one of the most supportive people I know and tirelessly offering his advice and support to this project. An author of two books himself and with a boxing portfolio of reporting, interviewing and writing large enough to warrant its own library, his style and quality of writing give me a goal to aspire to. I have a hunch those goal-posts will forever remain tantalisingly close.

One of my nephews, Alexander Hearn, for providing a permanent source of fuel for my inner boxing fire with his technical support and design for our website, www.homeofboxing.com. Your support quietly spurred *Ungloved* on too. Also to your fiancée, Amy Cole, for tolerating my invasions of your home! My family – Anthony and Camilla Benda and their 'Firm'; Nicholas, Jonathan and William. Henrietta, Simon, Harry, Olivia and Issy Hearn; Ceci, Antonio, Lorenzo and Alfredo Calder-Smith; Victoria, Bobby, Bert, Imogen and Bridie Leach and Daisy and Max Calder-Smith. A particular mention for Simon's sister, Miranda Hearn, for her valuable insight into getting a book ready and prepared for publishing and passing on some priceless advice. A published author herself, it was time constructively spent listening to her.

To my lifelong pal, Sam Hoexter, his never to be forgotten mother, Sarah, his father, Nick, and his two sisters, Harriet and Hannah. A special thank you for a special family. The same applies to Justin Sims, his son; my godson Louis, and my trusted old schoolfriend, Ben Trimble.

A poignant mention for the late John Fulkes, for passing on his passion for the English language, its words, its prose and its meaning to me. He was my English teacher at Lord Williams's School in 1990 and was instrumental in igniting in me a passion for the written word. I was saddened to recently hear of his passing. May he rest in literary peace.

My friends at B1, you will never know how much your passing words of interest and encouragement have meant. You've played a part in keeping the dream alive. Thank you.

I thank Richard Chapman for supplying me with fight footage as and when required for my research. I'm sure there needs to be another cheque in the post by now! Thank you also to Nobby Reeson for inviting me into his home to grill his son on his career and to Champagne Jaye for her assistance and support in setting up my meetings with Mark Prince. The work they both do for the Kiyan Prince Foundation is utterly inspiring.

For showing me that smoke signals, two twigs and carrier pigeons are no longer particularly advantageous in this day and age, Clint McCutcheon deserves a big thank you. Submitting this to the publishers would not have been as smooth without your help.

My friend and writer of my foreword, Richard Clark. Rochester's Two Brewers served as the perfect place for me to learn about much of British boxing's past from a true aficionado on the subject. A professional boxing manager and friend of proven quality, Richard also pointed me in the direction of a vacancy with the British Boxing Board of Control, so…I would like to give an extended thanks to Mick Collier, Les Potts, Bill Edwards, Cecil Ross, Peter McCann, Helen Oakley, Richard Barber, Nick Laidman, Brett Bowles, Nigel Thomas, Steve Larman, Herold

Adams, Gary Roberts, Barry Freeman, Dr Anthony Buckland, Bret Freeman and all at the Board of Control who have made my position as an Inspector thoroughly enjoyable. I do not consider this position as work; more a fantastic privilege.

You would be hard pressed to encounter a more genial, hospitable man than Phil Sharkey, who allowed me access to his remarkable archive of boxing photography. A passionate boxing enthusiast, this drive is equalled by his photographic expertise. The son of a man who once fought the legendary Jackie Turpin, I will never tire of his boxing recollections. Who knows Phil, one day I may make it on to your office wall!

Richard Whiting at Action Images for his generosity and support with a number of the photographs. A better service from a more reputable firm, would not be possible to come by.

A big thank you to Ed Robinson at Sky TV. Welcoming me into your home for tea, mince pies and phone numbers was more than I could have asked for. You helped fire the gun to start me off. Thank you.

For their time, phonecalls, messages and support, I thank Julian 'The Hawk' Jackson, Charles 'The Hatchet' Brewer, John Ashton, Richard Williams, Jose Ribalta, Sean Murphy, Johnny Armour, Richie Davies, Bob Williams, Steve Holdsworth, Steven Bendall, George Danahar, Gary De'Roux, John Westgarth, Alec Mullen and Beau Williford.

A big thank you to Don McRae for his recommendation of going with Pitch Publishing. His messages took time and thought and, being a world-class sports writer of undeniable depth and stature himself, I felt incredibly confident that going against his advice would be nothing short of foolish and detrimental.

To Paul and Jane Camillin at Pitch Publishing for justifying my faith in Don. Their belief and support in my book has been humbling. Duncan Olner deserves a big credit for the cover design which has received the highest praise from those who have seen it and also to Derek Hammond for his part in publicising the whole project. Also to Gareth Davis and Dean Rockett for being instrumental in presenting a book which has been subjected to the most detailed scrutiny and, thankfully, the utmost integrity. My appreciation for this is immense.

To my beautiful girl, Claire Elizabeth Chapman and her two daughters, Katie and Millie. My excursions from family life to get this book done have been, at times, trying on her and while we've been a bit like George Foreman against Ron Lyle in the process, I hope she can see that the satisfaction I've garnered from writing this book has been proportionate to the appreciation I have for her support and commitment. I love her lots; not least because she gave me my little fellow, Thomas George Dempsey (yes, my own piece of Manassa!) Calder-Smith. Simply put, my raison d'être.

This book is dedicated to them and to the memory of my parents, Rosemary and Robert, for showing me how, and how not, to be and I miss them both terribly.

Benjamin Calder-Smith
Rochester
March 2015

Foreword by Richard Clark

MY love of the noble art was first ignited by a series of programmes aired by the BBC in the early 1980s called *A Fight to Remember*. Presented by that doyen of British boxing, Harry Carpenter, and featuring the likes of Henry Cooper, John Conteh and Dave 'Boy' Green, I was hooked. 'Our 'Enery' had long since retired, nevertheless, his autobiography was the first of many I borrowed from the local library. And so began my lifelong fascination with boxing and boxers; active or retired and anything else connected with the business.

Fuelling my new-found interest, I watched or recorded any fight broadcast on television and read as much as I could. The 80s unfolded and brilliant fighters graced my screen and bookshelf. Across the Atlantic were Hagler, Hearns, Leonard, Duran and the young, irrepressible Mike Tyson. At home and of greater interest to me were the likes of Magri, Kaylor, the 'gifted one', Kirkland Laing and, of course, not forgetting Barry McGuigan and Frank Bruno. The stories behind the men who had pulled, or were pulling, the strings fascinated me too. There were characters aplenty; Solomons, Levene, Duff, Lawless and Frank Warren, who, back then, was the newest young face on the block.

All this in an era devoid of Facebook or Twitter, when a boxer's thoughts or opinions weren't globally accessible at the mere click of a mouse. Back then, social networking meant standing at a bar, or sitting in a cafe swapping stories of fighters and fights. Apart from a 30-second, 'training's gone well' before a contest and 'he was a good, strong boy' afterwards, one rarely heard a boxer speak. I was interested to hear first-hand what boxers and those associated with the business had to say about their experiences. I wanted to know more about them. What made these brave, young men and their advisors tick? Their exploits inside the roped square were on record for all to see but what had fashioned them? What were they really like and what became of them at the final bell and beyond?

It seemed to me that most autobiographies only scratched the surface. Likewise, all the best biographies were sugar-coated and carefully sanitised. Those that were not, by definition, covered only one subject. Thankfully, *Ungloved* addresses all those shortcomings perfectly. Within its pages, we meet a broad range of fight characters, covering many aspects of the business.

Benjamin's encyclopaedic knowledge, allied to his tenacious yet sensitive investigative skills, has seen him delve deep. In doing so, he enables his subjects to reveal their innermost thoughts and emotions to him. For instance, one cannot help but be moved at the sheer pride of Rod Douglas, as Benjamin describes him standing in the new gym he has built. A gym constructed out of love for the sport that almost killed him three decades earlier, robbing him of the fame and fortune he was so very close to achieving. All that is tragic and triumphal about boxing can be summed up in Rod's chapter, where one man's battle to reconstruct his life outside the ring is all too apparent.

The author and I first met, by chance, nearly 15 years ago when working in the same building in Limehouse. He introduced himself to me, 'Hi, I'm Ben Calder-Smith, pleased to meet you.' Ben's articulate and eloquent manner made him seem somewhat out of place in that grubby, run-down corner of Cockney London. The shadow of Canary Wharf loomed large over us and I first thought he'd be better suited to sitting in one of the posh, shiny new offices over there. My initial assessment couldn't have been wider of the mark – I'm pleased to say.

The name 'Calder-Smith' rang a bell with me. The unbiased fight reports of Dominic Calder-Smith featured regularly on the pages of *Boxing News*, which I was (and still am) an avid reader of. 'Any relation to Dominic?' I asked. 'Yes, he's my brother.' Our shift passed in the blink of an eye as we swapped opinions and thoughts on our shared interest, or obsession if you asked our families! Benjamin's observations of the current scene, at home and especially in the US, left me in no doubt that I was talking with a young man who, as they say, 'knew the game'. A much valued friendship was born that day.

My life in boxing spans four decades, as novice amateur (of very average ability), Board of Control inspector, timekeeper and, most lately, as manager of a talented stable of champions. Despite my close involvement with the business, I am a fan first and foremost and always will be. I remain as fascinated as ever by the men (and now women) who inhabit the hardest, loneliest sport of all. Benjamin's work is a labour of love, written out of respect and admiration for those same people. It is my privilege to have been asked to pen the foreword to a book that will be at home in equal measure in the hands of the casual observer as it will be in those of the most knowledgeable of fight figures.

Richard Clark
Rochester
March 2015

Introduction

I MENTIONED in my 'acknowledgements' a gentleman called John Fulkes. I was heavily influenced by his grasp and portrayal of the English language while taking my exams at school. So much so, in fact, that from this early age, the idea of putting pen to paper to create something imaginary or otherwise strongly appealed to me. I would start absorbing my surroundings, taking in people's mannerisms and tones, the way people held themselves, the way they looked. I'd look for influences and inspirations to feed my idea of writing. During one particular school holiday, I wrote a story entitled *A Pot of Marmite*. The general crux of the story surrounded a war child from the 1940s who was evacuated from the inner-city and all he had time to take was a pot of yeast extract. He lived on it until he became sick so he stopped having it until he returned home after the war. Finding a pot of the stuff on his doorstep, he opened an accompanying note. It was from a friend who he hadn't seen since before the outbreak of war. The friendship was rekindled.

I still can't recall WHY I wrote it or what inspired me to but I love writing and have always taken pride in it. Maybe I find expression easier written than said. Sadly, my Marmite story has been lost over the years. I have since started a number of fiction novels but, unfortunately, the self-doubt in me was strong enough to overcome my self-belief and they were never proceeded with. I was always, and to a degree still am, my own worst critic. I would get disillusioned easily until my love for boxing developed into an all-encompassing passion. I'd found my niche and my self-doubt was going to be blown away by a sudden surge of energy. It was a mismatch, pure and simple. When the bud appeared to start my writing for this book, it blossomed and the urge to see it through got more and more intense.

Working it around my day job, I started to travel around the United Kingdom and meet up with many boxers from this country's past. A selection have been chosen for this maiden voyage of mine. Neither preference nor personality were allowed to decide which pieces to include. They were chosen at random and I simply opted for the age-old theory that less really is more. I want these people's stories told and by holding many back for, hopefully, future publication, I hope the reader will be able to better focus on those presented.

My research into this work commenced in October 2012 and it will therefore come as little surprise that a few of the book's principals' circumstances have changed since the final word was scrawled.

Rod Douglas is no longer at the Arches Gym in Bethnal Green, largely due to the unmanageable rates and maintenance costs being demanded. He is still training and I have little doubt that his services and expertise will assist him in making a champion one day.

Dr David O'Callaghan remains as a doctor for the British Boxing Board of Control. I was working at ringside for a recent Steve Goodwin show at Bethnal Green's York Hall where Surrey-based light-middleweight Chas Symonds suffered a shocking knockout loss to Michael Lomax. One huge right hand deposited Symonds on the canvas in the seventh round and when his head hit the floor, his eyes stared in my direction but I was certain, and very worried, that he wasn't seeing anything.

Dr O'Callaghan and his two colleagues were in the ring within seconds and Symonds had been placed into the required recovery position and was hooked up to an oxygen supply almost before the white towel, that Symonds's corner had thrown into the ring, had settled. The speed and professionalism with which crucial first aid was administered was absolutely second to none. With doctors like these, the Board of Control can rest easy, knowing it has the best personnel, resources and facilities available in the event of an emergency. His take on the sport is fascinating and is massively relevant to the past, present and, most importantly, the sport's future.

Both Tony Conquest and Steve Goodwin remain plying their trade so while the nature of the book is to explore past fighters from the domestic scene, Tony's story to date provides a measure of calm and offers the reader a piece of light-hearted reading about a genuinely pleasant, upbeat man. The piece was originally used in a programme for a fundraising event for Dagenham's Police and Community Amateur Boxing Club in February 2013. Since completing his chapter, Tony has since gone on to win, and in turn lose, the Commonwealth cruiserweight championship. He is currently fighting his way back up towards title contention once more.

Steve Goodwin gives a brutally honest view of the sport in the current climate and the challenges posed by a relatively new promoter. To this day, both his daughter, Olivia, and son, Josh, are actively involved and with Kevin Campion on board as Goodwin Promotions's matchmaker, the future of British boxing will be hugely complemented. Their shows continue to provide competitive boxing and attract good turnouts across the southern area. With an ever-growing stable of fighters, 'They Never Stop'!

James Cook is carrying on his tremendous work with the local community at the Pedro Club in Hackney. Living a short distance from the club, James reaps enormous satisfaction from the mentoring seeds he sows and the popularity of the club goes from peak to peak.

Herol Graham continues with his boxing training project and has informed me of a few youngsters he is training who he believes are worth marking as potential future champions. An opportunity has also arisen for the Sheffield-nurtured guru to possibly become a trainer at the North London Boxing Club on Wood Green's Truro Road. I can feel nothing but the most driven optimism for those that traverse the four corners of the ring under his guidance.

Billy Schwer goes from strength to strength with his motivational speaking and relating boxing's gospel to individual and corporate ways of life.

Colin McMillan continues his success with his various ventures and can be seen frequently at many shows across the southern area and at many charity fundraising boxing events.

Sammy Reeson continues to travel from Bournemouth to Mitcham, splitting his time between his home on the south coast and looking after his father, Nobby.

Jim McDonnell's domestic star, James DeGale, was shining brightly and ready to dazzle American audiences with his challenge for the vacant IBF super-middleweight title against Andre Dirrell in Massachusetts on 23 May. While narrowly missing out on becoming a world champion, McDonnell could be on the verge of training one.

Horace Notice still exudes the friendly, amiable demeanour he showed when I first met him. We have hooked up since and he still has a highly positive outlook on life despite his heartbreaking exit from the sport in 1988. He takes pride in his role as a London cabbie and is content and happy with life. Being one of British boxing's 'what ifs' no doubt made many potential opponents breathe easy.

Mark Prince has since returned to the ring under the auspices of the Maltese Boxing Commission and has notched up three wins. His last win saw him lift the Maltese international cruiserweight title. His remarkable story goes from strength to strength as does his work with the Kiyan Prince Foundation.

The majority of the photographs used in this book have come from the private albums of the boxers included. It was always my intention to make this book as personal an account of those individuals featured as I could. Their contributions made this book. I therefore wanted their personal touches added.

The times I have spent with these boxers and many other of the sport's personalities, have left me in little doubt that boxing doesn't just develop individuals into champions; it breeds and develops a vast array of personal attributes in people that are to be found sadly lacking in many other walks of life. To instil discipline through boxing is to ingrain in those involved, the possible consequences one faces if short cuts are taken, if the commitment, drive and will to succeed falter. Ironically, it is with taking those well-documented risks that the fighter strives to hold off defeat and live out their personal goals.

Their paths have led them through many varying obstacles and successes but, most importantly, they're still standing. The final bell is still a long way off.

Benjamin Calder-Smith
Rochester
April 2015

1

Rod Douglas

'YOU go on in mate. I've just got to finish off out here,' the middle-aged, muscularly set man said to me as I introduced myself outside his recently acquired, and appropriately named, boxing establishment – Arches Gym. Situated under Bethnal Green's railway arches, it sits diagonally across from the main underground crossroads of Bethnal Green from the renowned York Hall, undoubtedly east London's most famous boxing venue, which not only inhabits an atmosphere of bygone times, but also finds itself steeped in the richest of boxing history and tradition.

The man smiles at me with a wide, beaming grin and, with gardening tool in hand, turns to finish off the uprooting of a stubborn bunch of weeds sprouting through the pathway directly outside his gym's front entrance. The sense of personal pride in what he does is clear. The strip of Mr T-esque, short, tight, black curls that swept up and over the centre of his head have long gone but the face of Rod Douglas hasn't changed hugely over the course of time. There is no mistaking the man who started to blaze a trail of serious intent towards the peak of the British middleweight scene in the latter part of the 1980s. It was a trail that came to an abrupt halt on 25 October 1989, five days after his 25th birthday, at London's Wembley Arena, after a courageous attempt to lift Herol Graham's British middleweight title ended with Douglas suffering a ninth-round stoppage loss, incurring life-threatening and, ultimately, career-ending injuries in the process.

As I entered the gym, I saw a young lad in the ring at the back of the main training area thwack, thwack, thwacking the sparring mitts held up by Solomon, Rod's right-hand man. Immediately inside the gym opposite the reception desk was a wall, adorned with press cuttings of

Rod in his fighting prime, both in his amateur and professional days. One picture stood out. At first, it appeared to be that of 'The Greatest' himself. Rod had his arm stretched around the shoulders of Rachaman Ali, brother of the former three-time world heavyweight champion and, arguably, the greatest fighter of all time. Rod's face was contorted with unrestrained emotion and tears were visibly building in his eyes. 'Incredible, unbelievable,' Rod exclaimed as he looked at the pictures taken months prior to our meeting, in the build-up to London's third hosting of the Olympic Games. He grinned with pride as he ushered me through to another training area of similar size through an open doorway next to the ring. This room consisted of an open padded-floor area with speedballs along one end and shower cubicles against the far side. 'Step into my office,' Rod said with a sense of jovial humour, pointing to a bench under a window.

It became apparent to me very soon after we sat down to talk, that one of the most prominent chapters in Rod's fistic sojourns was inflicting the lone loss on Nigel Benn's amateur boxing résumé.

Towards the latter parts of the two fighters' amateur careers, Rod and Nigel Benn had grown well accustomed to each other, fighting one another twice with one win each. Before their paths crossed however, Rod had picked up the Junior Amateur Boxing Association light-welterweight title in 1980, the same year that Frank Bruno won the senior ABA title in the heavyweight category. In 1983, Rod was to pick up his first of four senior ABA titles, defeating future fringe professional middleweight contender Johnny Melfah in the final of the light-middleweight class. This feat was repeated in 1984 when beating Neil Nunn in the final. That same year, Rod travelled to Los Angeles to represent Great Britain in the Olympic Games under the tutelage of the national coach, Kevin Hickey. After receiving a bye in the first round, Rod posted comfortable victories over a Kenyan followed by a Japanese fighter in the second and third rounds of the tournament respectively. In the quarter-finals he faced eventual losing finalist and future budding professional Shawn O'Sullivan of Canada and was outpointed 5-0 to curtail his Olympic dream.

It was at Los Angeles that the United States of America had one of their strongest teams on record with fighters such as Tyrell Biggs, Evander Holyfield, Meldrick Taylor, Pernell Whitaker, Virgil Hill, Mark Breland and Frank Tate going on to make a big impact on the professional circuit with all but Biggs lifting a world title. With Rod, however, the temptation to turn to the professional ranks after the Games was one which he found relatively easy to resist.

'I think I was anti-professional at the time. I had a really good Olympics in Los Angeles and gave a really good account of myself. There's always one athlete the media want and it was my turn for boxing. There was a lot of pressure on me and when I came back a lot of people wanted me to turn professional more than I wanted to. The enthusiasm they showed me was a bit scary because I questioned why they wanted me to turn pro. You know, I'm the one taking the punches! I've always been wary of what I call "quick friends". Growing up as a young man, people in the know with experience always warned me of bad managers and those that could rip you off and take the piss. It was drummed into me more and more as I was growing up and my promise started to show. I really wasn't interested in it. It was my decision. Now, though, I look back at the history of boxing of those turning pro with lots of exposure and hand-picked fights and, yeah, I should've gone that route. At the time though, I was treated like royalty after Los Angeles and I wanted to experience it again in four years' time!'

The amateur wheels, therefore, continued to roll on and his hat-trick of ABA light-middleweight gold medals was complete in 1985, defeating Gary Phillips in the final. It was in this competition that Rod inflicted the one blemish to Nigel Benn's amateur record. By this stage Rod was developing and growing and he comfortably grew into the middleweight division the following year.

'I moved up to middleweight in 1986 and my first opponent? Nigel Benn!' A smile spread across his face as he geared up to address a fight which he contests to this day. 'That year, he beat me. I beat him in 1985 in the ABAs but I couldn't make the weight no more.' Rod pulls in the hollows of his cheeks and widens his eyes to illustrate what effect the light-middleweight limit had on him. 'I had a bit of a break and came back at middleweight and had a really close fight with Nigel Benn. I still dispute the decision to this day but anyway, I had to prove myself at middleweight and show I could still win the ABAs. You have to remember, I'd won three ABAs on the trot so you had all these old codgers, ABA officials and so on. They want to see some new blood come in. These new guys are a couple of years younger than me and just coming into the ABAs. Then there's me! Nigel Benn gave me a good fight but like I said, I still question the decision. I give him 100 per cent for effort. He trained to beat Rod Douglas. He deserved it.

'When Buster Douglas beat Mike Tyson, he did it because he TRAINED to BEAT him. Nigel Benn TRAINED to BEAT me. At that time, I was unbeatable, untouchable so Benn had it in his head, "I'm training to beat Rod Douglas." I was his hurdle. I dispute it but he beat me and to be honest, it was a great relief that I lost the fight. I hadn't lost a fight for five or six years so it got to the point where everybody was expecting me to win. You miss a day, it starts playing on your mind. You question yourself. Am I fit enough? Am I good enough to go the distance? When the ref raised Nigel's hand at the end, he let out a "YAYYYYY!" Funny story though. Nigel was a kickboxer too. It was at the York Hall and afterwards I come out and as I was coming to the top of the steps, Nigel Benn was at the bottom talking to three or four guys and I was shouting, "Oi you, you c**t!", just humorously as I just got beaten and I'm unbeatable right?!! I run down the steps towards him and as I get closer, you see his feet take on the stance of a kickboxer! He's ready to kick me or punch me!

'I went right up to him and said, "Nigel, well done. You done really, really well. I hope you go all the way." He's gone on to greater things and good luck to him. He then got thrown out of the English boxing team for the Commonwealth Games in '86 because he'd done something wrong outside the sport or whatever so they put me in the middleweights and it was cool. I went and won the gold medal! Benn's upset at this. When I get back from those Games in Edinburgh the national papers are all saying that Benn will fight me anywhere, anytime and that he'd put up 50 per cent of the gate money. He wanted to fight me as I'd supposedly taken his gold medal at the Games. The ABA got involved and said there's no way they'd allow this fight to take place as it was too professional-orientated and the amateur board weren't having it.'

Rod defeated Australia's future two-time WBC light-heavyweight champion, Jeff Harding, in the final and the occasion isn't lost on him. 'After our fight, I was in the dressing-room under the ring and I was looking in the mirror for any marks or scuffs. I sensed this person standing next to me and I turned and saw Harding there. I genuinely felt as if he had hurt me more than I'd hurt him so I was still pumped up. I looked at him and shouted, "WHAT?" I was pumped up and ready to go again there and then!'

It was around this time too that Rod Douglas fought and defeated another middleweight who would go on to have a highly successful professional career, including two wins over the aforementioned Nigel Benn. 'I fought Steve Collins over in Ireland and won it on points. He obviously wasn't well known back then but I remember it being a tough, tough fight!'

While missing out on a place in England's team for Edinburgh, Nigel Benn turned to the ABAs and won the middleweight gold himself, defeating Johnny Melfah in the final. At the start of 1987,

Nigel Benn turned professional and embarked on a blistering trail of devastating knockouts that ultimately earned him the moniker 'The Dark Destroyer'. Witnessing Benn's early promise in the professional ranks proved thought-provoking for Rod. 'He turns pro. Knockout, knockout, knockout,' he said, slamming his left fist into his right palm while emphasising 'knockout'. 'I was still amateur and I was thinking to myself, "I'm twice better than him. Why don't I just turn pro?"'

One boxer who Rod fought three times as an amateur was Alec Mullen, who now runs the Irvine Vineburgh Boxing Club in Scotland. They fought a number of times with Alec winning once in a BBC1 televised Scotland v England International in Dundee in January 1986. He recalls Rod's fighting style clearly, 'Rod was a machine. He had a non-stop punching, come-forward style. An always-in-your-face type of fighter. His footwork was also impressive with a very muscular physique. The guy was relentless.'

Rod remained in the amateur ranks for a further eight months after Benn switched and managed to win the gold medal in the ABAs once again, only this time at middleweight. It was something of a milestone in the sense that it was the 100th ABA tournament and such a landmark in amateur boxing history may have seemed a fitting way to wave farewell to the amateurs and step into the professional arena. One last opportunity arose prior to turning to the professional ranks. In June 1987, Rod stepped into the ring at the Lonsdale Gym in London with another budding British middleweight prospect who had just returned from the United States of America where he notched up five four-round points wins to start his own professional career. The prospect's name was Chris Eubank and the sparring session they had was so intense that, had it not been for the training vests and headguards, it could have passed as a genuine crowd-pleasing professional scrap. A couple of years after the fight with Herol Graham, Rod attended a garden party at Buckingham Palace. Chris Eubank was also present and Rod thinks back to a brief conversation the two fighters and Rod's wife had that day.

'I went up to Chris and said, "Chris, tell my wife how our sparring went."' Rod then put on an impressive impersonation of Chris Eubank's now defunct lisp. 'Eubank said to my wife, "It was very difficult and I thought to myself, no, I don't need this kind of sparring!" A couple of weeks ago my son bumped into Chris Eubank in Oxford Street and Chris had a long chat with him and spoke to him in detail about our sparring and complimented me!'

On 30 September 1987, Rod Douglas began his assault on the professional circuit with a first-round knockout of Dave Heaver, a veteran of 46 fights, and by the end of the year he had racked up four quick knockouts to kickstart this new episode in his career. In 1988 he was stretched to the distance in two eight-round bouts, the latter of which took him to the shores of Atlantic City, New Jersey. Both these fights, against Jake Torrance and Lester Yarborough, proved highly beneficial in his development and both opponents were deemed to be valuable gatekeepers for promising up-and-coming prospects at the time and thereafter. Closing out the year with a first-round knockout over John Keys back in London, he began what would prove to be his final year as a fighter full of confidence. In January 1989, Rod looked sensational when blasting out Ralph Smiley in little over one round at the Elephant and Castle. Showing excellent speed and power, Rod utilised a ramrod left jab to whip repeatedly into Smiley's face in order to set up the finishing blows.

'My aim at this point was still a fight with Nigel Benn. This was the time when Ambrose Mendy was his manager. We tried to get a match through him for about 18 months but they weren't having it. I was a better all-round boxer than Nigel Benn but as a puncher, yeah, he could hit really hard but they knew I could take a punch and probably outpoint him. Why ruin what they've got? They could build him up so why risk me? So we set about fighting his last opponents!'

The sole opponent in common that Rod Douglas and Nigel Benn fought was Reggie Miller. In February 1989, Miller was stopped in seven rounds by Rod, the same round in which Nigel Benn had finished him in December 1987. After three more fights, including a one-round knockout over Paul Wesley who would also prove to be something of a measuring stick for the top domestic level of fighters for many years after, the call came for Rod to challenge Herol Graham for the British middleweight title in October.

Prior to his title shot, Rod Douglas sparred with, amongst others, the dangerous and awesome-punching John 'The Beast' Mugabi. Famed for his frightening punching power which had left many an opponent literally lying in his wake, Mugabi posed a serious test for the pending British title challenger, even in sparring. 'I had to stay on the outside to spar with him because, let me tell you, he had some SERIOUS power in those fists. You would touch his arms and it was like tapping a brick wall! He was that solid.' I asked him which punch, in particular, was the hardest in Mugabi's arsenal of weapons to which Douglas's eyes widened in surprise. 'Which punch?!' he asked me back in surprise. 'WHICH punch? EVERY punch! It didn't matter what he hit you with. I was staying well back because I did NOT want to get hit by THEM!'

Herol Graham was participating in his first fight since an unsuccessful attempt that April in resting the vacant WBA middleweight title against the famed 'Bodysnatcher' – Mike McCallum.

McCallum had previously reigned as the WBA light-middleweight champion with impressive and unexpectedly short knockouts over Julian 'The Hawk' Jackson and Donald 'The Cobra' Curry among his title defences. In his first attempt at winning the middleweight title he lost a decision to the underrated yet technically excellent Sumbu Kalambay. His second chance against Herol Graham swung in his favour and he defeated 'Bomber' by split decision.

When Rod stepped into the ring at Wembley to challenge for the title, there was a feeling among various sections of the boxing fraternity that, while he may not be guaranteed to dethrone the champion, he had what it took to stretch Graham to his limits and perhaps be in the right place at the right time to catch a champion many deemed to be on the downslide after the defeat by McCallum. Tim Mo of *Boxing News* wrote in his preview of the fight, 'Douglas is essentially a pressure fighter, though a classy one, and he is a solid puncher with either hand. He has plenty in the other departments as well.'

After a fairly positive first round where Douglas landed a brace of left hooks followed by a heavy right hand which backed Graham up, the champion slowly took over and used his superior defensive skills to leave Douglas swiping at the air while shipping a continuous repertoire of combination punching. The contest was finally terminated in round nine when referee Billy Rafferty led the courageous challenger back to his corner after being floored twice.

Events took a sinister turn a few hours after the fight when Rod collapsed and was rushed, first to Mile End Hospital, and then to the Royal London in Whitechapel where surgery was undertaken to remove a blood clot from his brain. Incidentally, he was operated on by Dr Peter Hamlyn, who just short of two years later would be carrying out a similar operation on Michael Watson after his fateful rematch with Chris Eubank at White Hart Lane.

'I remember a few months after my fight with Herol Graham, when I was still in a bad situation not being able to walk properly, co-ordination not quite there, memory pretty terrible, speech still slurred, I remember going out of my house. I was walking down the road and I heard this "beep beep" and when I looked round, I saw this white Porsche and when I looked closer I saw Nigel Benn!

'I hated him so much I thought we were going to fight! He asked if I was going down the road and said "jump in". We were talking and he turned to me and said, "Rod, all those things I said, I didn't mean it.'"

Bad blood and animosity between rivals plays an almost tangible part in the sport. A chance meeting between two rivals in a hotel, a confrontation at a press conference, a weigh-in or ringside at a fight where either both are spectators or where one may be in the ring, can frequently become out of hand and need the assistance of others to prevent a full-scale melee from erupting. The atmosphere can become prickly and very tense, leading bystanders to anticipate the possibility of impending chaos. A lot of rivalries are also, however, coated in a healthy swathe of irony. Rivalries increase spectator interest and subsequently heighten the demand for tickets at the fights and subscription/pay-per-view fees for live TV. In turn, this generates money in the pockets of the participants.

'It was just publicity and exposure between us. There was no animosity really. It's a business. Of course it helps further our careers.'

With his professional career cut brutally short just as he seemed to be poised on the brink of championship level, Rod found the desire that most fighters harbour, was still very much alive inside him.

'I finished boxing and it took me about 18 months to get over it with the injuries and the recovery. I always had that drive and ambition in me to achieve my aims. It didn't happen with the boxing but I started to practise and participate in kickboxing. I'm in my 30s at this time. I ended up training the kickboxers to use their hands. Within about 18 months, I ended up with about four world champion kickboxers! I was sitting in a bar one day and I noticed this bloke staring at me. He came over and introduced himself. His name was Bill Judd and he had a gym on Globe Road, Bethnal Green called the KO. I started training once or twice a week. He was really well known on the kickboxing scene.'

Indeed he was. Bill Judd won world championships in kickboxing and Muay Thai and earned black-belt status in other forms of martial arts such as karate, wu shu kwan and judo. The Globe Road site is just one branch of the KO gym and it stretches to foreign countries too. Thirty-four world champions in Muay Thai and kickboxing fell under his tutelage and his expertise has been utilised by such international stars as Madonna and Pink.

'I went down to Bill's gym on Globe Road and trained there for about five years. For about four of those years, I did two boxing classes a week. Just simple stuff but it got really, really popular and the gym got really packed on those days. I never ever took a penny for it. I did it because I love boxing. It wasn't for the money. It did get to the stage where it got a bit harder and age is no longer on your side. One day, Bill called and said, "Rod, come and see me. I've got something to show you." He brought me down here to this site. All it was, was an empty shell. He said to me, "I reckon you could do a lot with this." We had a look around and I was kind of agreeing with what he was saying. We came out, shut the door and he turns to me and says, "Here you are, that's yours!" He put the keys in my hand! I was in shock. Just as I was about to smile and show some appreciation, he says to me, "I've got cancer." I was dumbfounded. Speechless.'

Rod's voice slowed down to illustrate the proverbial rollercoaster ride of emotions that charged through him on hearing this piece of news. 'Anyway, a couple of days later, I came in with a broom, marigolds and paintbrushes. On the Tuesday the ring came. On the Thursday, the bags came with the brackets and for about six weeks, I was here every day. Hammer, saw, drill, paintbrush. On my own. All day and all night. I built this. Sorry, I'm gonna have tears in my eyes now...'

Rod's voice trailed off as his eyes started to well. The feeling of achievement and what this meant to him after all the years since his near-fatal encounter with Herol Graham was crystal-clear. The more I got to converse with him, the more I encountered human achievement and what it means to the individual at its most raw and untinged. Rod continued to talk but only through a cracked voice, heavily charged with emotion.

'Day and night, night and day. I'd get up in the early hours and I'd get home about ten o'clock at night. All the floors I put down, the bags, the ring took me a whole day and I did it on my own. It was brilliant. At the time I was doing some security work too for about two months and I remember, I finished work the morning the gym opened on a Friday and had to get back for about eight o'clock, got all the kids out, got them done. I went to the gym and on the first day, the gym wasn't big enough. There were so many kids.'

Rod jumped up at this point and paced around in front of me, unable to contain the feeling of joy he experienced. It was a feeling he was reliving in front of me now. Rod threw punches at invisible opponents. The eyes narrowed and his lips tensed as he demolished the space between us. I sat there on the wooden bench not uttering a sound. To have done so would have been to fracture one man's moment of unblemished intimacy with his past. Rod had been taken back to his fighting days and he was relishing it. I let the mood take him. It would return him when it was good and ready and it was incredibly moving to witness. The double jab, the hook, the uppercut, the cross, the feint, the head movement. For 30 seconds, I travelled back almost 30 years. As the combinations slowed and the eyes focused back on the present day, they appeared watery. The beast never dies; it simply lies dormant. 'I went home later that day, sat down and just cried. I've done it! I've done it! Such a great feeling.'

Of all the achievements Rod had in his amateur career along with the name he was quickly making for himself in the pros, one got the feeling that, at the very least, this achievement ranked up there with them. 'It SURPASSED that. Surpassed it. That feeling of seeing people coming off the street from scratch, don't know nothing about boxing. You become a social worker. You see people making progress. They win fights. It is so rewarding. Can you believe this, the Olympic Games this year, I get a message that Muhammad Ali is coming to my gym! I'm running around shouting, "Muhammad Ali's coming to my gym! Muhammad Ali's coming to my gym!" People are looking at me strangely! After a while I stop telling people in case I end up looking stupid. He then got ill and I get a message from him. He said he's sorry he couldn't make it. He's sending his brother.'

His voice faltered again. 'It's hard. The rent here is very expensive and the bills are big. I'm still not making any money but I'm sure it'll get better in time. It's a lot of work but I'm in it for the love. It's been brilliant and I pride myself on ANYBODY can come into my gym. They are all nice people and they come from all walks of life.' His willingness to speak and help anybody would appear to be a common trait with most boxers. Being enshrouded in agents and handlers and others who exist to simply boost the individual's public image is certainly not in Rod's make-up.

'That's why I love boxing. Most boxers are really nice people. They're not arrogant at all. They will go up to anybody.'

I mentioned the reaction of the local residents in the vicinity of the Royal Albert Hall, the site for Douglas's challenge to Herol Graham, on London's affluent Kensington Gore, who were displeased with news that the sport was attempting to return to the venue. The locals claimed they did not wish to have 'such people' on their doorstep. Rod's reaction was blunt. 'These people don't know what they're talking about. There are big football grounds there so why not ban football?! Boxing people are some of the nicest people you could meet.'

The outpouring of emotion shown by Rod, while talking about the creation and success of the Arches Gym and his recovery from his ring injuries, was soon replaced by a more melancholic bout of reflection. Being born and bred in Bow and having grown up within the close local vicinity, he had been surrounded by the strong boxing culture of the East End and was a proven fighter of impressive standard when at school.

'I was the best fighter in my school. I wasn't a bully but every year I was the best fighter. I was a sportsman. I was always competitive. I was about 13. I was out running the 100 metres one day and I dipped to get in front of the line. I was neck and neck with this guy. I dipped just a little bit too much and I bent over and crashed on to my shoulder. I broke my collar bone and a bone in my back where it joins so I was in hospital for about six weeks. Part of my physio was to give me a punchbag. That's how I started. It was in my first season that I won the Junior ABAs in 1980.'

For a fighter whose boxing career was instigated and ended by varying degrees of injury, Rod Douglas achieved a commendable amount and has a healthy number of amateur accomplishments to show for his blood, sweat and tears. In the professionals, he was making a serious name for himself. Had the defeat, or indeed the fight, against Herol Graham not occurred, there would have been a number of alternative options for Rod to choose from. The European title-holder was Francesco Dell Aquila from Italy and Britain's own Michael Watson held reign over the Commonwealth title, courtesy of his thrilling six-round war with Nigel Benn in May 1989. At world level, the Panamanian legend Roberto Duran held the WBC title, Michael Nunn held the IBF title, Doug DeWitt held the WBO title while Mike McCallum (after whom Rod's youngest son, Callum, is named) held the WBA title. It's a fantastical 'what-if' but what would have happened in the future was clear to Rod.

'Listen, listen, there is no doubt in my mind that I would have been at least British champion. Most of the guys I went to the Olympic trials with won British titles. Me and Watson couldn't fight because we had the same manager, Eubank had just come on the scene and we'd had that two-day sparring and Benn was avoiding me. None of the top fighters wanted to fight Herol Graham because he was boring and not a crowd-puller so they'd have a hard fight and not make any money from it. It was the only fight open for me. As for the world champions, I reckon I could have outpointed most of them if not knocked them out. None of them I looked up to. At the time, I tried to model myself on being "Sugar" Ray Leonard. I used to watch him on television and watch his jab and I tried to get my jab faster than his jab but I didn't really look up to anybody in my weight division at that time who could have beaten me. Nowadays, I don't really follow the sport much.'

While the current batch of top middleweights battle it out to see whose head breaks the surface of the ever-increasing murkiness of the infamous alphabet soup, Rod is not overly familiar with the likes of the current crop of 'world' champions. You detect very strong vibes that the former four-time ABA champion was extremely proud of his accomp'ishments as a fighter and could have achieved much more had the har ds of fate dealt slightly differently.

As we stood up to end our chat, Rod led me back through the main training hall. As we passed the ring, Solomon was tutoring a young lad in the basic art of maintaining your defence with one hand as the other shoots out a jab. As we passed them, Rod suddenly lurched over towards the student with a tense expression, clenched fists and pumped-out chest and barked, 'Keep those hands up. DON'T drop them.'

For those few seconds, the relentless nature of the man which Alec Mullen had referred to resurfaced but as quickly as he tore into the student, he came back to my side, his eyes and mouth smiling once more. Something on the wall caught my eye. A long board overlooked the gym. It was entitled 'Arches Combos'. In four separate sections, lines of numbers were scrawled to denote a particular combination. One section for three-punch combinations, one for four, one for five and one for six.

'They remind me of Kevin Rooney and Mike Tyson,' I said to Rod as we stood in the immaculately weeded pathway outside. The images of Kevin Rooney bending down to Mike Tyson between rounds during 'Iron' Mike's heyday in the mid-late-80s, bellowing numerical sequences into his ear that would be transformed into combinations created with a frightening combination of speed and power, were iconic. Rod didn't say anything. He looked at me and smiled. A smile that had an air of expectation about it. As he turned and walked back inside his gym, I walked off unable to shake the belief that, were Rod to fill the role of mentor and find a prodigy who would go on to achieve great things in the ring like the aforementioned Rooney–Tyson partnership, it would be nothing short of what he would deserve.

2

David O'Callaghan

IN 1956, Dr Edith Summerskill CH PC, feminist, Labour politician and writer, had a book published titled *The Ignoble Art*. It was a book of just over 100 pages of anti-boxing propaganda which took an unobstructed aim at those who deemed the sport of boxing to be an appropriate and socially acceptable choice of career and walk of life. Dr Summerskill endeavoured to prove that the sport had no place in the society of that day and that those involved in the sport should either be prosecuted for assault or aiding and abetting such a practice. As I read through the pages in an attempt to see the sport through others' eyes, one quote of the author's stood out, 'The point in boxing is to render your opponent insensible.'

Boxing fans are renowned for their passionate, forceful debates such as to who would beat who and their various reasons why, who should fight who, the latest issues in and out of the ring, how unfair it is to dig deep for pay-per-view fight coverage when you subscribe monthly to that channel as it is etc. On the subject of defending the sport against the anti-boxing establishment, it is brought up in several conversations that there are more injuries in other sports such as motor racing and rugby yet they don't come under such intense criticism and scrutiny, in terms of safety, as boxing. While, statistically, this may be true for the amount of injuries incurred, it must be remembered that the intention in boxing is to hit your opponent. We can only hope this will never come about in motor racing or rugby. Yes, the intention IS to hit your opponent but to 'render them insensible'?

'No, no, no,' exclaimed Dr David O'Callaghan, giving no doubt over his views on the issue. 'It's a weak argument. Certainly in amateur boxing, the point is definitely NOT to render your opponent insensible.

It is to outscore him. In terms of professional boxing, yes, the intention is there to hurt with your punches. That is part of it and it may stop your opponent but you don't stop your opponent only by rendering them insensible. That is one of the ways it CAN happen.'

I met Dr David O'Callaghan, an NHS doctor whose expertise is utilised by the British Boxing Board of Control at a number of their shows, in the home fighters' dressing room at Bethnal Green's York Hall in September 2012 while he was giving London's middleweight journeyman Duncan Cottier his pre-fight check prior to him winning a four-rounder against Kevin Greenwood, his first win in five years. We subsequently arranged to meet in the ground floor cafe of St Thomas' Hospital on London's South Bank where he is a Doctor-in-Training, seeking the grounding required to be made a full consultant with further stints at St George's Hospital in Tooting, Hammersmith and St Mary's, Paddington. Involved specifically in neuro-anaesthetics and intensive care, there is an obvious connection to boxing's welfare and the potential risks involved. Having a healthy interest in both these fields, Dr O'Callaghan is able to provide a relevant and fascinating insight into how this knowledge can impact on boxing and be applied to make the sport safer. He also explains how the two opposing fields of boxing and medicine crept into his life.

'I grew up in Sheffield in the 1980s and early 90s,' he explained. 'I ended up doing science A Levels but never had an overwhelming desire to be a doctor. I did those A Levels and then thought about what was the most interesting thing I could do with them. It was borderline whether I could get the grades or not so I moved to London in 1996 where they accepted lower grades. I went to medical school then and have never looked back. Growing up in Sheffield back then, there was a lot of boxing going on at the time with Prince Naseem, Johnny Nelson and before that there was "Bomber" Graham. There was always that interest so I revisited that when I left medical school. I didn't have much time for hobbies when I was at medical school so once I got through it, I kind of thought, right what can I do? I didn't go through medical school to be a ringside doctor but it was one of those things where you start to think about the hobbies you had and really enjoy.

'I used to do a bit of sparring. I wasn't the most flexible chap but I could give a few punches so I was quite keen to get back into boxing. I couldn't really turn up to work with black eyes, missing teeth and bruises so I thought of other ways that I could get involved. The obvious way was to get involved in the medicine side. A long time ago, I had a friend who was helping out at The Ring, which was a white-collar boxing gym in Southwark. He ended up organising the medical side to a few of those shows so I turned up. My friend said I should contact the board to try and get involved in the pro shows instead of just the white-collar stuff. I sent my CV off to the board in Cardiff and they invited me to observe a couple of shows. When they're happy that you're safe, that you know what you should be looking out for at a boxing show, they let you start to practise independently. I've been with the board now for about four years.'

Dr O'Callaghan speaks with a matter-of-fact, sincere and articulate manner. His views are corroborated with strong supporting evidence as well as a deep interest in a sport he is committed to safeguarding both in conversation and in practice. The argument that raises its relentlessly inquisitive head is that of the risks undertaken by the sport's participants and the comparisons drawn between those in boxing and other sports.

'I give a talk I've given a few times to various different groups of doctors about boxing. From a purely independent point of view, if you were to look at the statistics and ask if boxing should be banned on the basis of how dangerous it is, it's quite difficult to interpret the stats. Do you go on number of head injuries per boxer, per rounds boxed or per minutes boxed? Obviously you can therefore alter the statistics as to how you look at that. How do you then quantify a head injury? Do you say a head injury is something very severe like a brain bleed or do you classify every concussion as a head injury? How does that then compare to sports such as rugby, horse-racing, diving or parachuting?

'I've seen statistics that can be manipulated to suggest boxing can be more dangerous or less dangerous than those sports. From a purely statistical standpoint, I don't think the evidence stacks up to ban boxing. I think where people sometimes have a point is when they say that in none of those other sports do people go out to injure the other person, which clearly in professional boxing as opposed to amateur boxing could be argued is the case. As doctors, we aren't there to control people's lives. We are there to inform people of the risks and they then make informed decisions on how they live their lives. As long as all people in boxing have an understanding of the risks, and I think all boxers do, I have no issue with boxing and have no issues with squaring my position with the British Medical Association (BMA) which is very anti-boxing.'

During the years I have followed the sport, I have witnessed many fights where the defeated fighter has had to absorb terrific blows to the head, sometimes when the contest should perhaps have been terminated sooner than it was. Being 'too brave for their own good' is a saying commonly used to refer to a fighter with too much pride to retire from the fight and too little defence to ward off the blows flying through the air in their direction. It is usually in the later rounds of those particularly intense, fast-paced fights where the level of injury would appear to make itself morbidly apparent. The cases of Gerald McClellan against Nigel Benn (round ten), Michael Watson against Chris Eubank (round 12), Johnny Owen against Lupe Pintor (round 12), James Murray against Drew Docherty (round 12) and Bradley Stone against Richie Wenton (round ten) are points in question.

'What causes problems in boxing in terms of catastrophic head injuries are blood vessels breaking and bleeding into the skull which is a fixed box. Inside your skull you have your brain, blood and cerebral spinal fluid. If you have an expansion in the amount of the volume of the blood, then it's going to compress the other tissues. The pressure inside your skull builds up to a point where cells start to die. The thing that causes those bleeds is called rotational acceleration. When you get punched, your head will go one way and your brain will go with it BUT there will be a delay. So the blood vessels that go between your brain and the veins on the inside of your skull will create tension as the punch lands, a bit like pulling on a rope. So these vessels can rupture as they twist. It's that rotational acceleration that causes those head injuries and what causes them is that twisting motion, so headgear for example wouldn't make a huge difference.

'The things that would make a difference are making sure the boxers aren't dehydrated in the build-up to a fight because the brain then shrivels in size and also ensuring there aren't huge fluctuations in weight. That is what causes change in your brain's tissue volume and your risk of injury is much higher if you have been knocked out and the risk of you being knocked out gets higher, the more rounds you go. What you could look to do is bring down the number of rounds.'

The introduction of preventative measures to safeguard the wellbeing of the sport's combatants is a matter that will never have its limits and boundaries. Working tirelessly to ensure the safekeeping of the fighters themselves should always be the priority and the benefits are obvious. Of the utmost importance is the fighter's health. Following on from that is the need to maintain the longevity of the sport and to fight the anti-boxing lobbyists with evidence that the number of serious injuries incurred is on the downward slope and that everything is being done to reduce that statistic further. The sport is monitored and assessed continuously for ways to improve its image to ensure enjoyment for a fan base which, globally, is constantly on the increase and also to attract new fans and followers.

'It can be looked at on two levels. You have the primary measures. Everybody goes out wearing seatbelts when they drive and people put on their crash helmets when they ride their bike. In boxing, what you can do is keep an eye on your hydration status and your weight reading. What we can do as the British Boxing Board of Control's medical arm, is to sort out the secondary measures. If you get punched and get a bleed to the brain, there really isn't very much we can do to stop the problems that are caused. What we can do is limit the secondary problems so we can control things like blood pressure, oxygen levels and carbon dioxide levels and then minimise the amount of tissue damage done to the brain. That is why, after the Michael Watson fight, they introduced this idea of a doctor who was skilled in the management of an unconscious patient having to be at ringside the whole way through. That's why there are now paramedics there with oxygen and who have the means to put artificial tubes down the windpipe and do the patient's breathing for them if they need to. That is also why when we do our pre-fight preparation, we go through the evacuation routes at the building to find the best route and which hospital to go to. When I go to the York Hall or wherever, that is the side which I have much more involvement in.'

The issue surrounding the injuries incurred by Michael Watson in his heroic effort against Chris Eubank on 21 September 1991 at Tottenham Hotspur Football Club's ground in north London for the vacant World Boxing Organisation super-middleweight title, is one of the most-used examples of a fight in which the plot adopted a violent twist and took one of the participants to within an inch of his life. Three months previously, Eubank made the third and final defence of the World Boxing Organisation middleweight title with a very close and highly contentious points decision over Michael Watson, a fight which drew derision from the press in the subsequent days' coverage. Eubank remained stoic in his affirmation that he had done enough to earn the victory while Watson reacted in the way most of the fight fraternity and British public did; with bemusement and shock that he had been dealt, not so much a short straw, more the stalk's root. A rematch was a natural to clear up the ambiguity of the first contest.

In a fiercely contested rematch in which the fortunes of both fighters swayed, the ending seemed near in the 11th round when Watson threw a combination, capped with a vicious right hand which lowered the self-styled 'Simply the Best' to the kneeling position. Upon rising, Eubank walked forward to face what many thought would be his timely demise. Instead, he hurled a perfect right uppercut that sliced through Watson's defence, sending him tottering back a few steps and then falling back on to the canvas, the back of his neck connecting with the bottom rope, causing his head to snap backwards with the knockdown's full momentum assisting. The damage had been done at this point. As the bell rang to start the next, and final, round, Watson walked slowly out where Eubank met him with a fusillade of hard blows against the ropes next to his corner. Referee Roy Francis waved the fight off with Watson in no position to defend himself. At the time of the stoppage, Watson was ahead on all three judges' scorecards. While being tended to by his cornermen, Watson collapsed in the ring and what transpired has been well documented and publicised.

At the time the British Boxing Board of Control's duty of care to its licensed boxers was not provided sufficiently and as a result the board was subsequently fined £1m in compensation to the stricken fighter, though this sum was ultimately reduced to £400,000. The board winced at the impact of such a blow to their finances and had to sell their London headquarters for a more economically viable location in Cardiff.

'My understanding was that there was an ambulance there but that they couldn't find it so they couldn't get him out of the ring. I don't know whether that was a result of poor planning or because there was chaos at ringside. There were fights breaking out around the ring and there were also a lot of people in the ring which makes it much more difficult to get the fighter out. The other problem was that as the fight was in north London, he was eventually taken to North Middlesex Hospital who turned him away because they didn't have a neurosurgery unit. He was then taken to Whitechapel Hospital in east London. Nowadays, I can't see that sort of thing happening.'

Spotting signs that a fighter is in distress before a contest is a crucial factor in preventing possible injuries and even tragedies in the ring. There are endless stories of fights being called off for all manner of reasons ranging from a boxer having caught a flu bug to suffering from spells of dizziness, constant vomiting, damaged retinas, failed MRI scans etc. There is also the opportunity for something untoward to be spotted by the Board of Control doctor while he is giving his pre-fight checks to the fighters in their respective dressing rooms.

'I have never been in a position where I've had to declare a fighter unfit before a fight. That would be a very different position to be in. All boxers will have had their annual MRI scan, eye and hearing test as well as annual HIV, Hepatitis B and Hepatitis C blood tests. They also have check-ups with their GP to monitor their blood pressure. When we see them at ringside what we are looking for is evidence of something having happened in sparring. Have they got an obvious fracture in their face? Have they broken a bone in their hands? You are also looking for any abnormal neurology signs. Are their pupils the same size? If they aren't, it can mean that something catastrophic is going on.'

There have been occasions when a fighter has shown signs of serious distress during a contest that would be reason enough to give the referee, or ringside medical officers, cause for concern and indeed justification for bringing proceedings to a close. When Michael Watson walked out for the 12th round of that fateful fight with Chris Eubank, he hardly moved but seemed to shuffle over to his right to the ropes and slowly lifted his arms to try and stave off the torrent of punches aimed at him. When the fight was stopped, he was assisted back to his corner but had a vacant expression on his face and his feet appeared unsteady. It seemed the fight was stopped because he was unable to punch back against Eubank as opposed to most of his adversary's punches getting through. On a separate occasion almost three and a half years later, Gerald McClellan was seen blinking furiously after he was floored against Nigel Benn in the tenth round of that titanic duel they put on for the London Arena crowd. By that stage, sadly, the damage had been done.

'It's very hard from ringside,' David explains, 'you're hugely reliant on the referee who is obviously the only person who can stop the fight. If you have concerns as a doctor, you clearly communicate with the referee and all referees would pretty much stop the fight. The referee has the best view in the house. Even though we are sitting at ringside and we have the best possible view other than being in the ring, we can be obscured by one of the fighters, by the ropes or by the corner. What you are watching for is engagement with the referee. If the referee tells them to break, are they focusing their attention on the referee and are they interacting appropriately with him? Are they co-ordinating their movements and their gait properly and can they walk in a straight line and a steady manner? When the bell goes do they know where their corner is or do they walk off to the opponent's or the neutral corner? In the corner between rounds, does the fighter show signs of nausea? Is he vomiting? These can be signs of an impending head injury. Are there signs of distress in between rounds? Are the cornermen struggling to interact appropriately with their fighter and struggling to get the boxer's attention? These things can give you cause for concern.'

It is arguably the most important aspect of the health and safety of the sport's participants. To protect them and look for signs which encourage the intervention of a third party to ensure they are able to fight another day. Whether it is the referee's arms wrapping around a thoroughly beaten and demoralised fighter, that very same official accompanying the climactic announcement of 'ten' with a wave of his hand, the corner's towel being thrown into the ring or the referee being called to a corner to be told that the fighter does not wish to continue, the decision to terminate a contest is one which is taken with, solely, the fighter's wellbeing in mind. Maintaining the health of a fighter after a contest is one thing but what of the fighters who are believed to have continued their careers when they are deemed to be comfortably past their peak? So much so, that they become accustomed to being beaten comprehensively by fighters who, to use Larry Holmes's opinion of Rocky Marciano's chances against him, 'couldn't carry their jockstrap' if they fought in the fighter's prime? The fighters whose performances have deteriorated so much, that even the slightest glimmer of them from their peak days has faded like shadows into the night?

Attention can be drawn to the distressing sights of Muhammad Ali going through the motions against a list of, at best, average heavyweight contenders after the infamous 'Thriller in Manila' with the late, great 'Smokin' Joe Frazier in 1975. The 1978 defeat to Leon Spinks, a seven-fight novice going into the fight and the deplorable decision to pitch him in against his ex-sparring partner Larry Holmes for the latter's World Boxing Council title in 1980 were fights that convinced everyone but Ali himself that his fighting career was over. In the Holmes fight, 'The Greatest' attempted to cover up his greying temples, turn back the hands of time and float and sting his way to a fourth world title. What he discovered in place of this hugely ambitious attempt, was an opponent who repeatedly turned to the referee and beckoned him to stop the beating so he didn't have to continue humiliating his idol and former boss in front of a worldwide audience. An audience whose numbers probably started diminishing by the middle rounds with viewers wiping the tearful mistiness from their eyes and changing channel, not wishing the last image of their hero in a boxing ring to be a pathetic impersonation of what once was.

Over one year later at the Queen Elizabeth Sports Centre in Nassau, Bahamas, Ali fought for the last time against heavyweight contender and future world champion Trevor Berbick. Ali lost on points in a fight most widely known for having a cowbell to start and finish each round. Ali finished with a record of 56 wins, five losses with 37 knockouts. This writer is of the belief that Muhammad Ali's professional career would have been capped perfectly after George Foreman was bemused, outfought, out sped, outpunched and knocked silly by the finest right hand Ali threw in one of the finest performances ever seen in a boxing ring. In this instance, three of his five losses would never have happened and he'd have defeated everyone he'd have fought. In his next fight, he fought the 'Bayonne Bleeder', and the inspiration for the *Rocky* films, Chuck Wepner. Allowing this fight, during which Ali suffered a body-shot inflicted knockdown, to go 15 rounds before the referee intervened, perhaps should have made Ali realise that the time was nigh to go out while ahead. Just six years and one month after retiring, he was welcomed into the ring in Atlantic City prior to Mike Tyson defending his world title against the fighter who hated hurting Ali in 1980, Larry Holmes. Acknowledging the crowd's raucous ovation, he waved to the fans. Distressingly, a minder either side of him held his hands up.

Other examples can include the case of Evander Holyfield, whose natural cruiserweight physique was beefed up to enter the heavyweight echelon in 1988. 'The Real Deal' progressed to show an almost superhuman appetite in handling the biggest and best fighters this new division had to offer. He held various segments of the world title four times and now comfortably sits in most pundits' top ten heavyweights of all time. However, when the sensible time came for him to retire, he answered his detractors by saying that he would yet again win the world title, a belief which, worryingly, seemed to get stronger and stronger the more fights he lost.

Danny Williams, the former British and Commonwealth heavyweight champion, stated BEFORE he lost his British title for the last time to Dereck Chisora in 2010, that he believed he was shot and that this would be his last fight. To date, he has fought nine more times; losing to fighters he would have handled with ease in his prime. This was the fighter who took the murderous punches of Mike Tyson in the first round of their July 2004 bout and rebounded to knock 'Iron' Mike out in the fourth. While Tyson was so far over the hill at this stage that this particular landscape feature had all but vanished over the rear horizon, his power remained and Williams's jaw always seemed susceptible. Another crushing first-round finish for Tyson had looked imminent.

'I don't sit on the board of medical meetings. The chief medical officer for the southern area would do that. There was one occasion however, where there was a young chap who fought in London. He was knocked down in the third round. After the fight, I asked him what round he was knocked down in and he said the first round. He continued saying this for several minutes after the fight. This could be a sign of anything when a fighter shows this sort of amnesia after a fight. It could be a pending catastrophe in the head. We took him to Charing Cross Hospital in an ambulance and on the way there, his girlfriend said to me,

"This happens every time he gets hit in the head." I told the boxer that I would have to report this to the board because I was a bit worried. As far as I'm aware, if there is any doubt with regards to a fighter's health, the board may revoke that fighter's licence. There always seems to be more controversy over taking away someone's licence when other people don't think it should have been than vice versa. The other thing which I have a bit more of a hands-on with is, what happens if their MRI (Magnetic Resonance Imaging) scans are unusual. If there are any concerns with these, they are sent off to x-ray experts like radiologists and then sent off to a couple of neurosurgeons who then write reports to the board and that case is then discussed at the next medical meeting and if there are any concerns, the board has a tendency to take their licences off them.'

The issue surrounding a fighter who has prolonged his career to the stage where he needs to be protected from himself is a sensitive one. It's a damned-if-you-do, damned-if-you-don't position for anyone with such authority to be in. You either risk having your fears and concerns being realised by allowing the fighter to continue or you protect the fighter, from what is likely to be further anguish, but then bring the curtain down on the dreams and ambitions of the individual.

When the 'Punching Preacher', George Foreman, embarked on his second coming in March 1987 after a ten-year sabbatical, critics almost rioted to get on board the medical bandwagon. They stated fears that 'Big' George's once feared power and effective cross-armed defence would do precious little at his advanced age to hold off the aggression and ferocity of the world champion at the time, Mike Tyson. Foreman made it clear that Tyson was clearly focused in his artillery's sight picture. Tyson, in turn, alluded to the former champion's swollen girth and newly-shaved pate by ominously declaring he'd 'kill the old Buddha'. At the over-ripe, ancient age of 38, Foreman defied the critics and tucked into a diet of cheeseburgers washed down with an oversized helping of hand-picked journeymen. As present-day boxing manager Richard Clark correctly points out, 'George got it right in his comeback. He'd been out for ten years and realised he had to have the attitude of starting over. He started with four-rounders and worked his way up, the way a new pro would, to title contention.'

A heroic losing effort against Evander Holyfield for the world title in April 1991 resulted in *Boxing News* to lead the fight review encouraging its readers to 'salute the sport's time machine'. Over three years later, Foreman won the world title with a tenth-round, one-punch knockout of Michael Moorer. At the age of 45 he ripped the record of the oldest world heavyweight champion from Jersey Joe Walcott by an extraordinary eight years and, more importantly, Foreman showed no sign of physical deterioration.

Another record was again broken in May 2011 when Bernard 'The Executioner' Hopkins defeated Canada's Jean Pascal for the WBC light-heavyweight title at the age of 46, hence becoming the oldest world champion in any weight. Hopkins's career was deemed to be on the slide after losing his middleweight world title to Jermain Taylor in 2005 but rebounded to totally dominate leading light-heavyweight Antonio Tarver in such a fashion that one could be forgiven for believing he had almost planned the Taylor loss to make the subsequent resurgence appear that much more incredible. When he lost to Joe Calzaghe in a disappointingly scrappy affair over 12 rounds two years later, it was finally believed that the slippers, rug and honorary invitation to Canastota could be seen moving in his direction. These were ushered back into his retirement plans with his next performance. In a showing that is not only deemed by some to be his finest career performance but also one that enhanced the credibility of Calzaghe's prior win over Hopkins, the 'Executioner' exorcised Kelly 'The Ghost' Pavlik to such an extent that his confidence evaporated and what was left was more a mild wisp than the spectral powerhouse that had demolished Hopkins's past conqueror the previous year. The Jean Pascal performance came two years after this and Hopkins is still active and chasing world titles. Again, with no sign of any harm done.

Admittedly, these examples are of two fighters who have never been repeatedly beaten. However, to introduce an age limit to the sport would undoubtedly curtail the risk brought to those who find it hard to hear the loud chimes of father time. It would, however, hinder the historical significance and potential greatness deserved and earned by fighters such as Foreman, Hopkins and, to name another, 'The Old Mongoose' Archie Moore, who won his final world title at the age of 44 and who still holds the world record for the most amount of knockouts in a career; 131 knockouts in 218 fights. His final fight, aged 46, contributed to this tally.

'My gut feeling is that there should be an age limit but this is a very ambiguous area. Those who get injured more tend to be a bit older. That's just because your reflexes aren't quite as quick as they once were, your hand-to-eye co-ordination isn't quite as quick as it once was and you therefore have a tendency to ship more punches. The difficult thing is how do you say it should be 40? How do you say to someone who has been a professional boxer all their life that they've got to stop when they are 40 if they're relying on that money? There is clearly a difference though between various fighters. Look at the difference at Bernard

Hopkins who is fighting at 46 and at Ricky Hatton who came back at 33. You have Hopkins who lives at the weight and then someone who balloons up in between and who pushes their body to physiological extremes.'

The issue of weight and the sport's requirements when the fighters clamber on to the scales in the official pre-fight weigh-in the day prior to the fight, is an issue which is heavily debated and as closely fought as two come-forward sluggers in the proverbial telephone kiosk. There have been numerous occasions where fights have developed into painfully gruesome mismatches as a result of one fighter feasting on a banquet after the weigh-in due to the physically draining rigmarole of forcing their weight down to ensure they arrived within the stipulated weight category. Do you therefore have the weigh-in shortly prior to the fight to ensure, weight-wise at least, an even contest or do you prevent last-minute weight-shedding to stop the fighter's energy and hydration levels lowering to a dangerous depth by having the weigh-in days before the fight, thereby opening the door to substantial weight gain before the first bell has rung? The late Arturo Gatti's second-round knockout of Joey Gamache in 2000 is a brutal illustration of what can happen as a result of this final option. Both former world super-featherweight champions in the same weight division, Gatti weighed in at just half a pound heavier than his adversary only to look, alarmingly, a whole weight division bigger come fight time.

'It's very difficult,' Dr O'Callaghan stressed. 'I think the solution to the problem is not to have single weigh-ins, rather than weighing the person 24 hours before the fight and saying, "Right, you are this weight," and letting them put on a number of pounds before the fight. Now, that clearly is bad. Not just for the person who has had to lose the weight and then put it back on after the weigh-in but also for the guy who is going to get punched. The other point is that boxers dehydrate themselves to get down to the weight so the chances of your brain swivelling around and stretching those blood vessels is high. The risk of sustaining a head injury by being dehydrated going into a fight is very high. If you have the weigh-in the day before, they then have the chance to rehydrate but you then have the risk that their weight will go back up. What they need is probably to have their weight monitored several weeks before a fight and kept at a safe limit. Certainly for championship fights, I think there should be weigh-ins three or four days before the fight and this is something that the board and the organisations can look at. I believe this is something that Barry McGuigan brought up on *Ringside* recently so I think it makes a lot of sense.'

The one weight category that is not bound by specific weight-related regulations is the heavyweight division. So long as the fighter enters the ring with a recorded weight of at least 14st 4lb (200lb), he will be permitted to box an opponent the size, for example, of the 'Beast from the East' Nikolay Valuev who weighed in at over 300lb so the possibility exists that a heavyweight could share a ring with someone weighing one and a half times their weight.

'What is interesting is that heavyweights are relatively well protected from suffering catastrophic head injuries. There are a couple of reasons for this. They're not dehydrated from having to make the weight so you don't get these huge fluctuations where your weight drops. Secondly, we talked about the rotational acceleration of your head spinning around. Heavyweights have got massive muscle mass. They have this big block of neck so when they're hit, their heads don't whip round quite as much as fighters in the lower weights. When I was doing talks about this, it seemed to me that somewhere around the middleweight and super-middleweight areas, boxers were more vulnerable. They seemed to be in that category where boxers are striving to make the weight but also able to impart a very high velocity of hard punches. In the lower weights, yes the need to make weight and the velocity is there but the punching power isn't at the same level.'

While listening to Doctor O'Callaghan, what struck me was how clear the risks are and how effectively the risks involved to fighters' wellbeing could be minimised. The treatment and response by the emergency services, in the terrible event that something should go drastically wrong during the course of a bout, now have clear guidelines. It is just a sad irony that it took an event of near-fatal proportions like the Michael Watson incident to bring these safety issues to the forefront of the sport's conscience. The primary measures and secondary measures are both crucial to the survival of both the participants and the sport itself.

Dr Edith Summerskill's ghost of ideals past will never impede on the development of boxing's future. For that, we owe a huge appreciation to our medical and support services. A body of people and regulators who, like the oft-used duck's feet cliché, are working tirelessly behind the scenes to develop the sport's support mechanism for the enjoyment and entertainment of others.

3
Tony Conquest

'IT would be devastating,' Tony 'the Conqueror' Conquest said. The natural smile that seems a permanent feature on the face of the fighter currently ranked number six in Britain in the cruiserweight division by the independent ratings, temporarily hibernates as we discuss the issue surrounding the possible closure of Dagenham Police and Community Amateur Boxing Club. 'It's helped out a lot of tearaways get in off the street. It's terrific. It would be so detrimental. The kids don't just come from Dagenham, they come from other areas and it's so central, right by the train station.'

Established in 1950 on the grounds of the old school, the potential of the club took no time in making itself apparent. In 1951, it boasted its first National Amateur Boxing Association champion in Johnny Maloney, who lifted the welterweight title. Maloney repeated this feat the following year under the club's banner. This same year, all ten of the national champions went on to participate in the 1952 Helsinki Olympics, the tournament where a certain Jens Ingemar Johansson would lift the silver medal and move on to become Sweden's sole claimant to the world heavyweight championship. Maloney himself was edged out on points, 2-1 in rounds, to Czechoslovakia's Julius Torma in the opening round. In 1979, the club moved site to the Old Boat House on Wood Lane, situated on the border with Havering. This move resulted in the club being accessible to a wider audience and young, aspiring boxers were drawn to it from all over north-east London and west Essex. The club moved along at a respectable pace, collecting a number of youth, schoolboy, junior, senior and NACYP (National Association of Clubs of Young People) titles. In 1993, the club moved again to where it can be found today, at 218-224 Dagenham Heathway, up on the first floor nestled among a mall of various retail outlets. The emergence of Kevin Mitchell was soon hitting the boxing headlines, courtesy of numerous amateur accolades and, subsequently, a successful professional career which has included two challenges for various segments of the governing bodies' alphabet soup. The club is currently run, on a day-to-day basis, by its honorary secretary Danny O'Sullivan.

The smile returned once more to its rightful place as Tony re-lived the times he had before he got into the sport and his first impressions with the club. 'Before I started boxing, I was round my mates' and we'd go to pubs and clubs. You know, smoking and drinking. Looking back I'd dread to think of how you would end up if you didn't have something like a goal, a purpose. I don't know where I'd be now if I didn't start boxing. I tried football but I was useless at that. I got my first teeth knocked out playing rugby.' Tony pauses, chuckles and directs his attention to his friend who sits next to me in the Romford cafe we have met in, 'He knows all about that. He's the one that done it!' His friend smiles unapologetically as if to emphasise that being involved in a game of hard knocks will always have the potential to deliver just that.

'My dad said, "You got to do something." I had a friend at the time who boxed. It kept him out of trouble so I thought I'd give it a go. I took myself up to Dagenham. At first, I was a bit ill-disciplined but I was at the age where I wanted to go clubbing but I had five or so bouts when I was about 16 or 17. I then didn't box for three years as I had terrible acne so I was on medication for my skin. During this time, my weight went up to in excess of 20st. I shed a bit of weight and went to Hornchurch. I had a few fights for them and won the North-East District for them twice at heavyweight and cruiserweight. I then went back to Dagenham and done the ABAs in 2009. I got through to the semi-finals and lost to the eventual winner, Robert Evans. He's a model now for Calvin Klein. Every time I buy a new pair of pants, I see his face!'

Boxing took a hold on Tony from an early stage and Dagenham ABC was a club which grabbed his attention and held it to such effect that its influence went beyond that of simply boxing tuition. 'Boxing was something I tried and liked. It was like a drug to me. You can never get away from it. Once it's got you, it's got you. I love every aspect of it. I was lucky to be trained by Mickey Kilmurray Sr and the O'Sullivan brothers who were like brothers to me. They were involved with me from the age of 15 or 16. They don't just show you how to box, they show you how to be men as well. It's just how they are. It's not just boxing, they pass on their life experiences to you. I'd be heartbroken if the gym were to close. It's a very disciplined club, very strict routines. Not another club like it. It's a fantastic club. It's where I started. It's where my heart is. Two rings, loads of training space. Until you travel around and have a look at other clubs, you don't realise just how good a club it is. It's turned out quite a few champions too.'

In 2009, Tony left camp with Dagenham ABC and embarked on a professional career under the tutelage of manager Richard Clark, the Metropolitan Police's amateur boxing Lafone Cup winner at light-middleweight in 2000, and trainer Jason Rowland, the former undefeated British light-welterweight champion from 1998 to 1999 and former World Boxing Union light-welterweight champion from 2000 to 2001. This camp saw him streak towards ten straight wins with four wins coming inside the distance before suffering his first loss last time out at the ExCel arena in London's Docklands against Neil Dawson on Frank Warren's 15 December 'Three Kings' show, the title referring to the Commonwealth super-middleweight champion George Groves, the Commonwealth middleweight champion Billy Joe Saunders and Tony himself.

In Tony's third professional outing, he earned a tough six-round decision over John Anthony, a fight which saw both men on the floor in the first round. 'This was probably my hardest fight. Big puncher. I actually caught him and had him over but then obviously I got a bit carried away and a bit gung-ho and he put me over. First time I'd ever been on the floor. When I got up I was quite badly gone and I fought back. I'd just stopped Nick Okoth in a round but I was told to take my time with Anthony as I wouldn't be able to hurt him. I went out and hurt him and thought, "Lovely, another first-round stoppage." I tore in like a madman and I thought the referee was going to jump in but he slung this right hand and it caught me on the back of the nut, right behind the ear and he just frazzled the brain a little bit and I ended up bouncing off the canvas but that was a big learning fight. That's what Jason was telling me. To break them down, break them down. If they're going to go, they're going to go.'

Two fights later, he faced off with 79-fight veteran Hastings Rasani. Rasani, by this point, had mingled in such company as David Haye, Terry Dunstan and Tony Bellew. Tony outpointed Rasani widely and repeated this victory in a rematch two fights later, both by scores of 60-54. A matter of months later, Rasani was deemed unlucky to receive just a draw against the huge Polish fighter Albert Sosnowski, who only a year previously had taken Vitali Klitschko ten rounds in a challenge for the Ukrainian's World Boxing Council heavyweight title. These fights were supplying Tony with invaluable experience and his next outing allowed him to display his ever-developing fighting maturity in a solid, workmanlike performance against Toks Owoh in November 2011. Winning a comfortable decision over Owoh afforded him not just the vacant Southern Area cruiserweight title, but also the knowledge and self-assurance that he could still throw sharp and accurate combinations in the later rounds against a tough opponent, renowned for lasting the course.

In his first defence of this title, Leon Williams stood in the opposing corner. The fight itself was short and brutal with Tony landing a series of arcing right hands to the side of Williams's head to register a first-round stoppage victory. Facing someone who Tony also deemed to be a good friend of his outside the square ring, didn't pose him any unique problems and his approach to the fight wasn't altered because of it. My mind drifted back to 18 March 1991 where, in a world welterweight title unification fight, the WBC champion Maurice Blocker squared off with the IBF champion Simon Brown. Outside of the ring these two were as good as best friends and it was reported that they had been to each other's homes for dinner and their respective partners were also great friends and occasionally socialised with one another. What transpired within the ropes on that Las Vegas night on the first Mike Tyson–Donovan Ruddock fight undercard was as compelling a fight as one could wish to witness. Brilliant boxing combined with a fast pace from start to finish resulted in a tenth-round stoppage victory for the IBF champion. Afterwards, Brown was asked why the fight was so relentlessly fought to which his reply was, 'He's a friend of mine so I wanted to try and get it over with as quickly as possible.' Ten rounds later…

'The Conqueror' explains his approach to the Williams fight, 'He's a good friend of mine, Leon is. He stopped me as an amateur around 2005 in a London final. Since then we've been really good friends and we talk on the phone. He's a nice fella. I became emotionally detached at that time. I wasn't even thinking about it. I just concentrated on what I had to do. I knew what I had to do. At the end of the fight when I looked at him and said, "You'd have done the same thing to me," he gave me a big smile and said, "Yeah, I would!" You want to give your best. You never want to leave them thinking, "What if?" You want to leave it all in the ring, give it your best and have no repercussions about it. It went really well.'

This was then followed in September 2012 with a contest against the Republic of Ireland's Ian Tims for the vacant World Boxing Organisation international cruiserweight bauble. Something of a home fighter to this point, Tims had won his first nine professional contests in Ireland before travelling to Finland in January 2012 to fight Juho Haapoja for European Union cruiserweight title only to be conclusively outpointed. Style-wise, Tims appeared tailor-made for Tony and he recorded a straightforward seventh-round corner retirement win after flooring Tims in the dying seconds of that round. It appeared the restraint and control shown against Owoh and the ferocity and conclusiveness of the Williams performances came together against Tims and the result was an impressively mature and crowd-pleasing showing.

'I just need to get my mindset right. I've suffered terribly with hand injuries over the last year and a half. I went to see a hand specialist in London called Ian Winsburn and since I've seen him I've had no problems. When I had bad pains and when I was throwing big punches I was worried about putting everything into every shot. Now obviously I can whack with both hands and I've got no problems. Jason says I've got world-class fitness, the punches are coming along. He's confident in what I can do and what I can do in the gym. He knows what I'm capable of. The way they are confident in me makes me more confident in myself. Jason doesn't beat around the bush. He says it like it is so I'm very well behaved!'

There is little doubt that Britain's brightest cruiserweight stars since the division was recognised in this country in 1987 have been Glenn McCrory, Johnny Nelson and David Haye. Other notable names who flew the Union Jack for the cruiserweights are Sammy Reeson, Derek Angol, Dennis Andries, Carl Thompson and Enzo Maccarinelli. The day I spoke with Tony, John Lewis-Dickinson outpointed Shane McPhilbin to wrest the British cruiserweight title. This time-honoured Lonsdale belt is clearly one of the next targets to be conquered. 'That Lonsdale belt would mean the world to me even if in the next couple of fights I get a shot at the English. I just want the traditional titles and belts, the British, European, all them. I'd say in 18 months to two years I'll be right up there at the top level. There is still a lot more I've got to do in Britain and Europe first. Another couple of fights and I'd like to think I'll be at European level and add my name to that list of Brits.'

While chatting, I noticed Tony eyeing some notes I'd scrawled outlining the current crop of world champions at the weight. With Guillermo Jones (WBA), Krysztof Wlodarczyk (WBC), Yoan Pablo Hernandez (IBF) and Marco Huck (WBO), he faces an accomplished group to test his mettle against. One name among these stands out though. 'He's a big lump that Marco Huck. All he wants to do is throw that right hand. He sits back and looks to sling it. If it don't land he throws the left. He seems very basic. Give him angles, a bit of speed and a lot of movement, he'll struggle. He's very hittable but he's so strong and game. I think Hernandez is the best of the bunch. Guillermo Jones, no one wants to go near. He got a draw with Johnny Nelson. He's so awkward. An absolute headache to a lot of people.'

Tony hopes that, sooner rather than later, he gets a chance to, not just redeem himself against Neil Dawson, but also prove a headache to the champions on the domestic and continental levels followed by those on the world scene. Confidence in his own ability does not appear to be a problem and the team around him would appear to corroborate that. He is also, however, a man with his feet firmly planted on the ground. For someone who needed a well-timed reminder from his father that he needed to get out and 'do something', his ambition, commitment and dedication to the sport cannot be doubted. This attitude and outlook on his chosen profession, but also in the way he conducts himself, would seem to be largely thanks to the tuition he received at Dagenham Police and Community Amateur Boxing Club and the mentoring of the training and coaching he benefitted from while there.

A short while after I met him, I had an opportunity to meet Danny O'Sullivan at the gym itself. We spent a while chatting about the fighters who frequent the gym and the seriousness of the potential closure of the place unless the required funding could be found. As I was about to leave the gym, the phone rang and Danny entered a lengthy conversation with the caller. Upon finishing the call, Danny explained that the caller was from Hopewell Independent Special School based in Dagenham. The school deals with children who have been permanently excluded from mainstream school and then excluded from the local borough's Pupil Referral Unit. Their motto stands proudly; 'Restoring Hope, Releasing Potential, Rebuilding Lives'. As I left, I thought back to what Tony Conquest stated about what the club does for youths in the local community and the surrounding areas. I wondered whether that motto should be adopted for the club too and be used as a reminder of what can be achieved and how the community it serves, and the people it gives hope and ambition to, would suffer were the gym to cease to exist.

4
Steve Goodwin

IT was 15 September 2012 and I was fortunate enough to have a ringside seat for an evening's boxing at Bethnal Green's York Hall, hosted by Steve Goodwin, a Hertfordshire-based promoter. Headlined as 'London's Calling', it was only my second visit to the famous venue for a boxing fight and the poignancy of the occasion was not lost on me. Being an avid fan for as far back as I can remember, I used to watch fights that took place at York Hall when they were aired on network television. Sitting there on that September evening was special. The famous rock hit by The Clash thundered and the venue was alive with the anticipation that comes with a high-quality show at an historic location. The banter and chatter was animated among the spectators at ringside and up in the tiers. Their opinions on the fight they had just seen in the ring, their views on the round-card girls and spirited chanting are, reliably, the most common forms of passing the time while awaiting the ring walks of the next scheduled bout's participants. As the fidgeting and milling about continued, the lights dimmed and half a dozen girls stepped forward into the ring and took up position. The crowd's attention became more focused and, with the inevitable wolf-whistling and rapturous applause, the dancing commenced to the sounds of loud music booming from the surround-sound speakers. Under the watchful guidance of Olivia Goodwin, the promoter's daughter, the performance uncovered a hidden gem. This wasn't just about boxing. This was about entertainment.

'We had a five-piece band playing on Saturday with their latest single being performed,' Goodwin said in reference to the show at the Brentwood Centre he hosted a few days prior to our meeting at a bar/cafe on Finchley Road. The midday custom in the bar wasn't busy so we had space and minimal noise to hinder our interview. 'Some people don't like it in boxing but you've got to develop the entertainment business. I look at Germany as the way it should be done. They have massive, sold-out arenas and they do the corporate side too. They have entertainment outside of boxing. If you don't change it, it's never going to get fixed. We did ringside interviews so I brought a girl in from the BBC. After the show, the inspector advised us to stop as it was deemed to be slowing down the boxing. That was back in December 2011 but I do, however, seem to be having a better relationship with the board now though and they seem to be more accepting of us with what we are doing.'

There is little doubt Steve Goodwin is out to show that, in a sport that embodies its fair share of shady characters, varying levels of corruption and baffling matchmaking, he can deliver quality shows that will leave the spectator satisfied with what has been delivered as well as eagerly awaiting the next promotion, safe in the knowledge that it will contain as evenly-matched contests as possible. To date, Goodwin plies his trade with a promotional banner that is gradually increasing in size and gaining national recognition. Galloping alongside his boxing promotions is Diamond Racing, his horse racing syndicate, and a fervent business acumen forged by an early career in insurance broking and as a financial advisor.

'I started insurance broking in 1983 and then went on to be a financial advisor. I decided that was more lucrative and more skilled. It seemed a natural follow-on and I actually passed my last exam last month so I can enjoy life again!' he said, relieved that this particular grind had been successful. 'In 1992, I started Diamond Racing with my father. He was a previous bookmaker and a professional gambler. He got ill with Parkinson's. He wasn't well but he always wanted to do something with me so I really did it for him rather than myself. I'm an ideas man. I remember sitting in this caravan in Wales with my wife and my family and I just came up with this idea of a horse-racing syndicate. I went back from Wales and went straight to my dad's place and said, "Dad, I have this idea." It was innovative at the time so we just started. We've had 170 winners! We've being running around Europe with horses in France and Italy. It's been fantastic.'

With obvious success in the equestrian field, the subsequent move into the boxing business came about through similar circumstances. Establishing Diamond Racing as a means of satisfying his father's wishes, the move into the world of pugilism was conceived through a desire to support and create something of a vocational nest egg for another family member.

'What happened was, I was a fan and I went to see a lot of the 1980s and 90s fights. My daughter, Olivia, became quite a big fan too. We went over to see the Lewis–Holyfield fight in Vegas and Olivia liked it. I like boxing but I needed the aggravation of boxing promoting like a hole in the head!'

Goodwin entered the world of promotion without, it seemed, much doubt as to the characters and political shenanigans that existed; ones which he would have to come up against and stand his ground with. It soon became clear that while the boxers did the physical fighting, the sport's other personalities had their share of duelling to see to in various backrooms, boardrooms and courtrooms. The political and cut-throat culture of boxing that is kept between the fighters and power-brokers of the sport was something which gave Goodwin cause for pause relatively early on.

'When I got into horse racing, you're dealing with jockeys, corruption and whatever else there is to deal with. We ran a horse a couple of months ago and I know, I KNOW, something was untoward. Somebody involved was making sure that horse wasn't winning. I can't prove who, what or how but in my heart I know it. I have enough experience to know when you're being stitched up. When I got into boxing, I thought nothing could be as bad as horse racing but I would say it is worse. I have been asked by a manager, who wanted this boxer to fight on my show, "How much is my separate fee?" My background is in financial advising and it is a very ethical business and I am totally transparent in everything I do. People might not like what they see on paper but what I say is what I do. I am doing it to try and make in-roads into the sport but by doing it the right way.'

Goodwin's first venture in promoting came in March 2010 with a four-bout show in Milton Keynes's football stadium. Featuring four bouts, two scheduled for four rounds and two for six, the headliner saw middleweight Harry Matthews score a fifth-round stoppage over Terry Carruthers. A little over two years later, both these boxers would contribute to the professional development of Chris Eubank Jr. The son of the former WBO middleweight and super-middleweight champion outscored both fighters over six rounds in consecutive fights in what proved to be valuable learning experiences for the young professional. It also showed how much importance Goodwin attaches to evenly matched fighters in good, competitive bouts that can be counted on to give the paying customers their money's worth; a trait which he has maintained and passionately adhered to in all his subsequent shows. What this initial toe-dipping into the frequently murky waters of the sport's business also exposed were the fears Goodwin hoped couldn't be topped from his dealings in the horse racing industry.

Being a newcomer to the world of boxing promotion, Goodwin was seen by some as something of an unknown quantity that could be influenced and moulded into a persona more conducive to others' idea of how someone in his position should be rather than what Goodwin himself aspired to.

'I was from outside boxing and I think they thought I was going to be an easy touch but I'm not. I had people shouting at me and threatening to break my legs but I don't get intimidated by that sort of stuff. Don't forget, when I got into boxing, I knew nobody. I didn't know who was who and what I found in boxing was that if you went to a particular gym, they would tell you that this person and that person was really bad. They were scumbags, they were this and that. I'd never experienced anything like this bad-mouthing in my life. I had a situation where this boxer would sell 100 tickets for £3,500. I'd pay him a purse of £1,100 and the £2,400 would go towards covering the cost of the fight. This particular manager had signed a contract for two boxers on my show. This guy turned up with £1,500 worth of tickets on the day, telling me the day before they'd sold out! I said to him, "What are you doing? The fight can't even go ahead. We haven't even covered the fight." This manager turned to me and said, "You're staging that fight and you're also paying me the £1,100." He hadn't even covered the fight. I told him that he had signed a contract and he said to me, "I don't care about contracts. You are going to do that or I will never, ever do business with you again." So I said to him, "You know what's going to happen? I will never, ever do business with you again." To this day, this particular manager slates me off and tells people I stole off him. I didn't. He broke a contract and I lost money. I shouldn't even have staged the fight. That's what I don't like about boxing. People go around tarnishing your name with no substance whatsoever. I still have that contract now and after that show, that was going to be it. I can't deal with people who are unethical and don't keep their word.'

My mind went back to an incident, highlighted in Mickey Duff's book, *Twenty and Out*, that the late promoter had with American promoter Bob Arum in the early part of the 1980s. Agreeing prior to a fight that Duff would be paid $125,000, the British promoter approached his opposite number after the show to obtain his money. When Arum asked for the contract, Duff stated that they'd both opted for a gentlemen's agreement. Arum simply replied, 'Who says I'm a gentleman!'

The dissent and disappointment that Goodwin felt during these times came through in his pitch as if they had been experienced only a short while before I'd met him. It was something of a baptism of fire for him when entering this new field but the flames' intensity weren't strong enough to dissuade Goodwin from continuing on the rocky road to securing his daughter's future.

'Not everyone in boxing is bad though. I recently went to the Southern Area for my manager's licence and afterwards Mick Collier, the head of the Southern Area, said I was a breath of fresh air. That was nice to hear. Most people who become promoters are from boxing. I am a financial advisor so I come from outside the world of boxing. We aren't cancered with the whole thing so in boxing I think everyone tries to steal from everybody because they think somebody is going to steal from them first. I've come from the outside as has Miranda Carter, who runs some Sunday shows. She comes across as a thoroughly decent human being.'

Goodwin's successful career as a financial advisor not only established him as a promoter with his business head screwed tightly on but also gave him the monetary foundations needed to set up Goodwin Promotions and enable him to confront the risks which face every promoter, regardless of media stature or banked profit. The list of shows in the sport's history which have collapsed, suffered poor ticket sales and those where the promoter has had to swallow the realisation that the occasional show won't net the expected profit, are plentiful and therefore accepted as something of an occupational hazard.

'I lost £8,000 on my last show, I lost £4,000 on an Audley Harrison fight [where the former Olympic champion scored a fourth-round win over another Goodwin fighter, Ali Adams] and I lost £4,000 on my last TV show so this year I have lost. However, what I did over the first two years was build the company up and invest a certain amount back into it. We did two TV shows so I am able to tolerate that. What I can't tolerate is investing in boxers and TV. If I'm investing in TV, I can't invest in the boxers. Realistically, I couldn't sustain losses indefinitely and I wouldn't want to do that. It's a case of make a bit, put a bit back in, make a bit and so on. We had our first show two years and nine months ago and I would say we have made massive strides in London. I consider myself just below the level of TV promoters. We've broken away from the ones underneath.'

A tactic used by Goodwin to encourage success at the gates is the allocation of tickets to the individual fighters who feature on his shows. 'Absolutely crucial at this stage,' Goodwin says without hesitation. 'A show with no TV and no advertising would cost roughly £12,000. That is including the ambulances, security etc. That money has to come from somewhere. That last show in Brentwood, we sold 11 tickets to the general public. The truth is the public don't buy unless you have a very big fight these days. Boxers are selling all the tickets. I have to recoup the £12,000 so you have to work out what fights you have and how much they could make. If we break even, we are doing ok at this level. If the boxers don't sell their tickets we have a problem. With reference to that manager who I said I would never work with again, I now ask to see the money the boxers have made from their tickets 48 hours before the fight. If you haven't sold, the fight's off. If their opponent is foreign, they don't fly. People now know they can't get away with it. If you don't like that, go and sign with someone who will tolerate it. I won't.'

The obstacles involved in selling tickets to the general public without using the influence of the individual fighters can be said to exist partly because of the numerous mismatches arranged to pad out a fighter's record and regurgitating fighters who have a household name but are simply no longer the force they once were. It is a tool used to attract the boxing spectator to shows where, while the winner will no doubt look highly impressive despatching his inferior foe, the winner will have been practically rubber-stamped from the moment the contracts were signed.

'You know who is going to win a lot of the time before the fight starts. One of my fighters, Lee Markham, was losing until the sixth round last Saturday when he landed a punch and knocked the guy out. The other fights were all 50-50 fights. Lower level, yes, but at least they're 50-50 fights. I watched Mikkel Kessler against Brian Magee. I mean, really? Magee had been knocked out by a body punch before so it was obvious Kessler would go there. This is the problem with boxing. Nobody is prepared to put out 50-50 fights. We get criticised. People say, "You're bringing in foreign imports. You should be giving the work to British journeymen." Why? British journeymen do not entertain the public. The fans get fed up watching it. Another fighter, Joe Mullender, had two fights against journeymen. This time I brought over a foreigner and he gave Joe trouble for two rounds and then he took over. Joe would have learnt something in that fight. The guy was outboxing him at the start but he stopped him in the fifth round. We have quality control with our foreign imports. I go over them and check them. I make sure they come here and won't just go over. They will put up a fight. If I show fighters who are going up to six rounds from four, I tell their managers that they are not having a journeyman bum. I am not having a six-round snoozefest on my show. Four rounds, yes, do as you wish. Six rounds, you will be stepped up on my shows.'

This determination to keep a clear conscience and urge to be known as an honest and open promoter is something which is unlikely to wane with time. He makes his intentions clear with everyone he deals with, thereby giving them the option to either work with him or go elsewhere where their ideals will be better suited.

'The first thing my attitude to my work will do is avoid the dodgy boxers who want to start lying to me. They know they won't be fighting so they don't come. What I do is, when the boxer sells, I pay really good money. I pay 50 per cent override on ticket sales. Other people pay ten per cent or 20 per cent. I get boxers who are on four-rounders who are earning around £3,500. They are well paid for over-selling. Our last show, we had a six-rounder who was paid £3,000. What I'm doing is attracting those who want to be looked after properly and want a fair deal. I saw another boxer who is with another promoter who sold 200 tickets and got paid £800. I'm totally transparent. I find that some people may not want to work with me because they make things difficult but you've just got to work within that. Listen, not everyone is bad. I recently had a foreign opponent who didn't want to fight. I phoned up Bruce Baker the manager and he got me one of his fighters almost straight away. He could have left me in the lurch but he didn't. He helped. I'm hoping eventually it all becomes transparent because it needs to be.'

Jack Solomons, the former British promoter who started hosting shows in the 1930s and whose résumé includes promoting Randolph Turpin's stunning world middleweight title victory against 'Sugar' Ray Robinson at Earl's Court in 1951, had one ideal which he stuck to unconditionally throughout his career. His shows would never be broadcast on national television. He wanted the proverbial bums on seats and anything that detracted viewers from walking into the boxing arena and planting their rears was seen as hugely detrimental to his way of working. Fast forward to the present day and this is a view respected and understood by Goodwin.

'My last show I sold just 11 tickets so my experience there is that is a negative. The people came to watch the fights but independent people said they'd just watch it on TV so not only am I paying £11,000 on TV production, I am also losing on ticket sales. While I have given them a taster of TV, that has got to be the taster over with. If they are not prepared to pay, I will go back to non-TV because they have at least got to cover the cost of production to move on. I can't suffer production and a 70–80 ticket loss at about £2,000–£3,000 which we would otherwise have got. It is a massive problem if you give TV but boxers have wanted TV exposure to become household names since the chicken and the egg. I think boxing on non-terrestrial TV is killing the sport because nobody knows who's who.'

While addressing the subject of fights benefitting the sport if shown on terrestrial TV, memories of me sitting in front of the TV with my brother at 2am to watch a live Mike Tyson world heavyweight title defence, presented by the likes of Dickie Davies, sprung to the forefront of my mind. Having become an avid follower of the sport during the early part of the 1980s, my passion for boxing was conceived and developed by watching such fighters as Lloyd Honeyghan, Barry McGuigan, Nigel Benn, Herol Graham, Frank Bruno, Kirkland Laing, Dennis Andries and many other household British names. All these were on terrestrial TV in the days prior to the media invasion into our living rooms of Sky television. Walking into your local convenience store and mentioning one of these names to the shopkeeper would most likely result in a measure of recognition, if not a passionately fought but well-spirited debate. Trying the same task these days could well leave them at a total loss.

The other, much-publicised, issue which results in the average boxing fan or indeed the general public not knowing 'who is who' in the boxing world is the multitude of 'world' titles on offer. Combining the various titles to be won with the lack of terrestrial TV coverage would seem to cause alienation between the sport and those who wish to, not only follow it, but also to make sense of it and have an idea who the real champions are and how they can be seen in action without the followers having to dig deep into their pockets.

'It's turned into a joke. They just invent title names now. They get sanctioning fees for making it a title fight but it means there may be no quality control over the opponents. On the world scene, there is the emeritus, the world and the interim. I've lost touch. It devalues world boxing. What titles ARE good for are for local boxers to sell more tickets. You have these titles but you will have one boxer fighting for one tomorrow and someone else fighting for the same one next weekend. It gives a title to a small-hall show but it's becoming diluted. Boxing needs a massive overhaul from top to bottom but that will probably never happen, both domestically and internationally.'

The idea of injecting alternative entertainment into his shows and offering the paying customer something alongside the boxing is something which Goodwin attaches significant importance to and plans are afoot to cater for a wider audience to attract higher numbers. The introduction of alcohol to the arena is a matter which Goodwin is also giving considerable thought to and the benefits to him are clear.

'I would like to see ringside tables with alcohol and the area done out with some plush carpeting. The rest of the hall is then for the standard ticket holders. The problem you have got, is you are not getting the corporates taking their clients out for a great evening because they know they're going to get a cramped bar. It's very difficult to get them in. You would just have to have an area put aside for them where they feel they are having a nice evening. They wouldn't necessarily take the seating space away from the hardcore boxing fans who may know more because boxing doesn't sell out so there is plenty of room for the corporates.'

Boxing fans have attracted, on the whole, good press and are not looked upon as groups of people who are constantly simmering and looking to square up to their opponent's followers. The atmosphere at any given boxing venue generally seems in high spirits and well-natured. Of course, there are always exceptions and the riots at the Alan Minter–Marvin Hagler world middleweight title fight at Wembley in 1980 is one such example but the ratio between those shows that remain peaceful and those that erupt into riotous behaviour must surely place boxing nearer the strawberries and cream of Wimbledon end of the disorder spectrum than, for example, many football matches. This is not to tarnish one complete sport with the same brush. After all, a number of champagne-fuelled horse racing fans participated in their own glad-rags at dawn fracas in 2011. What is inescapable is that boxing fans tend not to advance their rivalries with opposing fighters' fans beyond playful banter. Very rarely does disorder spill out into the streets after an evening's boxing and a police presence at a show is almost unheard of. The physical fighting is confined to within the roped square.

'We've done shows now for two and a half years and we've never had any trouble,' Goodwin says emphatically. 'They can get rowdy but that's it. Things get rowdy in football and other sports but with boxing it doesn't go beyond that.'

The ultimate ambition of Goodwin is to feather the promotional nest for his daughter, Olivia. With her wish of boxing promotion clearly stated during her illness, her father was clear where their respective strengths lay and where each of them could most benefit the partnership. 'My better skills are going to be in the management side. I don't want too many boxers. I want a selection but my skills are better served in management.'

His heavyweight protégé, Ian Lewison, is a fighter where Goodwin's management skills have appeared to flourish. 'Ian Lewison, who was ranked four in the world in the amateurs, was going nowhere,' Goodwin told me in earnest. 'I sorted out a new trainer for him, I speak to him regularly and try to motivate him and organise him. I'm good at relating to them and being honest with people. "Come on, that's not good enough!" After his first fight with me, I went round to see him at his home in Brixton and sat with him. I said to him, "If you don't do what I'm telling you, I'm firing you. This is not good enough and you are letting yourself down." He is now getting there so I believe my role is that of a straight-talking people person. Olivia likes to do all the promotion with all of these different ideas. That will be her role.'

In a sport that is historically, and in all probability always will be, male-dominated, Olivia would appear to be up against some stiff opposition. On the 'London's Calling' show, however, she seemed to project an impressive air of confidence and this enabled her to produce an attention-grabbing spectacle with her female dancers. Regardless of one's views on such things, what could not be denied was the effect this alternative source of entertainment had on the crowd. It was positively received and is an accurate mark of what the paying customer is willing to fork out for. Her impressive conception into the boxing world has laid the foundations for a future whereby she could be seen as a force for other promoters to treat with sincerity and also to reckon with.

'She is really polite but she will not stand nonsense from anybody,' her father states. 'She is the best friend in the world to her friends but if she hears one talking badly about another she will have them coming together to talk about it. There is no back-stabbing. I'm not either. We do the face-to-face thing and I've brought my kids up to do the same.'

There have been women in the sport who have reached the dizzy heights and have garnered worldwide acclaim with their male counterparts. Kathy Duva, the current CEO of Main Events Promotions in the USA, is an example of a woman launching herself into a testosterone-riddled minefield and being more than equipped to handle the pressures and obstacles it brings. In an article in 2007, Duva explained what one of her most effective tactics is in order to survive and be heard. With the loud, boisterous and extroverted demeanour of Don King, for example, Duva will wait patiently until the frenzied poetry-reciting, history-quoting and sometimes personally offensive typhoon has petered out before quietly asking if he 'is done yet'. One big plus side to being a female promoter, Duva stated, is the chivalrous act of her male associates footing the bill when going out on business!

'Olivia believes she will be up there in the next ten years,' Goodwin says. 'I'm building a really good plan. We have boxers coming to us all the time and I am able to take on the ones I want. I helped Tony Conquest get that fight with Leon Williams [which Conquest won conclusively in the first round]. That is what you get to be known for and in time more and more people will get to know that you are like that. You can then build up.'

In terms of his current stable of fighters, one fighter stands out in Goodwin's eyes. One fighter who, given the right encouragement, could go far enough to propel Goodwin Promotions to the next level. 'The one that COULD take us into the big time is Ian Lewison. He promised me this in May, "I am going to do for you what Lennox Lewis did for Frank Maloney." Let's see. He was ranked fourth in the world in the amateurs. He beat Odlanier Solis and Robert Helenius. He fought David Price in the ABA finals and lost a contentious decision. The thing with Lewison is, you can't manage him softly. He turned up late for the weigh-in on Saturday. I sent him a text yesterday that said, "When I give you a deadline, you are to make that deadline. You are never to be late again." I gave him a rollicking and he sent me an apology.'

With that, Steve Goodwin was off to his next appointment. Like he states at the end of his company's social media updates, 'We never stop.'

Since I met Goodwin, Ian Lewison took part in the Prizefighter tournament at the York Hall on 23 February 2013. While he got pipped in the semi-finals to Derric Rossy on points, he registered a stunning first-round win over the 49-fight German veteran, Timo Hoffman. Being a series of three-round fights, the well-established Prizefighter tournament leads many fighters to adopt a more aggressive stance without the worry of having their endurance called into question. While the tactics may differ from those used in a longer scheduled fight, the truth remains that Lewison destroyed a fighter who went 12 rounds with Vitali Klitschko, Henry Akinwande, Paolo Vidoz and Frans Botha and registered wins over useful names such as Mike Dixon, Michael Sprott and Ross Purrity.

With Lewison reaching for the elevated status previously enjoyed by Lennox Lewis and Goodwin being the force behind his daughter's rise through the ranks along with Josh, his son who is also making his mark in the world of boxing promotion, the future of Goodwin Promotions appears bright. While it may not become a one-horse race in years to come, one gets the hunch it could draw neck and neck with some of its more experienced competitors.

5

James Cook

STANDING outside the Pedro Club on Rushmore Road in east London's Hackney borough, I looked at the various pieces of graffiti scrawled on the outside walls to the entrance of the site. However, this wasn't graffiti of the criminal type where the perpetrator shakes and sprays his aerosol while deploying the senses for approaching sirens or police officers. In adjoining Gilpin Square, there is indeed a neighbourhood police office so only the foolhardy would brave such a thing. This, more importantly, was specific street art, brilliantly displayed within a designated area next to the main entrance. One particular mural screamed from the brick and mortar, 'SAY NO TO GUNS AND KNIVES OR SUFFER THE CONSEQUENCES.' This wasn't nonsensical scribbling on the sides of tube trains and neglected, derelict buildings. This art portrayed a positive message, illustrated by the area's youthful population, the part of society most exposed and vulnerable to the dark and criminal influences that exist in the world of street crime and gang culture. A father figure to provide a stable platform for youngsters to look up to and respect is much needed to compensate for the amount of broken homes and deprived childhoods in the area and the benefits of the Pedro Club and what it offers strives to achieve just this. At its helm is the former Southern Area middleweight and European and two-time British super-middleweight champion, James Cook.

Founded in 1929 by Baroness Harwood, the Pedro Club has become something of a byword for the regeneration of a particularly deprived area of Hackney and also for the refocusing of the local youths' outlook on life and offering the opportunity to make constructive use of their time. The club was temporarily revived in the 1960s with the support of Dame Elizabeth Taylor but upon facing a subsequent generation of neglect, James Cook formed a new management committee and re-opened the club in 1993. In 2006, the club received a golden handshake as a result of being approached by the Channel 4 show's covert entrepreneur, the Secret Millionaire. The £20,000 donated to the club was used to construct a music studio. Cook's commitment to the club and his arduous efforts to bring about a sense of self-worth and well-being to the local communities was awarded with an invitation to attend Buckingham Palace in 2007 to receive an MBE from the Queen for services to Youth Justice in Hackney.

'That was a shock!' Cook said with a wide grin. 'When that letter come and I read it to my missus and it said, "I'm your servant," I chucked it inside the bin! I thought it was someone playing games. When the press and the boxing board started to phone me up, I thought it could be true so I went inside the bin searching for it! She was the only lady that frightened me. The leader of the country and she was asking me about three questions and I said, "Please ma'am, don't ask me no more because I'm so nervous!" I was sweating and she was shaking my hand. She was great and she told me that the area needed someone like me.'

Cook led me into his club where he poured me a coffee from behind a bar in the games recreation room. It was a welcoming sight. Not just the coffee, after my typically stressful rail journey up from Kent, but also what the club offers. The club was closed on this day but I could envisage it teeming with youths making the most of the games and other facilities on offer; not least the boxing ring set aside off the main area. The former champion then led me into his office which is a shrine to the sport he excelled in. Memorabilia of his fights adorn the walls, piles of boxing-related correspondence cover the furniture and his trophies and cups take up whatever room is left. The smile that is permanently stretched almost from ear to ear is evidence that you have one of those rare individuals who works to live as much as he lives to work. The passion is unmistakable.

James Cook was born and brought up in his native Jamaica under the watchful eye of his grandmother after his parents left the Caribbean island for Britain when Cook was very young. He recalls these early years in Jamaica with fondness and poignancy.

'The upbringing was very strict. You had to be suited and booted at school and the teachers would be waiting at the gates running a comb through your hair. At nine and a half I remember being so bright before I come to London that when I come the education system had so much time to play that the work went out of the window for a while. Jamaica was so strict. My mum left me pretty early when I was one or something like that to come here and look for jobs with my dad. I was brought up by my granny. When my mum came to look for me, my granny said, "James, your mum is coming over to take you to England." I said, "England? You crazy gran." I remember people saying that England was a cold place and I didn't want to go to that cold country. I remember stoning my mum when she come. I was actually flinging stones at my mum telling her I didn't want to go over there!

'On my last day at school, I said to the guys, "After school, let's try and trouble the teachers!" They said, "No, no, no, you're crazy, we'll get into trouble tomorrow morning." I knew I was flying out to England the next day so I said, "Nah, come on, let's do it!" I remember flinging stones at the teachers as they drove past after school. In the evening we sat round a fire and they said, "What's going to happen tomorrow morning?" I looked at them and said, "I'm flying to England!" I wouldn't think we're friends now!' He laughed at the mischief of his schoolboy antics. 'I got into trouble the next day with the weather though, when I was flying to England!'

While his move to England led to a successful career as a boxer, he had initial reservations about leaving Jamaica, the close-knit family environment of his birthplace still holding a special place in his heart. 'My fondest memory was something like when Easter or Christmas comes. It seems like people got together to enjoy themselves and at them times you will probably get extra food. Even if your parents or grandparents were struggling, there always seemed to be extra food on the table. Family and friends would all get together and holiday and festival times were my favourite. I was always running around and doing things. That's why I said when I come over to London, the education for me for a while went out the window because I used to play football, I used to play cricket for my school, I used to play rugby for my school. I always thought I would play rugby or athletics here!'

The eldest of his siblings, Cook became the brother to another three boys and two girls who were all born in England. The attraction to boxing wasn't solely with the eldest sibling. His last brother also tried his luck in the ring.

'My last brother, Brian Cook, had one professional fight and won [a second-round stoppage to one Peter Cannon in December 2009 at Caesars nightclub in Streatham, south-west London]. We lost my mother last year and it kind of upset him a bit so he hasn't had no fights since. He was the only one. The rest of them were football or cricket. My other brother was a centre for football. He has six sons and one plays for

Colchester and two just signed up for Arsenal, one who has signed as a goalkeeper at 17! I started the boxing in my family. My dad used to be a very, very good cricketer back in the West Indies. People would say he would win matches with his bowling. My father was a skinny bloke. He only weighed about eight stone. I remember him coming over and I used to test my dad with running. He was not a bad runner!'

Being a naturally sporty and athletic pupil at school, concentrating on rugby, cricket and football, the switch to boxing was a sudden occurrence. 'It kind of fell by mistake. It wasn't that I wanted to do boxing. I was playing other sports but a friend of mine asked me to go to a boxing club. We went to Manor Place Baths in Elephant and Castle. I went over there when I was about ten. I was very tall for my age. I saw this skinny little white kid so after being offered a spar, I climbed into the ring and this kid beat the shit out of me. I picked up my bags and told the kid I'd be back for him. I forgot about boxing for a while for about three or four months. A mate of mine told me there was a gym closing down in Camberwell Green. We went down there messing around and my trainer who ended being my proper trainer, Jimmy Redgwell, showed me little things and he said to me, "You know, you're not bad at this." My name was in the press and I thought, "I kind of like this sport!"'

In my experience of speaking with fighters to establish what the reaction was of their loved ones to their decision to step inside the boxing ring, a recurring pattern emerged. The father tended to be full of encouragement, willing their child to learn how to look after himself and to develop self-confidence. The mother, on the other hand, would almost retreat into a state of denial, finding it increasingly difficult to accept the reality that her son was willing to give and take punches and risk physical harm as a means of securing an income. The only acknowledgement would come during endless tense hours at home waiting for that call from her son to tell her that the fight was over and that he and his opponent were unhurt and able to live to fight another day. Watching the fight, either at the venue or on television, was not a favoured option. In James Cook's case the script, to an extent, wasn't read.

'I'm going to be honest, my dad was kind of a placid guy. Anything you do, he never said much. He was very quiet. Mum, she was the same thing. I remember bringing mum to me fighting in my first div's inside Manor Place Baths and I remember I was about 16 or 17 and I was walking towards the ring and it was the first time my mum and my auntie went to a fight. The guy looked big you know! I was inside the ring and my mum was coming up with her brolly. I turned round to her and said, "MUM!" She never went back to a boxing match! They were pretty quiet. Proud but quiet. The bully of my family was probably my mum. She was the one who teach the discipline. Dad was very placid. If mum says, "Leave that 'til your father comes, dad will beat you," dad would just say, "Don't do that again!" Mum would get upset but he was just that type of guy.'

After participating in two London Amateur Boxing Association tournaments, in which he was defeated both times by Johnny Graham, the decision to turn his eye to the professionals was strongly encouraged by Jimmy Redgwell.

'To be quite honest, I didn't know nothing about going pro, turning pro or getting paid for it. I remember Hal Hamilton who used to be with Frank Bruno at the time. Hal says to me, "There's a guy in Hackney who want to go pro," His name was Billy Winter and I didn't know nothing about Billy Winter and I says to him, "What do you mean turn pro?" He said, "You get paid. You get money." So that is when I went over. I like to think I am a fair judge of my fights and I remember the first time I fought for the London ABA's and Johnny Graham beat me on points, I didn't think he won it. The next year when I won the south-east division, I met him again in the ABAs and again he beat me on points and Jimmy Redgwell told me that I'd may as well get paid for it if I'm going to be robbed! I realised that Mickey Duff and Terry Lawless were looking at this Johnny Graham as a good amateur which didn't really mean nothing to me but I thought if I'm to beat this Johnny Graham I might have to knock him out. My mind was then set. I went pro and went with Billy Winter.'

With his reasons for going pro clear and with a team behind him who he knew well, James Cook emerged from the sport's amateur shadow and entered the paid ranks. Almost immediately, life as a professional taught him something altogether unexpected.

'We was up the gym training and I was sparring with Mick Courtney and me and Mickey was always sparring together. I got a call from Billy Winter and he said, "You're fighting tonight!" I asked who I was fighting and he said it was Mick Courtney. I said, "But we spar together." He turned to me and said, "So you're going to let your sparring partner beat you then?" This was the first time I started to realise that it doesn't matter if you spar together, you may end up fighting each other. We went to the show and I think he put me down and I put him down but I beat him but I realised that things like this can happen.'

The amateur side to the sport and the professional side have many differences, not least the scheduled duration of the fights that see the combatants duel over three two-minute rounds as an amateur with the extra protection of headgear (though there is a credible argument to suggest that headgear may minimise damage to the outer tissue of a boxer's head but the damage and impact upon the brain and other inter-cranial structures is no less affected). The fitness levels, training programmes and the styles of fighting are significant changes that can impact upon the fight's outcome.

'They are definitely different. I always saw myself as a good runner, very good inside a gym but when I went inside a gym as a pro and watching other people punching the bag, doing their groundwork and running for an hour, I thought, "This is what I got to do!" I started to do that and it's a massive difference and if you fell short you were in trouble. I thought my stamina was good. It wasn't too good in the early fights and my uppercut came to rescue me. Even then when I think I'm fit, the sort of opponent I was getting had been there and had been experienced and I probably didn't expect to win these fights. I realised that there were a lot of differences in what you got to do.'

With his professional career up and running, Cook racked up two more victories before facing a debutant in Jimmy Price. On 3 February 1983, Cook entered the ring in Bloomsbury's Crest Hotel and ended up losing a six-round decision after being floored in the third round. Price had been a two-time ABA champion, firstly in 1980 when he defeated Nick Wilshire in the light-middleweight final and then again two years later when he defeated Cy Harrison in the middleweight final. An impressive amateur pedigree garnered him a professional debut against James Cook. While referee Tony Walker scored the fight 59.5-58 in Price's favour, it was a decision which was believed to have gone to the wrong fighter according to Cook, an opinion which was to be held on numerous occasions throughout his career when various points decisions went against him in tightly-fought contests where the verdicts could have gone either way without the cause for outrage. 'The first fight I lost to Jimmy Price on points. Actually, I didn't think Jimmy Price won the fight. Then I realised he was with a big promoter, he'd won the ABAs and I knew that if I didn't knock him down I wouldn't get the win. I didn't think he won it.'

After defeating the comparable 38-fight veteran Willie Wright in his next fight on points over eight rounds, Cook brushed aside Croydon's Dudley McKenzie over eight rounds in what was to prove McKenzie's final professional fight. His next opponent was the experienced Eddie Smith. Smith had been once around the block in boxing terms and then for a few surplus laps. In 1978, he recorded an eighth-round knockout over future British and Commonwealth middleweight champion Roy Gumbs and a points win over another future British and Commonwealth middleweight champion Tony Sibson. Sibson also held the European middleweight title and challenged for separate portions of the world middleweight title twice and once for the light-heavyweight title. Sharing the ring with the likes of Tom Collins, Chisanda Mutti and Mark Kaylor suggested Cook was in for a hard test. Cook dismantled Smith in six rounds to bring about the referee's intervention. Smith subsequently went on to fight the likes of Jimmy Price and Pierre-Frank Winterstein before his career was terminated by way of a first-round knockout at the destructive hands of one Nigel Benn.

Two fights later, Cook found himself contesting the vacant British Boxing Board of Control Southern Area middleweight title against the unbeaten Tony Jenkins. The fight took place at the Royal Albert Hall in what was also an eliminator for the British middleweight title held by Mark Kaylor. It was a thoroughly controlled performance by Cook who measured his opponent in a tentative beginning before unloading with right hands to ultimately wear down the Brentford fighter to force referee Harry Gibbs's intervention. The fight was stopped in the ninth round after Cook's dominance was capped with two knockdowns in the final round. Now on something of a roll, a rematch with Jimmy Price was set up for the Empire Pool at Wembley on 25 September 1984 so Cook could set the record straight. 'The second time we fought, my mind was just set to go out there and hit him. That was my mindset. Every time that happened I get hit! My mindset was not to go out there and feel around as you do. He beat me so I want to give it back. I went to attack and as soon as I reach him, I got caught,' Cook said, as he slammed his fist into his palm and a subtle sign of a guilty smirk stretched the corners of his mouth.

Seeking revenge for an earlier amateur loss to Conrad Oscar, Cook stepped into the ring with him to defend his Southern Area middleweight title in London's Queensway. Oscar's professional career to date had been unflattering with a patchy résumé of seven wins, four losses and one draw. At the end of ten rounds, revenge was indeed Cook's. Despite touching down with a glove when cuffed with a left hook in the second round, Cook appeared to break away from the halfway point to register what appeared to be a surprisingly tight 98.5-98 score from referee Harry Gibbs.

Five months later, on 2 October 1985, he suffered a shock loss to Tony Burke by a second-round knockout to lose his Southern Area title and this brought about a change of heart and Cook brought on board Darkie Smith. His first two contests with his new trainer took place in March 1986. The first saw him travel to Cologne, Germany to face the unbeaten Graciano Rocchigiani. Participating in just his 16th fight, Rocchigiani would go on to become the IBF super-middleweight champion (a title he never lost in the ring) and the European and WBC light-heavyweight champion. Wins over world champions Thulane Malinga and Michael Nunn proved his calibre. Throw in a brace of fights with each of his compatriots, Henry Maske and Dariusz Michalczewski, and the level and quality of opposition that Cook sought to test himself against is only too apparent. Rocchigiani took an eight-round decision over Cook but it was, not surprisingly, a fight Cook believed he did enough to win. 25 days later, he travelled west to challenge the Dutchman and future European light-heavyweight champion Jan Lefeber. He was defeated in three rounds.

'Going abroad to fight these guys made me become a man. I realised you have to be tough you know. I had to go into their back yard. I put Lefeber down and then went over to him to congratulate him on a tough fight and then he hits me with a right hand and the referee looks at me and says he didn't end the fight! This was all learning stuff! It was the pro game and it was holding me in good stride. When I moved to Hackney I was reading about how good Michael Watson was. He's young and he's talented but I was quite happy with it because I realised I was not abroad. I'm over here!'

The Michael Watson fight was signed and confirmed for Wembley Arena on 20 May as a supporting bout to Duke McKenzie's fifth-round win over the European flyweight champion Charlie Magri. Also on that bill were a host of future stars including Lloyd Honeyghan, Chris Pyatt and Gary Mason. With just seven fights under his belt, Watson hadn't yet enjoyed the experience and valuable tuition of fighting abroad. The fight itself was a closely contested, gruelling affair with Cook edging the verdict with a big effort over the final couple of rounds.

'At the time, I think Mickey Duff looked at it and said that I was on my way out. I'd had these losses. I think I was still rated so it would be a good win for Michael. I said to Michael, "Listen, you can have your mum, your dad, your uncle, your auntie, you can have them all in the living room as referee and judge but I will still beat you." That was the biggest word I ever said to Michael. I remember, we used to train on Finsbury Park and we would try and avoid each other. Later, I said to Michael, "Beat Chris Eubank for us and we'll have that return," but then the accident happened. The fight with Michael was a tough fight. I knew I had to win it clearly as Michael was the up and coming guy. I had to perform well. I never realised how tough he was. I did hit him with some good shots and he was still standing up there.'

Nine months later, Cook travelled overseas yet again, this time to France to face the French-based Congolese boxer Mbayo Wa Mbayo. Two fights prior, Wa Mbayo had been defeated by Nick Wilshire on points, the same fighter who had lost to Jimmy Price in the 1980 ABA light-middleweight final. This fight also proved to be a frustrating night for the British boxer as Wa Mbayo got up on his toes and kept his distance to record an eight-round points decision win. 'I didn't think he was that good. I didn't think he really beat me. I knew by past experience that if I didn't knock out these guys I wasn't going to win. I got this into my head.'

Yet another learning experience which pushed Cook's tenacity to its limits was round the corner. He plumped for Italy as the fight's location and in the other corner stood the American, Willie Wilson. A scheduled eight-rounder, Cook returned to his corner after the fifth to hear some advice from his trainer which changed his approach to the fight. 'It was supposed to be an eight-rounder, I came over to Darkie Smith and he said, "They'll give you the same money if you let it be six but you're behind on points!" I said, "Don't worry, I'm gonna get him!" In the sixth round I knocked him out with an uppercut!'

Twenty-four days later, he appeared in the ring again in Finland to take on the unremarkable Tarmo Uusivirta. Again, the circumstances were unusual and the verdict was seen as disputable. 'We went over there to an ice-rink and they laid a carpet on the rink for the fight. After ten rounds, people were asking about the weather because he was sweating and I wasn't. We were trying to work up a sweat. He beat me but once again I didn't think he won the fight. I was just going forward like I did with the rest. I was getting into the groove and if you didn't get rid of me early, I know you're not going to go 12 rounds.'

In the three years between September 1984 and October 1987, Cook had built a record of six losses with just three victories. While Cook would like to state that these were the official recorded outcomes of the bouts, he disputes four of the losses with some element of legitimacy. The points losses to Rocchigiani, Wa Mbayo and Uusivirta were contentious in the sense that they were fairly evenly contested so an argument could have been made for either fighter with some justification, while Cook will tell you the Lefeber knockout was down to sheer miscommunication between himself and the third man in the ring. Disputable or not, contentious or not, the records stay the same and to progress to the level on which Cook was adamant he belonged, the win column needed to start leaving the loss column spluttering in its wake.

'My attitude started to change at this time. If I'm losing these fights abroad, obviously I was telling myself I'd knock them out. So my attitude was, if any British fighter beat me, they'd be lucky or good but I said I don't mind losing abroad because I know now how tough it is to win there. Over here now, anybody fight me and can't stop me before the end, I'm going to get them. I will stop them before the end. Now, a promoter or manager would take about six months or a year to get a fight for me. Somebody may think somebody will beat me before any fight come on you know. I'd be in the gym for six months or a year, running, training, sparring, just waiting for someone to pick up the phone and give me a fight. I used to run from here to Camberwell Green and then go to work so it was a sign of my toughness and attitude, since I can't get any learning fight, I gotta be ready anytime.'

In a routine, but unusually straightforward bout with Cliff Curtis at Basildon's Festival Hall in April 1988, Cook scored a fourth-round stoppage and moved on to challenge for the vacant British middleweight title against Herol 'Bomber' Graham on 8 June 1988. The *Boxing News* preview confidently predicted that Graham had beaten opponents who could both box and punch better than Cook and that the fight should be over in the Sheffield fighter's favour within the first half of the fight. It would also state how this would in all likelihood be the only British title chance he'd ever get. Time would determine the accuracy of this final statement. This was Graham's chance to win the British middleweight title for a second time after he knocked out Cook's old nemesis, Jimmy Price, in the first round to claim it the first time back in 1985.

'What I expected to happen was that if Herol Graham didn't stop me within the 12 rounds, I'd stop him. I knew I was fighting the best man in the country. At the time, Elephant and Castle had an escalator and I would run up and down. That was my mentality for that fight. If Graham didn't stop me, I'd get him before 12 rounds. I looked at Graham and thought there is no way he's going to catch me with those southpaw moves. I thought that if anybody drop their hands in front of me like he would, they'd get knocked out. I knew I could punch and I was quick. As I learnt though, he wasn't as easy as it looked! It was then that, if I'm to be honest, I knew I wasn't at that level. Barry Hearn said to me, "If you beat Graham, I'll make you a millionaire!" A couple of years down the line, I turned to Barry and said, "Well I'm champion now, you going to pay me the money?!" I think I got about £10,000 for that fight. The Graham fight was an experience for me and I said after that if another British fighter beat me, I'd retire. He was number one in the world then I think and I was unable to go 12 rounds with him so I said if I lose to another British fighter I'd retire. I'm still in touch with him. I saw him last week and we're good friends.'

The fight itself proved *Boxing News* to be accurate in its prediction. Graham fought an aggressive fight, flooring Cook twice legitimately and other times through pushing or mauling him to the floor. It was a generally scrappy performance by Graham but one which he ultimately won relatively comfortably.

For Cook, it was a case of rebuilding his stature after the defeat and a fifth-round win over the faded one-time hot prospect, Errol Christie, gave him a boost which, going by a letter he wrote to *Boxing News* which was printed in the 9 June 1989 issue, did his confidence no damage at all. Four months after the Christie fight, a huge tent was erected in Finsbury Park and former Cook victim Michael Watson stepped into the ring to challenge for the Commonwealth middleweight title against the devastatingly powerful Nigel Benn. With the general consensus within the fight fraternity being that Benn would add to his fearsome reputation with another chillingly conclusive early knockout, Watson fought the tactically perfect fight to weather the Benn tornado and move in for the finish after six pulsating rounds of back and forth action. The letter was an invitation for Watson to put straight the one blemish on his record. 'I was a better fighter than Watson at the time of our match and I STILL am today,' Cook wrote.

He stated that he approached Watson's camp after the Benn fight to issue a challenge and that if inexperience was the reason for his loss in their first fight, he could now step up to the plate with a subsequent three years' experience under his belt. The challenge was not accepted and the situation didn't change. They didn't fight again.

In September 1989, Cook posted a fifth-round stoppage over Liverpool's former Central Area light-heavyweight champion, Brian Schumacher. It would be little over one whole year before he would step into the ring again. When he did, it was to challenge Sam Storey for the British super-middleweight title, proving wrong the earlier prophecy by *Boxing News* that the Graham fight would likely be the only chance for a British title Cook would receive. Storey had beaten Cook's former conqueror, Tony Burke, and had defended it once against Noel Magee. His sole defeat had been against the former Irish, USBA, WBO middleweight and super-middleweight champion Steve Collins.

'One year in the gym waiting for that fight was unbelievable. Everybody had a warm-up for a fight. I wasn't getting a warm-up. I had to stay in a gym here in Hackney. I was going to work, back and forward. I was told that I couldn't get a warm-up fight as I may get cut. Everybody was worried about the southpaw thing but it didn't faze me. This was probably the first time I trained for a fight with southpaw sparring. I went over to Belfast with Barney Eastwood and the hotel we were staying in, we were woken up in the morning and told there was a Semtex bomb in the hotel. This was my preparation for the Storey fight! The only guns I'd seen up to this point was what I'd seen on TV. I'd never seen guns that close to me. The tanks and guns were following you down the street and the only time I felt at ease was when Barney Eastwood told them that we were boxers. That was the only time I felt sort of uncomfortable you know.'

The fight was described in *Boxing News* as 'a perfectly executed upset victory' and informed the reader that Cook's sights had been targeted towards the European championship. The fight was terminated by referee Mickey Vann in the tenth round after Cook had levelled Storey with a huge right uppercut. 'Even when I won, I did not want to celebrate because I didn't want to disturb anyone. In the morning when I was at the airport, these two big Irish guys come over to me and they says to me, "I see you!" I thought, "Oh hell no!" They said they'd seen the fight on TV and they bought me an enormous bottle of whiskey so it wasn't too bad!'

Winning his first British title was rewarded with a shot at the vacant European super-middleweight title the following March against Frenchman Pierre-Frank Winterstein in his own back yard of Paris. Winterstein had been a former French middleweight champion and held wins over former Cook conqueror Tony Burke, and former three-time British and two-time European light-heavyweight champion and two-time world light-heavyweight title challenger Tom Collins. Home territory combined with the mistaken belief that the number of losses on Cook's record showed him to be a severely limited operator was enough to install Winterstein as the favourite to lift the title. The fight had been postponed by ten days to allow the French Gypsy to recover from a bout of flu.

This was a fight he wanted to win impressively in front of his supporters without leaving anything to chance. What he hadn't bargained for was his opponent developing at a similar rate to that of a fine vintage wine. To use the oft-used cliché, he simply improved with age. The wisdom and knowledge gained from years of plugging away and taking on all-comers in all corners of the continent proved priceless. Winterstein had unfortunately become known as someone who would favour the softer opponents unlike Cook who relished the thought of a hard test. This attitude tended to alienate himself from many potential Gypsy followers. Indeed, the arena sold less than 1,000 tickets for the event.

'Winterstein wasn't the guy I was supposed to fight in the first place. I think that fight got switched somewhere along the line. I was supposed to box somebody else. On the plane I was reading about this guy with this record and I sat down and thought, "Damn, they've sent me out here to get killed!" When we sat down inside the hotel, one of the cleaners went up to me and said, "Don't eat inside the hotel." I went for a walk around the corner and found something to eat there. My trainer, who ate in the hotel, had the runs all day!

'Frank Maloney was out there and I thought to myself that winning the British title made me feel I had to go in there with a game-plan. The game plan was to box him and as soon as he came in to throw a big punch, hit him with a jab just to check him. I must admit I was doing so well up until the ninth round when I got put down. To be honest I didn't see the punch at all. All I can say is thank God for the referee [Daniel Van de Wiele]. He didn't jump in to stop the fight. He did give me a fair chance. He count me, let me get up and carry on with my job.'

With a steady workrate, nullifying the Frenchman's respectable power, Cook went into a lead and by the halfway point he was dominating the flow of the fight. Towards the end of the ninth round, Cook was caught by a swinging left hook which opened the way for a follow-up volley from Winterstein which dumped Cook down by the ropes. As he got up and was waved back in, the bell went to save him from a further barrage. Cook went straight back in during the tenth to reassert his dominance and aside from the occasional big shot getting through to his chin, he took over and finally brought the curtain down on Winterstein's effort with a blistering combination topped with a huge right uppercut which put his opponent down for the count.

'That was my pet punch. The right uppercut! People expected him to win the fight and he had a party laid on for after the fight. Winning the fight they invited me to the party. I remember going inside the room and saying, "He's not coming." There were a lot of people who got upset on the night. From what I have seen in and around boxing, win or lose, people will congratulate you and shake your hand but a lot of people outside the venue got up and I remember somebody, his manager maybe, said to the referee, "You cost me the fight because you counted for too long," so automatically I think they think I went over to make up the numbers!'

On winning the European title, Cook was closing in on a possible world title fight and the reigning WBA champion Victor Cordoba from Panama was eyed up as the potential opponent. 'Barney Eastwood had this guy, Cordoba and there were deals flying around. Like £30,000 for three defences. If I beat Cordoba why would you want me for three defences? I wouldn't mind giving him one defence but not three. The European title was like MY world title so I just didn't like the deal.'

Former British and Commonwealth middleweight champion Mark Kaylor was the choice for Cook's first European title defence. It was a classic match-up between the technical ability of the champion against the battle-hardened blood and guts style of Kaylor. Having 47 fights at that stage against Cook's 24, Kaylor had the advantage in age by two years. Kaylor had, however, been through the relative who's who of the country's middleweights and light-heavyweights. In fights against the likes of Roy Gumbs, Buster Drayton, Tony Sibson, Errol Christie, Herol Graham, Tom Collins and Mauro Galvano, he had picked up valuable experience but the feeling now was that he was on the wrong side of the hill and that years of tough brawls had taken their toll. And so it proved.

The fight was a clinical display by the champion who found his opponent easy to catch with jabs and hard crosses from the start. Kaylor never seemed to stop punching back but it was more like someone struggling to stay afloat when entering deep water than someone who was convinced they still had what it took to win. Kaylor's trainer Jimmy Tibbs threw in the towel in the sixth round to signal the surrender to referee Mickey Vann. Not only was Kaylor retired from the fight, he also bid an emotional farewell to the sport shortly after.

Cook was now looking ahead to his second European title defence against old adversary and conqueror, Tarmo Uusivirta. With a new lease of life coming about from signing a new managerial contract with Mickey Duff, having previously been with Harry Holland, Cook went about defending his crown in style. Opting to trade blows with Uusivirta throughout, fortunes swayed one way, then the other as each took it in turns to land hurtful blows. Cook's uppercut again played a key role in the contest, jerking Uusivirta's head back on his shoulders but then leaving himself open to countering shots which would momentarily shake the champion and lead to pleas from his corner to box more and not get too heavily involved. Ultimately, Cook ground the resistance out of the Finn and after almost a minute gone in round seven, the challenger turned his back and surrendered. For the second fight running, Cook's opponent announced his retirement from the sport. However, while

Mark Kaylor stayed retired, Uusivirta would come back for one more fight the following year to defeat the American Shannon Landberg on points over eight rounds, if only to go out with a win.

'My state of mind was if you beat me, I'm gonna get you back. I didn't think he beat me fairly so I went out to get revenge. I knew if he couldn't get me within five rounds, he'd be in trouble. I had good stamina and I will fight you from one to 12.'

After this fight, Mickey Duff announced that he would try to get a world title challenge with WBC champion Mauro Galvano of Italy for Cook. There were also whispers prior to the fight that the IBF champion, Darrin Van Horn, would be another route to pursue.

It was therefore a calculated risk that Cook and his team decided to plump with another trip to France on 3 April 1992 to face the unbeaten but largely untested Franck Nicotra. Unbeaten in 27 outings, the Frenchman had fought few fighters that would be deemed impressive on national level, let alone European level so while a largely unknown quantity, it was expected that another successful defence for Cook on his way to a world title fight was on the cards. Cook's previous manager, Harry Holland, had already been offered a world title fight for Cook, only for his fighter to opt instead on defending his European title. It was a decision which must have haunted Cook in the immediate aftermath of this fight as he had his treasured European crown ripped from his head in just over one minute of the first round. 'I'll be honest. I saw him fight a sparring partner of mine, Ray Webb. I thought this guy doesn't have anything on me. Anyway, I had a phone call the night before the fight that my mum was in hospital so all I wanted to do was go in and hit him and go home. I saw him look fierce and his girlfriend was at ringside in tears. Everything I learnt as a pro just went out the window. I just wanted to hit him and go home. I went out there and he got me.'

Cook was caught and floored with a big right cross almost immediately and he never fully recovered. He tried to retaliate after the first knockdown but two more knockdowns in rapid succession was enough for referee Marcel Roleau to wave the fight, and Cook's reign, over. Nicotra proved to be no 'flash-in-the-pan' champion. He went on to stop Ray Close, who would go on to claim the European title and take Chris Eubank to a draw and a split decision in two challenges for the WBO super-middleweight title, in eight rounds in his first and last defence. For Cook, it was back to the drawing board and the process to build himself back up into title contention developed with four routine wins over Tony Booth, Terry Magee, Carlos Christie and Karl Barwise over the next year. Cook was now in line to contest the vacant British super-middleweight title against Fidel Castro Smith, formerly known as Slugger O'Toole.

'Every time I lose a fight, I had to go back to the gym to work harder and harder. At this stage, everything was getting harder. I'd always freaked about Slugger O'Toole, thinking he was a white Irish guy and then I looked at him and saw a black guy! It was hard because I lost the world ranking and the European title which, like I said, was MY world title. I wanted the Commonwealth title which was held by Henry Wharton. He was managed by Mickey Duff so he wouldn't let me fight him.'

It was a fight which lacked the sparkle of many of Cook's more impressive performances. It contained a lot of holding and missing but while Cook's workrate may have been slightly busier, the Nottingham fighter appeared to have done enough as he looked to have dictated the pace with his more measured hitting. A more committed effort over the home stretch of the fight by Cook, however, ended up being the deciding factor in cementing referee John Coyle's score of 118.5-117. Many felt the decision was unjust to Smith.

'After fighting Slugger I said to Mickey, "I need a defence of the title." Cornelius Carr was rated at number 11 and asked Mickey about this boy. Mickey said, "James, I manage him, he's white and he's 21." I said, "No problem, I'll knock him out as well!" When the fight was made, I never had the best preparation for it, I was 34 and my body started to get tired. I trained for the fight just like them all, hard. I could have done things different as I was 34. Now as a coach, I know that! From round seven, I was looking at him and I was thinking, "A couple of years ago I'd have knocked him out." I then realised that things weren't going to plan. I wasn't as quick and I wasn't throwing the punches I wanted to be throwing. I didn't think I'd lose the fight on points but he put me down in round ten I think. He got the result, so I stuck to my guns when I said that if any British fighter beats me I'd retire.'

Looking back over his career, it is hard to dispute that you are looking through the career of a fighter who was prepared to keep coming back from defeat, was willing to travel to fight anyone regardless of risk and never took the soft route or cut corners. Southern Area middleweight champion, two-time British super-middleweight champion and European champion is an impressive résumé for a fighter who fought below the radar that focused more on the careers of the division's more marketable and crowd-friendly fighters such as Herol Graham, Michael Watson, Chris Eubank and Nigel Benn.

'My big strength was my big stamina. I always said that if you didn't get me quickly, you would struggle because I was just getting warmed up in those early rounds. You weren't going to find me short of breath in the later rounds. My weakness was getting caught early. I was keen to get out there. I had to survive the early rounds. In my head, I always wanted to get past that third round.'

In relation to the four other higher profile British fighters in Cook's weight, his opinions will not come as a surprise. 'With Eubank and Benn I think I would have beaten them both. Eubank would probably have given me a hard fight because he was very tough like Michael Watson. I would definitely have stopped Benn. There was no way Benn would have beaten me with his style. Benn's trainer, Ambrose Mendy would come around here and I said to Ambrose, "Won't you let me fight Nigel Benn?" and he said, "Jimmy, I'm supposed to look after my fighter. If Michael Watson couldn't beat you and he went on to beat Nigel Benn, Benn would never beat you."'

While this theory rarely occurs (Duran beating Leonard, who beat Hagler, who beat Hearns, who beat Duran for example), the view given here by Mendy is testament to the sort of respect other fighters and their teams had of Cook. 'Herol Graham would have had an easier time with Michael Watson because of his movement. With Nigel Benn, he'd have it a bit tougher because I think Nigel Benn would rush him. Graham would have beaten Eubank too. Nigel Benn would have given Graham the hardest fight. While he's not pretty, he's a swinger! He swings himself and because Graham wouldn't stand up to him, I think he would have been dangerous.'

The quality of Cook's opponents cannot be denied and picking through them to determine the toughest would not be an easy task. Cook, however, is in no doubt as to who his greatest adversaries were. 'Three people. Winterstein, "Bomber" Graham and Mark Kaylor. I used to spar with Mark Kaylor and I said Errol Christie was never going to beat Kaylor. Sparring with him, I knew how tough he was. I sparred with a lot of skilful guys and even when he fought Roy Gumbs, I sparred with Gumbs and I thought he may beat Kaylor. Some guy looked at me and said, "He won't beat Kaylor. He has no heart." Kaylor put on the pressure and won. He's definitely one of the toughest.'

While he chose to pursue the European title route instead of going for a world title at the start of the 1990s in a decision that backfired against Nicotra, were there any other regrets that Cook had about the course his career took? Cook was adamant that there weren't. 'You can't have regrets! In hindsight, when I turned pro, I would probably go with a manager who was well-known and I would probably become champion up there. No regrets though. Each trainer and manager I had, they taught me something about life and I'm still here and when you speak as well as me when you finish your career, you had a good career! Nothing was put in my way to be easy so I had to fight my way out of it. A lot was achieved.'

Looking back to when he arrived in England in 1968, there was the issue surrounding race and the environment that Cook grew up in. He will tell you that while it existed, he remained largely left alone by the whole thing until an incident later on in life when he was comfortably into his boxing career. 'I came here in 1968 when the National Front and the skinheads were rampant but I was never really touched by it all. It was never a problem. The biggest problem I had was when I was about 30. I was driving towards a petrol station and this man turned to me and said, "You're black," blah blah blah and so I turned to him and said, "Mate, I'm 30 years of age. If I don't know I'm black then something is wrong!" He walked out!'

When James Cook received his MBE from the Queen at Buckingham Palace in 2007, it was recognition for the hard work he had put into the Pedro Club and his work with youngsters to promote the need to stay away from crime and channel their energies into more worthwhile activities and to embrace a more positive lifestyle. 'One of my biggest things in life is that you can do something and achieve something if you look back at all those who have come before. These kids look at me in the papers and on TV. I have done it and come from the street like them. I never had rich parents like them so I say, "If I can do it, you can do it as well." THAT is the joy about it.'

That is what James Cook is working on at present. He has been officially recognised for his hard work. His past needs no further explanation. He was an accomplished, honest and gutsy championship prizefighter. What about the future? 'I would like to be one of the best trainers in the country. I look at people like Freddie Roach. I look at my life and I went from the south of Jamaica to Peckham to Hackney and up to Buckingham Palace and I thought I'm good to go but I may be looking for the next title that someone will say Jimmy Cook is the best trainer in the world!'

Cook is planning on going back to Jamaica with his father to meet up with his cousins and other relatives there. The people that Cook grew up with, however, have passed away so his interest in his place of birth has waned over the course of time. 'Since my grandparents died while I was over here, I lost all interest in Jamaica as they were the only people

I know who were looking out for me. They got sick and died and I lost interest. I go over to America and other places but I never really go to Jamaica. I'm going this year with my dad before it's too late though!'

As I finished up the interview and walked back outside to where the graffiti was, I looked at an image of the club's coat of arms with an inscription under it. In clear print were the words, 'YOU ARE WHAT YOU DO.' Having only been with the former British and European super-middleweight champion for a couple of hours, I had to disagree. I could safely disclose that, not for one second, did I deem James Cook MBE to be incredibly hard work.

6
Herol Graham

O N 23 August 1986, Mike McCallum defended his WBA light-middleweight title against a future world champion from the Virgin Islands by the name of Julian Jackson. McCallum ripped Jackson apart in the second round. Two years later McCallum would move up to middleweight and lose a 12-round decision to Sumbu Kalambay for the Italian-based African's WBA title. After three more routine wins, McCallum was in line for a shot at the vacant WBA title in May 1989.

Jackson, on the other hand, remained at the lower weight and had a very successful reign as WBA champion, defeating the Korean In-Chul Baek in three rounds to claim McCallum's old title. In November 1990, Jackson found himself in line for a crack at a vacant world middleweight belt too, this time the WBC version.

In both cases, McCallum and Jackson were paired with the British middleweight champion, Herol 'Bomber' Graham, to decide the new titleist. The 'Bomber' would lose both fights; one by the slimmest of margins, the other by the slimmest lapse in concentration Graham would have throughout his career. While losing both duels, Graham earned himself the moniker of 'one of the best never to win a world title'. while it appears a contradiction in terms, having the words 'best' and 'never' used in the same literary breath, it is a label which sits comfortably with the former British, Commonwealth and European light-middleweight and former British and European middleweight champion.

'It's complimentary in a sense. I had people at the time who despised me and were trying to bring me down. You know, "he'll never be a champion" and so on. There were people against me but I was able to lift myself above them, which I did in most cases. I could have been world champion three times in a row!' Graham said, exuding an ambience and humour largely unchanged from the grinning 'Bomber' that viewers at ringside and home would see in the ring after many of his career victories.

Still sporting a lean, athletic physique and with a goatee beard tinged with intrusive grey flecks, the former champion takes sips from his skinny hot chocolate as his partner, Karen, drinks her chai latte and then leaves to indulge in some retail therapy. Karen, as portrayed in Graham's book *BOMBER – Behind the Laughter*, has proved invaluable and of huge support when things went awry in his life after his career finished. Initially meeting in 1986 after Graham returned to the United Kingdom from a trip to America where he scored a first-round win over Ernie Rabotte on the undercard to the Barry McGuigan–Steve Cruz championship fight, the relationship collapsed less than a year later. Karen was to re-enter Graham's life many years later when the former boxer found himself in the throes of despair and depression and offered the support and affection needed for Graham to find himself again and turn his life around. The appreciation and affection Herol harbours for his supportive partner is not in any doubt and, while our conversation is naturally centred around his boxing career, the respect he has for Karen is vividly brought to life in his book. One only has to listen to the ex-champion talk about the darker periods of his life, compared to how he is today, and the lift in character and spirit is highly encouraging.

Needless to say, life was not always bad and the journey towards boxing stardom started in Nottingham under the stern guidance of his parents. '"You must go to university!"' Graham says, mimicking his parents. 'It was all about education. My brother and sister went to uni, so it was a case of me following suit. Whether it was sport or anything, it didn't matter. I was going to university! I didn't want to. I just wanted to be the guy about town and box and be sporty. I got a good education but I just didn't WANT to do it! I wanted to be a top sportsman and earn lots of MONNN-EYYY! An abundance of MONNN-EYYY!' Graham's grin spreads and his head bobs to the side to emphasise the word as if he's dodging an incoming salvo of punches in a manner reminiscent of his fighting days.

Once Graham's ultimate choice of occupation tightened its grip, the onus was still very much on him getting a solid grounding at school. As always, boxing had that lure of riches and fame but, more often than not, its participants would one day find themselves leaving the sport needing to find work through other means. Although possessing the oft-quoted 'richest prize in sport', very few boxers ever reach the dizzy heights of stardom and unimaginable riches. The rest would find themselves back in a 40-hour, five-day working week.

'They always wanted me to have the education just in case. So many boxers pick up injuries so if that happens, what are you going to do if you can't box? I took that dive though. I splashed but didn't drown! I should have done what my parents said and put education first.'

In 2011, Herol Graham published his book. A deeply sensitive tome, outlining his bouts of depression and adversity as much as his boxing achievements, it is brutally honest with a warm ending. When Graham was eight years old, he was befriended and raped by a family friend. Such an ordeal would have a lasting impact on anyone but Graham channelled this dark period of his life to his advantage.

'It did have an effect on my boxing career because that's the reason why I boxed because being raped, I wanted to defend myself and I didn't want it to happen again. It was at that age that I started my boxing. It was about me defending myself.'

The decision to take up boxing was made and it was Graham's godfather, Terry Miles, who encouraged him to go to the local club. 'Terry Miles,' Graham started, laughing with the memories, 'told me to go to the gym. It was him that called me "Bomber" as I ran or "bombed" around everywhere getting into fights. I wanted to be the kingpin, the toughie so I had to join boxing! It soon turned me around. I liked boxing and I was good at it. Roy, Alan and Frank Smith, who were my trainers at the time, loved me in the gym.'

Graham's amateur career got underway at the Radford Boys' Boxing Club in Nottingham. Graham went from strength to strength, developing a style and technique that would eventually become a trademark for Brendan Ingle's Wincobank gym in Sheffield. The art of hit without being hit in return was slowly being perfected to the point where it would be hard to get quality opposition. Other fighters' trainers wouldn't want their boxer going near Graham for fear of being humiliated and exposed as one-dimensional. It was normally more to do with the unique style of the Nottingham fighter than the pitfalls of the opponent.

In 1976, at the age of 16, Herol Graham got his girlfriend, Lilian, pregnant. By the time his daughter, Natasha, was born in October 1976, Graham was the Class B Junior ABA welterweight champion. It was in this year that Graham won the junior world welterweight championships, defeating the future WBC light-middleweight champion John Mugabi on points. It was also in 1976 that Herol Graham was introduced to Brendan Ingle. The 'Bomber' immediately displayed the style that would become his standard trademark. 'If I threw a handful of pebbles at you, not one would hit you,' Brendan Ingle said shortly after he first saw his new boxer sparring.

His progress continued but his southpaw style became something of an enigma. To some, it was the epitome of class and one for the connoisseur to marvel at and appreciate. To others, it was negative, uninteresting and unexciting. Such was the split in opinion when, in the 1977 ABA Midlands v Home Counties championship, Graham was defeated by Sandy's Jim Harrington. The fluid movement and rapier-like jabbing came from Graham while Harrington surged forward and landed his share of strong blows in the final round. It was simply down to how one interpreted Graham's style and what the spectators and judges favoured.

Not to be disheartened, Graham rebounded in the following year's ABA tournament. On 11 March in Birmingham, he knocked Ipswich's Junior Claxton cold in the first round of the English quarter-finals. On 5 April in Gloucester, he outpointed Finchley's Lloyd James and two weeks later, he outclassed Trostre's Robert Mogford on points. Despite Britain's *Boxing News* tipping Delroy Parkes to defeat Graham in the Senior ABA middleweight final, Graham fought on the back foot and jabbed his way to the title.

'They were all hard fights, those amateur ones,' he said smirking and looking off to the side as if amused by some sudden recollection. 'Yeah, they were hard! Jimmy Harrington! Ah, he was built like a brick ****
house. He hit me and, believe me, I felt it! It was a close decision but a really good fight. A HARD fight! Delroy Parkes too. He was hard! What stirred me up to win the ABA title was watching Terry Marsh winning his title before me. They were good times. Very good times!'

Graham's long-term gym-mate and, at the tail-end of his career, trainer, Glyn Rhodes, recalls the early days with fondness. 'I remember seeing him once in Nottingham. He was wearing a white vest with shorts and I remember thinking, 'f*****g hell, this kid's good!'

With two years to go until the Moscow Olympics, Herol Graham made the decision to turn professional after a rewarding amateur career. Going for gold in Moscow wasn't in his plans and, as he stressed, his style would have been better received in the pro ranks.

'The Olympics were too long away to wait and I was excited to turn pro,' Graham explained to me. 'My style was more suited to the pros anyway. The fights are longer in the pros so I have more time to do what I want to do, boxing them, frustrating them. This is what I wanted. Turning pro wasn't that straightforward though,' Herol said sternly when reflecting on the transition between the two levels. 'I was invited to go along to represent the England amateur team at the time at some big championships but I said no. I decided to turn pro.'

With his mentor and trainer Brendan Ingle in his corner, Graham set out on his professional journey on 28 November 1978 and his first challenge would come from one Vivian Waite of Cardiff. A wide points win over six rounds got Graham off the mark and over the next four months, racked up another five wins over similarly experienced boxers. With two knockouts in these initial six wins, Graham's slippery, elusive style was finding its niche in the professional game with success.

'There was a bit of pressure having won the ABA title. I had to do well. It was a case of, "Who is this guy?" Brendan would tell me it was no one special. I told him they're all special until you've beaten them! I needed to get off to a good start though.'

His seventh contest against Mac Nicholson in Newcastle on 27 April 1979 was, not only against a boxer who had lost his five previous fights, but also against a boxer who had already been in with some tough opposition, namely the future British middleweight title challenger Glen McEwan and Tony Sibson, the pending world middleweight contender.

'I lost to Sibson in the amateurs although I thought I won. Sibson had beaten Nicholson as a pro so I wanted to beat him even better!'

Graham posted an emphatic eight-round points win over Nicholson compared with Sibson's two stoppage wins, in the seventh then the first rounds. Not 'bettering' Sibson's performances against Nicholson wasn't of concern to Graham in the end.

'My runs during training gave me good stability and strength in my legs. I'd go out running at the age of 18 for an hour and a half easily. All this training was why people saw me whizzing around the ring. I had so much energy to do it and it proved natural to do that in the ring.'

Five more wins were added to Graham's record before he faced his first unbeaten opponent in Sheffield on 22 April 1980 in his 13th contest, George Danahar.

'George Danahar was strong and tall. Brendan was telling me to stay away from this guy and just to jab and move. "Easier said than done" I thought, but I ended up taking the Michael with him! It was a good fight but I was apprehensive because of his fighting family!'

As a result of some feverishly keen investigative digging, I tracked George Danahar, brought up in Rudyard Kipling's one-time home of Rottingdean, down to the Hillcrest Boxing Club in East Sussex. Winner of the Southern Counties middleweight amateur title in 1978 and being the nephew of Arthur Danahar, he of that famous brawl with Eric Boon for the latter's British lightweight title in 1939, we engaged in a phone conversation that lasted almost two hours. It could easily have gone on for longer if it weren't for the school run and other domestic necessities for me to accommodate.

'He was fabulous,' George began. 'I have nothing but respect for him, he was always destined to go somewhere. Our fight was originally set for the Crucible Theatre in Sheffield but they double-booked with the snooker championships! He had great reflexes and he kept his distance the whole fight. He was the only boxer I fought who had faster hands than me. When I did land the jab, he was already moving backwards. I'd take one step forward and he'd take two steps back. I'd love to have fought him as an amateur.'

Complimentary words indeed from a boxer who fell victim to the unique fighting style of the Brendan Ingle-tutored boxer who developed a habit of frustrating his opponents to the point of despair. George, however, summed Graham up perfectly by acknowledging the mentally-debilitating consequences of fighting 'Bomber'. 'He never shirked anyone,' he said with a quiet, sincere tone, 'people shirked him.'

Three more wins took Graham through to the spring of 1981 when he challenged for his first belt, the British light-middleweight title, held by Wales's Pat Thomas. Thomas had already won the British welterweight title and had claimed the Lonsdale belt in his previous outing before Graham with his second successful defence of the British light-middleweight title.

'A baptism of fire!' Graham said immediately. 'It was brilliant. He was touted as a good champion because he was a good mover, he was strong, durable and had good legs. I told him I was going to take him though. He asked me how and I just told him to turn up and see! I didn't want to talk before the fight. After, sure, but not before!'

What played out was pure poetry. Verse after verse of poetic mastery was presented to the spectators but so dominant was the display by the challenger, no chorus was needed to bring the contest to a final crescendo. Graham controlled the contest behind his snake-like jab and follow-up combinations that consistently kept Thomas off-balance and at arm's length as opposed to causing any real damage. Thomas, however, seemed lost and trundled after Graham for the majority of the fight in the hope of catching him with one big fight-ending punch. It was never likely. Graham ran out an easy winner on points over 15 rounds.

'I was very nervous in that fight though. I was fighting for the championship now. These were real proven men that I was in against.

He was a talented boxer, he knew his boxing and I had to do my utmost to win every round. That's the way it was but as the fight got closer I got really nervous. He was a come-forward fighter and I knew I had to be at my best.'

Fellow Sheffield boxer Glyn Rhodes told me, 'The buzz was unbelievable. You got this guy, Pat Thomas, a well respected champion and Herol Graham, a young kid from Sheffield boxing 15 rounds. Everybody knew Herol had talent but it's not until you beat a good fighter that people really sit up and say, "You know what? This kid's actually the real deal." For him to go and beat Pat Thomas over 15 rounds, yeah, there was a real buzz about town then!'

In its report of the fight, *Boxing News* described Herol Graham in the bout as 'unexciting to watch but clinically effective'. This was to be a recurring description levelled at the new British champion at numerous times throughout his career and gave a strong indication as to why many top-level boxers and even superstars of his weight division would opt out of fighting him in the coming years. From the early days, Graham's style was so effective, sleek and elusive, it presented risks to the sport's elite that were simply not worth accepting. While many would have fancied their chances against Graham's style, it was widely acknowledged that his style would, if not beat you, severely dent your image and force you into having one of your more unimpressive showings. More money and more compatible opponents could be found elsewhere. In light of being labelled unexciting but effective, the ex-champion did not seem perturbed by this.

'That's ok with me. I was the new boy on the block and to beat the champion you have to take the title away from him which is exactly what I did. I dominated the fight in my own way. He couldn't change anything because of my style smothering him. He kept coming into me and I slipped out the way. He was running past me. I'd switch styles and the result was technically perfect. Entertainment-wise, it was ok but like I always say, "Hit them without them hitting you!"'

It was at this time that, having won four fights in a row since being knocked cold by one left hook against 'Sugar' Ray Leonard in a challenge for the WBC welterweight title, Chatteris's Dave 'Boy' Green turned his attention towards Graham's British title. Green's manager, Andy Smith, claimed Graham's best paycheque would come about by fighting his charge, claiming his boxer was the big draw with the exciting style, the opposite, he stated, of Graham. Graham threw down the challenge with that time-honoured, but futile, winner-takes-all offer. Both sides were willing but Green would lose what would prove to be his final fight against the Guyanese-born American Reg Ford in November 1981. The Graham fight never happened.

'There was the possibility of that fight happening with that man from Chatteris!' Graham chuckled. His eyebrows rose as his mind went back to a time when they both met. 'I remember we sparred together as amateurs in the England squad. He was very strong but we were just messing around! Yeah, we could have but he was with Mickey Duff. They knew about me and maybe they thought I was a bit special and that I could mess him up mentally. He was very head-strong though, very tough.'

In a non-title fight three months after his British title win, Herol Graham took on Prince Rodney, a boxer with a respectable record who would go on to win the British light-middleweight title Herol would subsequently vacate. Never having been knocked out or beaten inside the distance, Rodney entered the ring with the new champion with confidence, believing he would beat Graham or, at the very least, provide him with a solid test. Graham despatched Rodney within one round and it was at this time that Graham became friends with a couple of other boxers from the Wincobank gym; Johnny Nelson and a very young talent spotted by Brendan Ingle called Naseem Hamed. The three of them would go on to become the figureheads of Brendan Ingle's training empire.

On 25 November 1981 in his third straight fight at Sheffield's City Hall, Herol Graham stepped into the ring and challenged the Commonwealth light-middleweight champion, the Brooklyn-based Guyanese boxer Kenny Bristol. It was Bristol's second defence but he had lost his previous two showings in non-title fights to the same boxer, Wayne Caplette. Graham completed the hat-trick with a 15-round points win. With just a single knockout win to his name, Bristol was faced with numerous problems. Without the power to hurt his Sheffield challenger, outboxing him would prove to be a big ask of any domestic-level opponent. Viewed as a lacklustre performance by both boxers, it was a classic performance by Graham who did as he pleased against the defending champion. Bristol didn't have the means to bring out the best in Graham so the challenger sat back and speared the jab through the champion's guard to slip and slide his way to his second title.

'Bristol was tall and it was a hard fight. I remember I hit him with a jab and his hair all came untied!' Graham said, laughing loudly. 'He had a high-comb style and it all went crazy. I thought, "Bloody hell, where did all that come from?!"' Graham laughed loudly as did I, imagining this mass unravelling in centre-ring. 'He had long, massive arms so I had to work inside his body. I had to bend my knees to get in. A lot of people bend the head but you have to bend the knees so you can still see what you're doing! He had such long arms so I had to spin him around. I was throwing more shots than him, busier than him and I won unanimously.'

Graham seemed to support Brendan Ingle's pre-fight boast that his fighter 'would lick Maurice Hope and I believe he'd take Sibson'. Leicester's Tony Sibson would make the second successful defence of the European middleweight title the day before Graham's win over Bristol. It was early days in Graham's career but already the Sheffield camp were looking further afield and taking note of developments in the higher weight division.

On 24 February, Graham stepped into the ring at Sheffield City Hall to face the unheralded Chris Christian from Stoke Newington. A points win over the former British light-middleweight champion Jimmy Batten and a win for the Southern Area title were rewarded with the shot for Graham's Commonwealth and British titles. Graham had stirred up a substantial amount of negativity with numerous followers, with accusations of him being boring, one-dimensional and even 'lacking commitment' as was mentioned in the immediate aftermath of the win over Kenny Bristol. He went into the Christian fight with a different approach and one which would leave a copious amount of egg on many faces. Ripping in combinations and showing an as yet unseen level of aggression, Christian was used as the proverbial punchbag, his face slowly degenerating into a bloody mess, his feet unable to shift him out of harm's way. The fight was mercifully terminated in the ninth round when referee Sid Nathan waved it off. Christian didn't argue. He made it clear he was dominated by a far superior athlete when he described Graham as 'the best I have ever met'. He was adamant about still going for a title but made it clear it would only happen if Graham moved to the bigger stage. The Sheffield fighter was slowly making believers out of those who were sure they could clearly see a tarnished armour, one that would be exposed when faced with an opponent who could land the big bombs and take Graham out of his comfort zone with effective pressure. The problem faced by those he fought was getting close enough to succeed. If the pawing jab wasn't enough in itself to keep his opponents at bay, Graham's reflexes would leave them chasing their own tails.

'He looked so much lighter than me. It was his looks and I thought I could walk through him. It was like I was being a bully to him. I laid back on the back foot and just jabbed him and jabbed him! This put him off balance and because of this, I could go forward easier. I was going in at different angles,' Graham exclaimed with a look of sincerity. He went on to explain to me the art of balance, movement and the best angles to approach your opponent from. This was clearly not just someone who was a defensive master but, now also, something of a wisened sage whose knowledge could prove invaluable to new generations of pugilists coming through. A sensei of the square ring.

A comfortable points win over ten rounds over France's Fred Coranson on 22 April set him up for a defence of his Commonwealth title against the Nigerian champion, Hunter Clay. It was Graham's first fight abroad and the experience made an instant impression.

'That was hard! We stayed in this hotel but I wished I stayed in a hut! There were lizards running around. This was primitive stuff. We could only drink bottled or filtered water. If the seal was broken on the bottle, forget it!'

The fight proved a test of the champion's resolve, tenacity and focus. Fighting in the country's capital on Nigerian Independence Day, feelings were running high for Clay to strengthen national pride and lift the title. Although being dropped with a series of body shots in the fourth round and having to weather repeated fouls by the ungainly challenger, Graham fought through and cruised to a unanimous 15-round decision to hold on to his belt. The injuries suffered to his left eye during the bout, courtesy of Clay's blatant infringements, led to the champion having to rest for a month before resuming training. Graham would be out of the ring for almost six months, his longest break to date.

To signal his return, Graham was given a place on the undercard of Charlie Magri's WBC world flyweight title-winning fight by taking on Pennsylvania's Tony Nelson. Graham scored a fifth-round retirement win to set up a challenge for the vacant European light-middleweight title. To achieve the title hat-trick, Graham would have to face the experienced African middleweight champion, the Belgium-based Congolese boxer, Clemente Tshinza. A veteran of over 50 contests, Tshinza had fought across the four corners of Europe but had usually been found wanting whenever the level of opposition was raised, seeing defeat against the likes of Colin Jones and Nino LaRocca. A solid win, however, over the former world middleweight title challenger Bennie Briscoe in 1979, told Graham that he was in with an opponent who was not to be taken softly. With Tshinza at the tail-end of his career and many expecting Graham to win, 'a stoppage win would be a good result', was the claim made by *Boxing News* in its preview issue of 20 May 1983. A stoppage win he would get too as he floored his 35-year-old opponent three times en route to a second-round knockout. Almost five months later, Graham appeared at the Royal Albert Hall and took Carlos

Betancourt apart in one round on the undercard of Jimmy Batten's final professional contest, a losing effort for the British title against former Graham victim, Prince Rodney. Graham had recently relinquished his British title to concentrate on higher, more lucrative honours.

Graham's second trip abroad took place for his first European title defence on 9 December 1983 against the veteran Frenchman Germain Le Maitre. In what was forecast as a certain distance fight, Graham excelled by finishing Le Maitre within schedule. It was agreed by those present that night, however, that this was all Graham exceeded in. Le Maitre fought a strictly defensive fight, leaving the Sheffield champion with few options to use. Flicking out his long left jab, trying to get his opponent to open up proved futile. In the eighth round, a fast volley from the champion opened a large cut over the challenger's eye and the fight was, to the relief of the paying crowd, waved over. Graham wasn't impressive and he admitted as much afterwards, saying the fight 'was a very bad night for me'.

'That was a lacklustre fight! He didn't come to make a fight of it so I was just moving and jabbing. I was keeping it simple because I was in France so I was going to make sure I was going to hit him twice as many times as he was going to hit ME!'

This last quote could be construed as extreme modesty; Graham was in no more danger of being hurt in this fight than he would have been had his opponent entered the ring with his hands and feet tied together behind his back.

In the immediate aftermath of the fight, talk turned to Graham's increasing weight problems and the suffering that comes from having to consistently shed weight in order to stay within your weight limit. The middleweight division was in Graham's and Ingle's sights and although *Boxing News* reported the Le Maitre fight with the headline 'Boring Bomber', the dominant Marvin Hagler was named as the ultimate target. Hagler had reigned supreme upon the middleweight throne for three years and earlier in 1983 had brutally beaten another Brit, Tony Sibson, to make his sixth successful world title defence. In time, Graham would find himself as the brooding champion's number one challenger but the business of money and marketability would pose a cruel obstacle and the golden opportunity to fight one of the division's best ever champions would be denied the slick operator from the city of steel.

The Le Maitre contest would be the last title defence for Graham at 154lb. His almost regal dominance over the light-middleweights was curtailed by his body's natural development only. The struggle to make the weight was too problematic. Gathering his quiver full of ingenious defensive moves and gifted reflexes that would elude the opposition like identical poles of a magnet, Graham eased smoothly into his new weight class.

What Graham left behind, however, were potential world title challenges against the WBC champion Thomas Hearns, WBA kings Roberto Duran and Mike McCallum consecutively and the first holder of the newly-established IBF title, Mark Medal.

'We came to the table so to speak and we wanted these fights against Leonard, Duran and whoever else for the big money but we were looking at Hagler. They didn't want to know me though. They'd heard of my name and what I did in the ring and it wasn't entertainment for them. They'd have to work harder than I would. They all said, "No, let's not go there!"'

Graham stepped back into the ring on 22 July 1984 to commence his charge towards middleweight title glory. Glaring across the ring at him was the mean-looking Lindell Holmes, the future IBF super-middleweight champion and one who would mix in world-class circles for the rest of his career.

'They gave me this guy Lindell Holmes to box and I was, "Yeah, no problem!" I trained and trained for this guy to get my fitness because I knew this would be a hard fight. At the fight, I looked at him and thought, "Shhhhhhite!"' Graham said as his laughter rolled across the cafe. 'You touched him and it was like touching stone. He was SOLID!' Graham again laughs aloud as he remembers the trouble he had in making a dent in the American.

'I hit him with a jab and I felt it all through my hand. You know when you hit a brick wall? That's what it was like! I wasn't gonna tango with him! I was NOT gonna mix it with this guy! I just went running. There was no way he was gonna hit me. If he had have done, I'd have...' I attempted to complete his sentence for him. '...felt it?' I offered, pre-empting the answer. 'FELT IT?!' Graham answered, clearly signifying the ludicrous understatement I'd made. 'He hit me with one shot and I felt it go from my chin, all the way down my body and into my toes! I just thought, "Freaking hell, I sure can't let him do that again because that is sure going to hurt me!" I just tipped and tapped him and it frustrated him.'

A cut by the American's left eye in the fifth round brought his visit to these shores to a disappointing end as Graham got off to a successful start in his middleweight campaign. 'As you can imagine,' Graham exclaimed to me, 'I was pleased because he hit so hard, you didn't WANT to be in the ring with him!'

Within the next eight months, Graham notched up a further four wins, all finishing inside the distance. Irving Hines, who was the first man to defeat Graham's last opponent, Lindell Holmes, by a knockout, was summarily despatched in two rounds. Graham then rounded off 1984 with knockout wins over Jose Seys, who had been the first man to defeat the budding British star, Errol Christie, in his previous fight, in six rounds and Liam Coleman, the former Northern Irish light-heavyweight champion, in three. A March 1985 win over Martinique's Jose Rosemain by a fifth-round knockout signalled his suitability to challenge for his first middleweight title.

The fight which many had been talking about now was the match with Tony Sibson. When 'Bomber' ascended to middleweight, 'Sibbo' was the reigning British champion so a match with the Leicester man was seen as a natural. The champion could get himself back into world title contention after the Hagler loss and Graham could immediately stamp his authority on the new division.

'The sooner we meet, the better,' Sibson was quoted as saying at the time. 'I can't wait to play piano on his ribs!'

The fighters were ready, the fans were ready but as is depressingly the case at times, the business machinations in finalising the contest hindered the deal. Promoter Frank Warren approached Sibson and offered his team the princely sum of £60,000 for their man to face Liverpool's Jimmy Price. Upon Sibson's team not looking favourably upon the champion boxing for Warren, the fight fell through. Sibson subsequently had to vacate the British title for not fighting Price and Graham stepped in. Price had been beaten just once; the former WBA light-middleweight champion Ayub Kalule had knocked him out in the first round.

The Graham–Price showdown for the vacant British middleweight title was set for 24 April in Shoreditch after Frank Warren won the purse bids to stage it. A 12-round points win for Graham was the prediction from the highly-respected *Boxing News*. While Price's record wasn't spectacular, this preview gave an indication that Graham was not expected to receive an easy pass from the bigger men. The speed and accuracy of Graham dazzled Price and the spectators watching as Larry O'Connell waved the one-sided drubbing off at the 100-second mark with Price falling to the canvas three times. Graham had received his easy pass.

'I watched it again only the other night!' Graham remarked. He was noticeably proud that his defensive style was able to produce devastating results when faced with the appropriate opponent. The Price demolition was a stark reminder to those potential adversaries who saw the new

British champion as little more than the proverbial 'Fancy-Dan'. When the opportunity arose, Graham showed he had many more arrows to his quiver and was able to deploy them with pinpoint accuracy.

'He was saying he was going to beat me and he was going to do this and do that. I didn't have to get myself up for that fight in the sense that I knew what I had to do. We got in the ring, he hit me, moving, moving, moving, jabbing, moving and then he let his hands down. I hit him to the head and he started reacting. He was moving forward into my punches and it was all over! This really takes me back!'

Graham's mind was firmly centred on his 1980s heyday. He was with me in body only and I therefore deemed it only right that the occasional brief lull in our conversation should be granted so he could live certain past moments again. Rubbing his chin, his eyes would veer away as he let his mind drift back. Graham was at ringside watching himself at Wembley Arena, Shoreditch Town Hall, the Empire at Wembley and the Royal Albert Hall. I felt almost intrusive being present at a moment of such intimacy between him and his past glory. Graham returned to the present with a characteristic chuckle.

'Price was yapping his mouth off beforehand. He was a nice guy but I had to take him apart. It took a couple of days for it to sink in as I was the new champion and I knew I was going places.'

Upon dismantling Price, words were again uttered over a possible match with the world champion, Marvin Hagler. While this would have seemed borderline ludicrous and premature to the limit, the new British champion was supremely confident of his chances and was certain he possessed the style to make the 'Marvellous' one's bald dome sweat.

'I was sparring with guys like Alan Minter anyway. I wanted Hagler. I wanted him! My movement would have frustrated him. I know he was a brilliant fighter at that time but I was going along with what I was doing at that time and that was moving a couple of centimetres out of the way. Those couple of centimetres were worth not being knocked out!'

Nine days before Graham's brutalising of Price, Marvin Hagler waged war with Thomas 'Hit Man' Hearns 6,000 miles away in the glittering backdrop of Las Vegas. Encompassing more raw mayhem and raging torrents of aggression than most other contests combined in living memory, Hagler won with Hearns sprawled across the canvas after three astonishing rounds of savagery. The simple presence of the referee stopped the contest from becoming a frenzy of relentless violence. Graham, however, was not put off by what he saw.

'That was a wicked fight! I was up early the next morning and out running, feeling elated. I wanted to box him. I knew I could BOX him!'

The developing at the new weight continued, however, and after a cut-eye stoppage win over Roberto Justino Ruiz of Argentina, he scored a dreary ten-round points win over America's durable Sanderline Williams.

'Sanderline Williams would spar with some of the top guys in America. I'm sure he sparred with Hagler and there were words said. He said there was no way I'd beat Hagler but I just said, "Yeah, but if I beat you there's always a chance!" He was a strong guy though, very durable and clever. He had to be to be able to spar with HAGLER!' Graham said, emphasising the world champion's name.

These two contests marked a new episode of Graham's career. With Brendan Ingle still in his corner, Graham had signed a managerial deal with Barney Eastwood. It would prove to be a deal which would have severe repercussions on the champion's career over the next couple of years.

While Graham may have looked sub-par against Williams, he found himself in position to challenge for Ayub Kalule's European middleweight championship. The Ugandan-born, Danish boxer held the WBA light-middleweight title from 1979 until 1981 when he was picked as the fall guy for 'Sugar' Ray Leonard in the former champion's quest to win a world title at a second weight division. Two fights prior to meeting Graham, he had lifted the European crown and had defended once against the Italian-based African, and future nemesis of Graham's, Sumbu Kalambay.

The fight with Kalule had already been delayed a number of times and it was under threat of happening again after promoter Frank Warren claimed he had a written agreement with Kalule to defend against his fighter, Tony Sibson. Kalule's manager Mogens Palle threw his oar in by deeming the fight to be void under European Boxing Union regulations as Graham's manager, Barney Eastwood, had already switched the venue for the fight from Belfast to Sheffield. With these contractual disputes threatening to overshadow proceedings, the EBU stepped in and, in support of Eastwood, threatened to strip Kalule of his title if his defence did not go ahead.

As it turned out, Graham's performance on that February night at Sheffield City Hall was near-vintage. Dominating the fight almost from start to finish, Graham added the European crown to his domestic title with an awe-inspiring tenth-round stoppage. He suffered some small nicks to his nose and mouth but these were no more than minor occupational hazards as he swept aside what efforts the African made on his way to a commanding win.

'I had sparred with him and ended up boxing him a year later. A comfortable fight, he was very strong and durable. I can remember the stoppage actually,' Graham said, again chuckling. 'I boxed him, boxed him, boxed him and he got so frustrated. In the tenth round, I punched him and he fell back into the corner and I just kept on pummelling him. The referee jumped in and said "no more". That was a brilliant night. It was winter but I was so warm it was unbelievable!'

Plans were now afoot to take Graham on the road and show his talent off to a wider audience and when Barry McGuigan stepped into the ring with the Texan, Steve Cruz, on 23 June 1986 to defend his WBA featherweight title for the third time, Herol Graham was given a slot on the undercard against the unheralded Eddie Hall. As fight time approached, Hall withdrew from the fight. Optimistically hoping that Marvin Hagler may step in as the replacement, Graham had to make do with Los Angeles's Ernie Rabotte who sported a wholly unspectacular record of four wins against 12 losses and one draw.

In preparation for the fight, Graham was informed after an early-morning dip that a sparring session with the legendary Roberto Duran had been arranged for later that day. Duran was a target of Graham's back in his days as a light-middleweight contender. That fight would never come off and if this sparring would prove anything, it was that Duran was well-advised to steer well clear of the elusive enigma from Sheffield.

'I sparred Duran but he sacked me! He couldn't hit me. He stopped, slapped his chest and said, "Who do you think you are? 'Sugar' Ray Leonard?" I was really taken aback by it. I wondered if he was really talking to me. This was ROBERTO DURAN! We did two rounds and he sacked me. He never touched me!'

Rabotte was picked specifically to make Graham look impressive in front of his new audience and he was plucked at the point of perfect ripeness. Rabotte was crushed within one round and Graham gave the American market a taste of what he could do.

'I did not want to be out there for long. It was SO hot,' Graham said, emphasising the searing heat that night in Las Vegas that Barry McGuigan would later fall foul to in losing his title to Steve Cruz. 'I got him in the first round luckily. He just came on to the punch but that was hot!'

Graham was finding himself moving up the world middleweight rankings and a shot at the world crown was starting to be seen as a strong possibility. Ranked at number three in the world by the WBC, Graham signed to meet the former British and Commonwealth champion, Mark

Kaylor, himself ranked one place behind Graham. For the winner of this contest, the world title surely beckoned.

'He'll give Marvin Hagler all the trouble he wants and may even beat him.' These were the words of Kaylor after he had been beaten into submission after eight one-sided rounds at the hands of the European champion. It was an increasingly frustrating night for Kaylor as he was slowly ground down and outclassed by the blurring hand speed and lightning reflexes of Graham. By beating Kaylor in such a manner, Graham had proved himself to be head and shoulders above the rest; a head and a set of shoulders which routinely swayed the rest of him out of harm's way, leaving his opponents lunging at empty spaces and thin air.

A seventh-round win over Charles Boston from the United States on 17 January 1987 kick-started a year which would prove to be a bitter disappointment for Graham. The environment he was training in became more and more suffocating and with an intense power struggle between Barney Eastwood and Brendan Ingle reaching a crescendo, Graham parted ways with his long-time trainer. Tempers flared, arguments occurred and Graham's concentration and focus suffered as a result.

A defence of his European title was booked against the capable African, Sumbu Kalambay. The next step in the champion's path towards a world title shot was expected to be a straightforward one but when 'Marvellous' Marvin Hagler was defeated in a stunning performance by 'Sugar' Ray Leonard in April, Graham's wishes of a fight with the long-serving middleweight champion all but evaporated. Hagler would not fight again. Personal problems away from boxing were also having an effect on Graham but with a lucrative carrot dangling agonisingly close to him in the form of a world title fight against Iran Barkley for the vacant WBA title later that year, Graham couldn't afford to let matters outside of the ring invade his objectives. Unfortunately for the defending champion, these matters didn't so much invade as simply terrorise his psyche going into the fight. Up against a Zairois boxer who fought out of his skin, Graham found it hard to settle into a rhythm, move fluidly or show those reflexes that thousands of spectators had become used to seeing. Kalambay was able to throw and land numerous combinations and the final round saw Graham pounded into the ropes by a ferocious onslaught from the determined challenger. Kalambay ripped the title away with a unanimous points decision and with *Boxing News*'s weekly newspaper sporting a picture of Herol Graham, with a badly swollen left eye, raising Kalambay's right arm in celebration, there was no reason to argue with the result. Graham had been beaten by the better man.

'My mind was all over the place. You don't mix girlfriends with boxing!' Graham exclaimed. 'Barney Eastwood and Brendan were arguing and it would sometimes happen actually in the ring! You know, who's fighting here? Me or you?! Barney was my manager and Brendan was my trainer but they would have this power struggle in the ring. There was probably also the old north-south divide! The less said there the better I think!'

'That was a shock, MORE than a shock to everybody!' Glyn Rhodes said animatedly to me. 'Nobody thought that guy was gonna beat Herol Graham. NOBODY. Herol had personal problems going on and it was also the time around then that Bomber and Brendan were drifting apart. People were sticking their oar in.'

With Graham installed as Marvin Hagler's next mandatory challenger were he to overcome Kalambay and, likewise, Hagler overwhelm the extraordinary 'Sugar' Ray Leonard, Rhodes has his own views on what may have transpired.

'I liked Hagler's style and I was a fan of his. I'd have put my house on it to say that Herol Graham would have caused anybody problems with his style. He was skilful as well and he could punch. A lot of people don't think Herol was a puncher but if you look at his record, he stopped a lot of guys. Listen, I sparred with him and Herol Graham could bang! These guys like Hagler and Leonard; I'm not saying that Herol would have beaten them but it wouldn't have been no easy night for them!'

When Barney Eastwood took over at the helm of the Graham camp, he brought Graham over to Ireland to train there. He went under the wing of Eastwood's trainers and Graham found himself taken out of type. His style was one which anyone would struggle to change.

'I read reports that my style was unique,' Graham explained. 'Well, I'm sorry but you can't train that. I was just doing it without knowing WHAT I was doing.'

Graham had wanted Brendan Ingle in his corner for the Kalambay fight. Once the dismal defeat sunk in, Graham got back in touch with the Sheffield-based Irishman and their working relationship was rekindled once more. Ingle was back in the corner for Graham's next fight, a third-round win over trial horse, Ricky Stackhouse. The win lined up a challenge for the vacant British title against Peckham's James Cook which Graham won with a convincing fifth-round win to reclaim the British title and put himself, once more, in a position to challenge for world honours. Graham seemed in command from the off, dazzling

Cook with his array of combinations and constant mobility. Another fifth-round win over Johnny Melfah in Graham's third British title defence brought him, not only the coveted Lonsdale belt, but also his first world title opportunity. In the other corner would be the feared and hugely talented and accomplished Mike 'The Bodysnatcher' McCallum. McCallum had reigned as WBA light-middleweight champion for almost three years when he moved up to middleweight and dropped a decision to Sumbu Kalambay for the WBA title. Three more routine victories over marking-time opponents set up the clash against Graham on 10 May 1989 for Kalambay's old belt. Opting for a fight with the IBF champion, Michael Nunn, Kalambay had his title stripped off him.

'I got a phone call on a Sunday from Eastwood and he said, "You know Herol, you got the black fella! You got McCallum!" Training for that fight, man, was tough. I was out every morning four or five o'clock in the morning running an hour and a half. My legs were tuned in, my body was tuned in. My weight situation was right on cue.'

Having already failed in one attempt to secure a large spoonful of alphabet soup with his loss to Kalambay, those in attendance at the Royal Albert Hall were hoping for a repeat. Their hopes looked set to be realised as Graham came out at the opening bell looking to trade with the Jamaican and match him punch for punch as opposed to adopting his more cautious approach. He swayed back from McCallum's left jab, putting his right foot forward and leaning back. His impressive reach allowed him to reach McCallum without receiving too much in return. It was a good start for Graham and his success continued into the second work as a left hand momentarily stunned McCallum. A couple of rights from McCallum to Graham's body then head did, however, remind Graham that he was in with a seasoned boxer, one who had proved throughout his career that he had the ability and the boxing brain to work out most styles. A return body shot from Graham towards the end of the round appeared to give him the round. Then came the third.

Both boxers stood toe-to-toe in some rousing, crowd-pleasing action when the round commenced. While Graham was holding his own, it was a surprise to the spectators and commentators that he was choosing to be more aggressive than usual, especially against a spiteful puncher like McCallum. A left from McCallum backed Graham towards the ropes where the normally elusive slickster had to ship some big punches flush on the chin. It was something of a surprise to witness Graham being caught with such blows but to say he should easily have evaded them would have been to deny McCallum the credit his skill and talent consistently justified and deserved. He was an excellent tactician and the way he cut off Graham's space to get inside in order to unload his combinations was admirable. It was a big round for him.

Graham kept up the pace, determined to stay in front of his opponent to start the fourth and snapping out his right jab with some success. Some got through McCallum's guard but the former light-middleweight champion found a way inside and scored with some short, hurtful punches to the body and hooks and uppercuts to the head.

As the bell rang for the fifth, McCallum met Graham in a corner and was turned round with what seemed a cuffing blow. As Graham's punched grazed him, he went down. The referee, Enzo Montero, started the eight count to the blatant disdain of the Jamaican. He motioned sternly towards the corner where a cornerman was wiping a pool of water off the canvas with a towel. A replay would show his foot sliding out from under him as Graham's blow was landing. McCallum had shipped more solid, accurate punches at other points during the contest so while the decision seemed a little harsh, the result stood and the round was awarded to Graham as it ended with him back on the move, circling his aggrieved opponent.

The next two rounds saw Graham build on his advantage gained in the fifth as he jarred McCallum with occasional left hands. McCallum attempted to get inside and bull Graham into the ropes where he would let his big shots go but, aside from a big right hand by the ropes in the seventh, Graham edged his way ahead by the round's end.

Round eight saw New York-based McCallum regain the initiative as he got through with points-scoring blows as Graham went on the move behind his right jab. Around the halfway mark of the round, Graham bustled McCallum into the ropes where he landed a glancing blow to the back of McCallum's head. Montero immediately deducted a point from Graham's score. The contest was tightly fought and was no doubt proving, as British manager Terry Lawless was saying for the commentary team, very hard for the judges to score.

Rounds nine and ten saw both combatants stand largely toe-to-toe with McCallum landing some hard blows and Graham sneaking in those clever right jabs and follow-up lefts to keep breaking McCallum's momentum. They both seemed tired going into the 11th as the surprisingly fast pace of the fight was catching up with them. The last two rounds were fought largely on the inside with Graham landing a good, hard left as he fought his way off the ropes in the 11th.

It is sheer irony that by adopting a style that wasn't typical of Herol Graham, he produced a thoroughly entertaining fight with a man who was willing to go into the trenches and respond in kind.

The crowd enjoyed the contest and the commentary team were highly complimentary at the fight's conclusion.

McCallum saluted the British crowd at the final bell and when the split decision was announced in his favour, the response was respectful and amiable. Graham, however, naturally believed he had clinched it. It was that tight.

'I thought I'd won that fight. He said to me, "Man, I had no idea you were so good!" When I asked him for a rematch, he said, "No chance. No way!" It was too close for him.'

In the immediate aftermath, Graham came under attack from the sport's media for not appearing to give the last drop of energy he possessed in his quest to lift the ultimate prize. It was believed that Graham still had reserves of ammunition which had yet to be fired. McCallum, on the other hand, was seen as having put everything on the line. This criticism was reminiscent of that aimed at Joe Bugner in the Hungarian-born heavyweight's challenge for Muhammad Ali's world heavyweight title in 1975. Ali was near exhaustion while Bugner went on a swimming spree in his hotel pool. Looking over the fight several times, this criticism is unfair. Both fighters were worn out at the end and while Graham may have had more success had he adopted his 'jab and move' strategy more, he surely can't be accused of not 'leaving it all in the ring'. He, along with McCallum, produced an excellent spectacle.

'The criticism doesn't affect me, it really doesn't,' Graham said with a matter-of-fact look, as if to explain his viewpoint shouldn't have been necessary.

'Listen, you put yourself in the ring with the main person, the number one, the cream of the cream and what would you do? Which one would you do? He who fights and runs away lives to fight another day. I'm moving around not to get hit. Yeah, you have to win by a margin but I thought I won that fight. He didn't do a lot. He was coming on to me but I was jabbing him and taking the rounds. I was moving around him and he actually said that he wouldn't give me another title fight. I was too tricky for him.'

With his world title hopes temporarily derailed, Graham could return to the domestic scene and concentrate his efforts towards defending his British title. He had pushed McCallum close; indeed many felt he deserved to receive the nod. Either way, he had shown he could compete, and belonged, at world level and a second opportunity would undoubtedly arise if his dominance on the British scene continued.

The former three-time ABA champion, Rod Douglas, guided by Mickey Duff, stepped up to the plate to challenge for Graham's honours at Wembley on 25 October. With a record of choosing the right time for his boxers to challenge for titles, one had to respect Duff's decision to put his swarming, marauding, pressure fighter in with a renowned slickster such as Graham. Inflicting the sole amateur defeat on the incomparable Nigel Benn, Douglas had trounced 13 professional opponents to cut a swathe of mayhem in the lower echelons of the domestic middleweight scene. Fighting as he had against McCallum five months earlier, one had to consider the possibility that Duff had seen a change in Graham from his usual fighting style that would suit his middleweight contender. If Graham were to stand and fight Douglas the way he did, for large parts, against the famed 'Bodysnatcher', his title may not be guaranteed to return to Sheffield. The risks and expectation of the contest were summed up by *Boxing News*'s preview. Tim Mo wrote, 'Douglas is essentially a pressure fighter, though a classy one, and he is a solid puncher with either hand. He has plenty in the other departments as well. Graham wins by one or two rounds in a bitter fight.'

For Douglas, the evening would prove utterly frustrating and, consequently, near-fatal. After a moment in the opening round when he caught the British champion with some hard shots, he gradually became more and more dispirited as Graham rattled him with his spearing jab and follow-up combinations. Slowly eroding his challenger's resistance and appetite, Graham put Douglas on the canvas twice in the ninth round shortly after Douglas needed the loose tape on his glove cutting. Upon rising the second time, the referee stepped in and stopped proceedings after the very next combination. Douglas sat in his corner being tended to by Mickey Duff and his camp while Graham gave his post-fight interview and addressed the crowd in celebration.

It was a gutsy performance by Douglas. Many others may have realised the futility of the exercise much sooner but the man from East London kept persevering and, attempting to land that one punch that makes boxing the most compelling, unpredictable and appealing of contact sports, only the intervention of the third man would curtail his show of courage. The evening would, however, take a turn for the worse and circumstances would lead the sport back up that dreaded path where the negative consequences of engaging in hand-to-hand combat were about to enter the sport's conscience once again.

Rod Douglas would collapse on his way home after the fight and was rushed to the Royal London Hospital on East London's Whitechapel Road where a subsequent operation, led by the renowned neurosurgeon Dr Peter Hamlyn, was carried out. The operation proved a success and Douglas would go on to make an excellent recovery.

'I wanted to get another fight done, no matter what,' Graham said. 'He was Mickey Duff's boy and before the fight, Duff was walking around the ring trying to upset our team. We would not get upset though and as the fight wore on, I KNEW I was winning. He was coming hunting for me but I was just titting and tatting him. They were sending him out to come and get me. It was like the bull and the matador. I had my sword in one hand which was my boxing glove and my cloak in the other. Every time he came into the cloak, I'd stab him and jab him! OLE!'

Douglas developed a strong empathy with many of Graham's past opponents as his frustration grew to dizzying heights. He lunged, swung and ripped the air in half in a desperate attempt to connect with any legal part of Graham's anatomy. His punches were loaded with power but simply lacked a target and, as such, his stamina waned as he was reduced to a gasping, trudging pedestrian.

'He was getting so frustrated. You could see it in his eyes. You could read his thoughts. But I was just jabbing him. I hadn't really hit him yet and he was suffering. Each round that he came out, things got worse for him. I couldn't envisage what would happen but I could see he was suffering.'

Graham's performance was given with such overwhelming superiority that the flip-side to the boxing community's mindset was engaged. From being attracted to the raw intensity of the sport, those watching this particular fight were soon hoping that compassion would be seen and the humiliation of the challenger would be brought to a timely finish. The champion was among those who housed such hopes.

'I liked taunting my opponents without battering them. He was suffering though and I was looking out for the towel to come fluttering into the ring. He'd had enough.'

Graham got the win he was after and did so by putting on a virtuoso performance. His domination of the domestic platform continued and he could look ahead to another drive towards the world stage. After the fight's worrying post-fight episode, Rod Douglas would make the recovery we all wished for. In the few months after the Douglas fight, Graham's appetite for the sport he excelled at dropped and the possibility that he may not fight again entered his head on numerous occasions.

With the support of his close friends and gym-mates, the future world cruiserweight champion Johnny Nelson and the former British middleweight champion Brian Anderson, he got himself back in the gym. His desire to fight again returned slowly and his next fight was arranged for the Dewsbury Leisure Centre in Yorkshire for 11 April 1990. In the opposing corner stood the New Jersey-based Puerto Rican

'Mongoose', Ismael Negron. Coming off a sixth-round win over the formidable Tony Thornton and a commendable performance in taking the future world champion, Reggie Johnson, 11 rounds was enough to ensure Graham didn't drop his guard, literally or metaphorically. A second world title fight was a distinct possibility and a slip-up could undoubtedly hinder the best laid plans.

Negron proudly announced in the pre-fight press conference that he would defeat Graham within eight rounds. Graham had to be on guard and at his fluid best. Unfortunately for the visitor, aside from the occasional big swing that got through, he was.

As Graham stood in his corner prior to the fight, commentator Jim Neilly referred to the crowd when he rightly stated that the 'object of their attention and, indeed I suspect, a fair amount of affection, is the man just shedding his white robe and that's Herol Graham'. The crowd's reaction to Graham's ring introduction fully endorsed this. It was rapturous.

An aggressive start to the contest by Graham immediately had Negron looking out of sorts. Graham mixed rapid punching with his slippery movement to leave Negron's back turned towards him. A slight shake of the head from Negron in the corner, soon after the start, could quite reasonably have been an acknowledgement of the accuracy Graham was showing with his offence as it could have been to the bemusement he was encountering. A clubbing right did catch Graham towards the end of the round as Graham was moving along the ropes but his movement took any sting the punch may have had.

The second round showed how one's offence can be one's own defence. Aside from another right which gave the Sheffield boxer a reminder of his own mortality as he was moving forward, Negron simply was not given the space or time to get any meaningful punches off. A big left hand by Graham backed Negron into the ropes and was teed off upon until the bell.

The end came in the next round. Cornered and helpless, Negron was teed off upon and blasted at will before falling heavily to the canvas to lie out the referee's ten-count. Graham was hugely impressive against a valid foe and he showed no ill effects from the Douglas incident five months earlier.

In June, the WBC announced that Herol Graham was to meet the former WBA light-middleweight champion, now campaigning as a middleweight, Julian 'The Hawk' Jackson from the Virgin Islands, for their vacant title. Roberto Duran had been stripped of the title he won in February the previous year with his win over Iran Barkley but had not defended it since. It was sitting idle. Facing pressure from the British Boxing Board of Control to defend his British title against the rising Chris Eubank, the options for Graham were plentiful. The world title was the obvious route to take and when Barry Hearn won the purse bids for the Jackson showdown to happen in Monte Carlo on 13 October, Graham's dream edged that bit closer. Jackson had been on the operating table on numerous occasions for detached retinas in both eyes and it was because of this that Graham couldn't have home advantage, the board refusing the thunderous-punching Virgin Islander a licence.

Towards the end of September, it was announced that the Monaco Boxing Association had followed in the footsteps of the British Boxing Board of Control and had declined Jackson's suitability to contest for the title in the principality on medical grounds. A month later, it was finally agreed to stage the contest in the Spanish resort of the Torrequebrada in Benalmadena.

It was a unique backdrop for a world title fight and with Jackson's oft-documented eye problems, the fraternity was quick to lay bets on the Briton recording a straightforward victory, if he could keep his defence tight and his wits about him at all times.

Jackson's power was legendary and keeps him, to this day, near the top of the sport's all-time one-punch knockout artists. His victims fell as if they had the customary carpet pulled out from under them or if a hatch-door had suddenly dropped down beneath their feet. His foes weren't knocked down. They were catapulted, momentarily frozen before toppling, violently short-circuited and stiffened before falling like Del Boy's now-iconic 'nice and cool son, nice and cool' bar-hatch scene. Jackson's punches were whistling bullets tearing through the air. They were detonators. They were explosive pressure pads which had a crippling and withering impact when encountered.

'He'd knocked out most of his opponents but he had these big glasses as he had problems with his eyes so that was in our favour. He couldn't really see! We had to be careful though but I was slick so why would he choose me when he could have chosen someone else?!'

Eddie Shaw, who managed Barney Eastwood's gym in Belfast, was quoted at the time as saying, 'Graham has turned defensive boxing into a poetic art. The trouble is, nobody ever knocked anybody out with a poem.'

Graham was near-impossible to hit and prior to the two boxers entering the Spanish ring, most favoured Graham's skills to overwhelm Jackson and his jabs to wreak havoc on the former world champion's already tender eyes. The fight went as anticipated from very early on with Graham taking immediate control of his opponent. His aggressive stance from the off seemed to surprise Jackson who was forced on to the back foot and made to ship quick, accurate volleys of punches. While not loaded with concussive power, Graham's punches were enough to keep Jackson preoccupied with defending his eyes and trying to find sufficient space to launch his missiles. Graham kept at close range though, denying him the chance to gain the necessary leverage. Graham fired off combinations accompanied by the occasional lead left hand, the mark of a truly dominant southpaw. Jackson was left to paw with his left and lunge with his right, searching for a way through his swaying target.

The next round saw Jackson show his first sign of distress. He covered up and dabbed at his left eye as Graham surged forward, his confidence increasing as his opponent's seemingly plummeted. Such was Graham's impenetrable self-belief at this stage that he found it appropriate to stand in front of Jackson and tee off. This was Perseus standing up to the Kraken. Graham's Medusa came in the form of his slashing fists and Jackson simply had no answer. The Briton's body slipped and swayed and remained out of harm's way as Jackson's wrecking-ball fists sliced through the air.

The third stanza followed suit and it soon became a matter of time before referee Joe Cortez would take a careful look at Jackson and decide whether it was humane to allow the contest to continue. Jackson's left eye was swelling and his visibility was rapidly diminishing. Graham repeatedly stung Jackson's face with his left jab and was caught with heavy shots which forced him back to the ropes.

Before the start of the fourth round, Jackson was inspected closely by the ringside doctor and when the bell went to commence the round, he came out knowing his title challenge would soon be at an end. After bundling Jackson to the floor seconds into the round, Graham continued his assault and the systematic drubbing of his world-class opponent carried on with Jackson backed into a corner. Graham surged forward and landed two pinpoint left hands straight through the middle of Jackson's guard. Ploughing forward to administer what may well have been the *coup de grace*, Graham pulled his left hand back once again and BANG! The punch landed with such savage force that Graham's body stiffened and slammed to the canvas with a massive thud. His eyes rolled on impact and he lay there, barely conscious. He was immediately rolled on to his side to adopt the recovery position as Jackson fell to his knees and prayed with his murderous fists reaching towards the heavens. Jackson's right eye was all he needed to spot the gap and his right fist was all he needed to fill it. The result was his coronation as the new WBC world middleweight champion.

'What can I say?' Graham turned to me and said with a look of genuine resignation. 'He hit me with a big punch and that was it. Yeah, it was just a lapse in concentration. I can't make any excuses. He hit me. He got through!'

Upon tracking Julian Jackson down and asking him for his version of the fight, he was in no doubt as to how hard it was to decipher the enigma put in front of him before lowering the boom.

'Herol was so skilful and awkward to fight, it was hard to work him out,' said 'The Hawk'. 'I really believe he was one of the best fighters I faced in the ring.'

After the fight, Graham experienced a period of contemplation and soul-searching. Two other boxers in the Brendan Ingle gym, Johnny Nelson and Naseem Hamed, were starting to attract attention for themselves and Graham wondered if it was a fitting time to pass the Wincobank torch on to the next generation of Ingle fighters. A year followed which saw Graham face indecision and uncertainty about his role in boxing and when he did finally return to the ring in December 1991 to defend his British title against Derbyshire's John Ashton, he was the first to criticise his performance.

Offering stern resistance to former Herol Graham conqueror Sumbu Kalambay for the European title in August, where he dumped the champion on the mat in the first round before being overwhelmed six rounds later, Ashton was able to mess Graham around for a short while before the champion took matters into his own gloves and forced the referee to bring proceedings to a close in the sixth round.

'That fight wasn't easy and it wasn't hard,' Graham stated. 'He'd given Kalambay a scare! It was a case of mentality. To get back to the top, I had to get through this. I was messing him around but it wasn't easy. He couldn't cope with it though,' Graham said, showing a hint of the relief that he undoubtedly experienced at the time. Indeed, as Graham stated in his biography, 'it wasn't a great win and I didn't really feel the buzz that I'd always had before.'

When I caught up with John Ashton with a follow-up phonecall, after touching base through the modern-day miracle of social media, the Derbyshire man was particularly open about the whole experience. 'I'd sparred with Herol about five years previously when I was in the ABAs and to be honest he stood me on my head! He was no use to me at all! It was like a dancing session. Five years on and had Herol stayed on his feet against Julian Jackson, I'd have boxed Tony Burke for the vacant

British title. Well, that all went down the pan when Jackson scored one of the greatest knockouts I've ever seen so I had to fight Herol again!'

While Graham had been clocked by Jackson, it was believed he still had time left to make another go at title glory. His chin had been tested but his skills hadn't diminished. 'I was never going to outbox Herol,' Ashton said. 'I thought maybe I could rough him up and land a big shot. I tried everything but with Herol, what you plan to do is very different to what you CAN do! He's either too far away to hit or he's behind you! People said he couldn't punch. Let me tell you, he COULD punch. I thought I was starting to get into it towards the end but I was cut and my face opened up so Terry O'Connor stepped in.'

To sum up the fight, Ashton laughed as he relayed a line Terry O'Connor gave him a short time later. 'Terry came up to me and told me he was on the verge of stopping it in my favour. "Why?" I asked him. He told me he was worried Herol was going to break his hands on my head!'

While seemingly disappointed with the Ashton contest, what the win did do was generate interest in a return match with his old nemesis Sumbu Kalambay the following March in Pesaro, Italy. Since that first duel five years earlier, Kalambay had lifted the WBA middleweight title in the wake of 'Sugar' Ray Leonard's win over Marvin Hagler in 1987 and had then won the European title in 1990. This return with Graham would be his fourth defence. Graham was adamant about exacting revenge on the Italian-based champion. To do so, he had to be at the peak of his powers. Kalambay was moving in on another world title shot himself and a repeat win over 'Bomber' could not be written off. Indeed, *Boxing News* predicted a contentious decision win for the champion. Unfortunately for the Graham camp, it was proved right.

After a brilliant start that saw the defending titleist on the canvas twice in the second round, Kalambay fought back and appeared to work out his old adversary's style. Graham threw a lot of leather towards the champion but it never seemed to staunch his forward momentum. Receiving point deductions from the referee in the fourth round for throwing the champion to the floor and in the twelfth for rough headwork, the decision was put out of his reach. There were those who felt Graham had done enough to both gain revenge and lift the title but the title remained in Italy and Graham was left to rue what he deemed to be a clear win.

'I thought it was easier than the first fight and that was in Italy on his own soil! That was a hometown decision. I knew I had to knock him out to win but it didn't happen. He was the champion so he got it!' As was the case in each of his first three career losses, Graham returned to the domestic scene to defend the British title, now regarded as something of a birthright for the Sheffield boxer. It was always a cushion for Graham to fall back on to to recuperate and take a back seat to assess the bigger fish from afar and plan his next global assault. He was like a traveller returning to his roots to rejuvenate with some home comforts before venturing out once again to tackle the sterner challenges.

When he stepped into the ring on 23 September against Bradford's tough Frank Grant, he was facing a fellow southpaw. Sporting an unspectacular record, Grant was on a run of six wins since losing a points decision to the capable Kid Milo. In short, Graham's dominance at home was expected to continue without the proverbial headache. While the headache never surfaced, it was brutally substituted with a full-on storming migraine in the form of Grant.

With Graham controlling the ring for the first few rounds, he was getting into the stride that he was used to against seemingly inferior opposition and Grant looked bemused by the constant stream of flicking blows heading his way. As the rounds progressed, however, Grant started to land more and more and even though his cheekbone suffered with the blows landing by Graham, it was ominous to see Grant not getting disconcerted or distracted from the task at hand.

As the rounds wore on, it was becoming apparent that Graham was tiring and Grant was remaining strong and confident. Graham was finding it harder to move out of the way of many of the Bradford man's punches. Graham had an encouraging eighth round, launching flashy combinations, giving shows of bravado and moving out of the way of the incoming artillery. It proved to be a momentary relapse back to his better, younger days. The ninth round saw the end as Grant landed a crashing combination to Graham's jaw which dropped him. A follow-up assault convinced the referee, Paul Thomas, that Graham's days of being undefeated against British opposition were now at an end.

'It was all too much. My sister came to stay in my house as she had some problems. I had to go back home to look after her but I had a fight coming up and I had to go to London to train. Mentally, it was all too much,' the former champion said. 'I had taken on too much again. I had the fight, I was winning it by moving around but, mentally, I just lost it.'

Graham announced his retirement after the loss to Grant and spent the ensuing months enjoying his time with his family. While, by his own admission, he had spent much of his hard-fought money over the years, he had enough left to sustain himself on. When his son, Oliver, went to pre-school, Graham had time to dispense with and he trained and worked out at the new gym on Carlisle Street, run by Glyn Rhodes, his former gym-mate.

'Those years after the Grant fight were spent soul-searching and having a break away from everything. Probably a bit of feeling sorry for myself too! The thing about boxing is that it is just one man,' Graham explained. 'Yes, you have your trainers and managers but in sports like football, you are part of a team when it comes to playing. In boxing, it is just you and you end up with the world on your shoulders. I took that break and got away from it.'

Graham contemplated the idea of running his own gym and even testing the waters of television. The pull of boxing, however, was what clung to him like a sweat-soaked vest and as he watched more and more youngsters pass through the doors of Glyn's gym, so the desire once again grew. Holding his own in sparring with the reigning British super-middleweight champion, Cornelius Carr, increased his desire to continue his career and led him to believe that he was still of able mind and body to contribute to the sport he had come so close to reaching the top of. The thought of giving it another attempt to attain the ultimate prize was to prove too much to ignore. After a series of stringent tests by the British Boxing Board of Control, Graham was finally issued with his licence in 1996 to box once more.

Performing under the promotional guidance of Frank Maloney, Graham's first contest back after over four years out was planned against Wisconsin's trial-horse Terry Ford in Sheffield. While the opponent was significantly underwhelming, Graham needed to get back to the ring, feel his way back round the four corners and shed the accumulative layers of rust that would have undoubtedly tampered with his boxing skills. With Glyn Rhodes appearing in his corner for the first time, he got the workout over eight rounds, gaining referee Mickey Vann's vote but the old magic wasn't there and it seemed as if the old fluidity of Graham's graceful repertoires of the past had gone flat.

'After the Terry Ford fight,' Glyn Rhodes said to me when I called him during one of his breaks in Sheffield, 'I'll put my hands up and be one of the first to say it was over because, you've got to remember, Terry Ford was just a blown-up light-middleweight. I didn't see anything of the Herol Graham of old. I, with many people, thought that Herol just didn't have it no more. I said that to him too but he just said, "Stuff you!" You can say that to your mates though!'

Another eight-round points win over fellow Sheffield fighter Craig Joseph followed in March at the Elephant and Castle. Just coming off a points loss to the future world light-heavyweight champion, Clinton

Woods, Joseph was seen as a suitable opponent for the come-backing 'Bomber'. Graham looked slightly improved against Joseph and as the fight wore on into the later rounds, he found his feet and started to work Joseph over. His performance suggested that Graham may have something left to offer and a challenge, once again, for bigger rewards became a possibility. His next fight would prove to be a stern yardstick with which to measure exactly how much Graham would have left and if his decision to return after four years out would prove to be one based on delusion or sincerity.

Chris Johnson, the middleweight bronze medallist at the 1992 Barcelona Olympics, was unbeaten in 18 fights and had recorded some solid wins over able opposition. By the end of this contest, Graham would know if he had enough left to pursue his dream.

Almost immediately, the signs were good. Johnson's pressure fighting suited Graham as he thwarted Johnson's onrushes with his slick head movement and peppered the visiting fighter with his southpaw jab and quick combinations. The second round saw Graham flicking out the jab more, making it increasingly difficult for Johnson to get inside. Johnson's left was sent sailing past Graham and he was repaid for his insolence by shipping punishment against the ropes. When Johnson did press forward, he was unable to land cleanly. Graham was able to dodge his punches with nifty little jerks of his movement, bringing back memories of the great Puerto Rican former world champion, Wilfred Benitez. After slipping near the end of the round, a heavy left-right by Graham only added to Johnson's increasingly lost-looking cause.

Graham's dominance continued through the fourth but the fifth saw Johnson land some clean right hands which appeared to have an effect on Graham, one in particular towards the end of the round which sent Graham reeling back into the ropes. The sixth, however, saw the return of Graham's dominance as he resumed control and put on what was becoming a highly impressive performance.

The seventh saw the beginning of the end as a big right cross, left hook combination floored Johnson heavily on his side. It was a round controlled by Graham and although they both brawled on the ropes until the final bell with both having varying degrees of success, it was as if Johnson was trying to hold off the inevitable. Graham fought with confidence, Johnson with desperation. The eighth round was all Graham as he took control from the outset. Towards the end of the round a huge left hook clattered against the side of Johnson's jaw and he sagged as a puppet would with one string left for support. The follow-up assault drove Johnson to a corner where the protective arms of the referee shielded him from further, unnecessary punishment. It was a stunning performance by Graham.

'I was asked by a mate if I was going to watch the fight,' Graham's former foe, John Ashton told me. 'I said no as I didn't want to see Herol get smashed to bits. Afterwards, my mate told me he'd only gone and stood him on his head. Absolutely incredible!'

A true sign of Herol Graham's modesty can be obtained with the strictly limited coverage this fight received in his biography. It got just three lines when the circumstances surrounding this fight, the manner in which he performed and the alarming reality that Graham had not recorded an impressive win for over seven years, simply fed bullets into the gun used to shoot down the critics and those who thought his comeback was based on delusion and denial. It was one of Graham's most impressive showings. Not only were the doubters back-pedalling; the hands of time were too.

'I loved that fight. He was being tipped by Mickey Duff to be the next world champion! I just did my thing and what I knew I could do,' Graham said with the same air of confidence now as he showed during the fight 16 years earlier.

Life was looking very rosy once again for Graham. He married his girlfriend of the time, Nina, had his two children and was once again moving in on a world title challenge. First, however, he had to defend the WBC international title he won with the win over Johnson against the flamboyant, energetic and relentless former world lightweight and light-middleweight champion, Vinny Pazienza (nowadays known as 'Vinny Paz'). Both boxers were hunting for the world title and the reward for the winner would either be a shot at the IBF champion Charles Brewer, or the WBC king Robin Reid.

When they stepped into the ring at Wembley Arena on 6 December, Graham once again had Glyn Rhodes in his corner along with the late, highly respected, Dean Powell. The fight followed a pattern forecast by many beforehand. Pazienza's almost frenzied rushes were swept aside by the elusiveness and accuracy of Graham. 'Bomber' controlled the action and would tend to hit the target as and when he wished and avoid the response with similar ease. Graham's biggest danger was being swept off his feet by the strong gusts that followed Pazienza's fists as they flew past his head. While failing to hit the target cleanly, Pazienza possessed speed of hand and the right hands were being thrown relentlessly. For the first five rounds, Pazienza seemed bemused by Graham's magic and only something not far short of a miracle would sway proceedings back in the Rhode Islander's favour.

This was a man, however, who fractured a number of vertebrae in his neck as a passenger in a friend's car when it crashed just days after he won the IBF light-middleweight title at the end of 1991 against Frenchman Gilbert Dele. The prognosis was not good. He was told his fighting days were over but 'The Pazmanian Devil' reminded the doctor that he 'don't know what sort of man I am'. Pazienza made a full recovery and he returned from a broken neck to box once more.

The sixth round of his bout with Graham confirmed this. He landed some hard single shots that got through and for the first time, Graham looked uncomfortable. Graham regained control in the eighth after another strong round by Pazienza in the seventh where a number of hard left hooks found their target. The gap in the scorecards was surely narrowing. Pazienza resumed his furious assault in the ninth and in the subsequent minute's rest, he leant over the ropes to the American commentary team and told them Graham was getting knocked out. His prediction, at this point, couldn't be entirely written off. Pazienza rallied in the tenth round to try for the knockout but Graham took command in the 11th before an exciting last round saw both fighters go toe to toe for the full three minutes. Graham received the unanimous decision but by scores far narrower than most had expected.

Heading into 1998, Charles Brewer had defended his IBF super-middleweight title once and had developed a reputation as a strong, stylistic puncher; a boxer able to do a bit of everything. He could move, had a dangerous punch, wasn't unfamiliar suffering knockdowns and was equally capable of bouncing back. He was dangerous and, to many, a severe risk to take. With Graham, however, time was of the essence and when he was offered the fight with Brewer for the world title on the undercard of Lennox Lewis's WBC heavyweight title defence against Shannon Briggs in Atlantic City on 28 March, he didn't need asking a second time.

Graham entered the ring that night full of confidence and it showed as he made his, now customary, fast start, exchanging hard left hands with the world champion. Classic lead left hands from Graham continued to sneak through Brewer's defence in the second but they were more accurate than loaded with devastating power. Brewer fought back, throwing fast combinations. The champion was quick and was able to match Graham in this area but while he looked to unload the heavier blows, Graham was settling into a rhythm of picking his shots and building up points with blows straight down the middle.

The third round was a big one for the challenger and the world title belt never seemed closer to his trophy cabinet. Working his way in behind his southpaw jab, Graham landed a cuffing left hand as he was spinning Brewer around by the ropes. Brewer went down but got up immediately and complained to the referee that he had stumbled and slipped. The referee, Earl Morton, continued to toll the standing eight-count as the champion shook his head in frustration. Going back in, Brewer walked into a brace of big left hands and fell to the canvas. Upon rising, Brewer acknowledged to Morton that he was able to continue. He seemed stunned though and Graham moved in, just one big punch away from that elusive world title. Getting to grips with that world title would prove harder than many of his opponents getting to grips with him. At the bell to end the third round, Brewer was fighting back. That particular moment had gone for Graham.

Needing to make a stand in the contest, Brewer crowded Graham into the ropes in the fourth and the pair of them stayed there for the majority of the round as they slugged it out, both trying to gain the upper hand at close quarters. Graham was tagged by a good right hand by Brewer in the sixth and the signs were creeping in that the champion was beginning to find more success in reaching his challenger's whiskers. Brewer pushed himself forward to get Graham out of there in a show of power and strength. Graham's legs were still serving him well and he was able to move around the ring fluidly, evading the bombs being thrown his way.

Graham dominated the sixth round as he outboxed Brewer from long range. A clear winner in this round, Graham showed precisely why southpaws are avoided by many orthodox boxers. Brewer was unable to negotiate the right jab and Graham's right foot stood firm in front of him, denying Brewer the space he needed to close the challenger down. Brewer's march continued to be stalled in the seventh and even when he was able to plant his feet by the ropes, Graham cleverly moved out of the way and increased the demoralisation that must have been creeping into the champion's psyche. The eighth and ninth saw Graham outpunching Brewer and the American commentators were complimenting Graham on his style and informing the viewers what they were witnessing for themselves; that Graham's agonising wait for world title glory was coming to an end. It was now within reach and he continued to expertly turn Brewer as he swarmed forward, thereby disrupting his momentum and breaking his rhythm. The tenth round would be the last of Graham's career. Jabbing well at the start, Graham moved around the outside of the ring where Brewer saw the opening and pounced. A right swinging round from Graham's left side crashed against his head and he sagged into the ropes. Follow-up blows from both hands left Graham sitting on the middle and bottom ropes. Several punches landed flush and, with nowhere to turn to and being trapped on the ropes, Earl Morton stepped in and waved an end to the fight, Graham's world title dream and, as would prove to be the case, Graham's professional career. For the fans of Graham, who had followed his career from his early amateur days in Nottingham and Sheffield, the dream was over.

'It was dubious how the referee jumped in. If you look at the referee when he stepped in, he stopped me from getting up off the ropes. I was sat on the ropes but I wasn't hurt. I was tired because I'd been running on a sand beach,' Graham points out. 'You going running on the beach, your feet go down further so it takes more out of you.'

When I caught up with Charles Brewer and asked him about his fight with Graham, he was in no doubt as to the Sheffield man's fighting qualities. Graham, he said, gave him his hardest fight. 'Well, Graham, for me, was the most difficult fight of my 16-year career. He's a crafty southpaw and in the third round, he caught me with a straight left hand. It put me down but also, I tore three ligaments in my right ankle as a result. I fought on and I was looking to land the home run. It came in the tenth round and I must admit, my ankle was hurting like hell! But for me, Graham was my most difficult fight.'

The professional boxing career of one of Britain's great enigmas was over. The unique capabilities of the Sheffield artist would never again be seen inside the ring swapping blows. The reflexes that could see seconds ahead, bamboozling opponent after opponent. The lithe, swaying physique which had an answer for every punch the Marquis of Queensberry could legislate for. The stance enabling 'Bomber' to reach his adversary and simultaneously denying them the angles and dimensions to respond in kind, hence promoting the time-endured adage of hitting without being hit. Yet, the big prize eluded him three times. It was a hat-trick that was seen as a mirage by his adoring fans and those appreciative connoisseurs of pugilism among us, to the point of us scratching our heads in wonder when realising the mirage was in fact a shocking reality; searching for the answers as to how Herol Graham could fall so molecularly short in his search for world title glory when he possessed the required assets to seal his place in the sport's circle of greatness.

Three months after the Brewer loss, Graham and his girlfriend, Nina, had their first child, Jessica. For work, Graham became a trainer at the new Rotherham Fitness and Boxing Gym and went on to establish Skip Fit with Nina where they would visit schools and children's organisations to promote health and fitness by means of skipping classes.

Three more children arrived but when an accident at work caused the gym to close down, work dried up and tensions at home increased with a young family to cater for and work proving scarce.

In 2007, Herol got divorced from Nina and he entered a dark period. He moved into a small ex-council house in Low Edges and didn't get to see his children as often as he wished. He sunk lower into depression and when his ex-girlfriend, Karen, re-entered his life, he encountered a new lease of strength and support. She visited him in his house and provided emotional support to him as he attempted to piece his shattered life back together. His loneliness and depression clung to him like Hercules's cloak of poison though and no amount of determination could liberate him from his tortured state of mind. Karen was in a state of helplessness too as she saw Herol slip further and further into emotional oblivion and the answers to his predicament became fewer and fewer. He was finally sectioned. It was as if a burden had been lifted from his shoulders.

Today, back on his feet and in a more content place, Herol is still with Karen and is putting his hand to training and offering his priceless expertise and knowledge to young amateur protégés whom he hopes he can nurture into promising future contenders. He may yet play out a role in lifting a world title.

'I just want to mention Don Charles. Without him, this opportunity really wouldn't have happened. He did mega favours for me. Herol says a big thank you for all he has done! He didn't have to but he has been really helpful. These new guys I wanted to help, I didn't have a gym to go to so I went to Don Charles's.'

To sum up Herol Graham's career in brief would be to do his style and accomplishments a genuine disservice. He was a boxer never before seen on these shores and likely to remain incomparable for many generations to come. Yes, the stylish likes of Johnny Nelson, Naseem Hamed and Ryan Rhodes emerged from his shadow shortly after but, as Glyn Rhodes says, he has a unique place in the boxing heart of Sheffield.

'There weren't no boxing in Sheffield until Brendan and Herol came along. When Brendan started putting these shows on at City Hall, they became like an event! Nobody else were putting shows on so it gave a chance to a lad like me to box on the undercard of people like Herol Graham. Being in the gym at the same time as Herol Graham was one bonus but then I was boxing on his undercards! I have a lot of time of Herol Graham. Before him there was no boxing in Sheffield, just a handful of pros at most. He was a PIONEER.'

People nominate Herol Graham and Kirkland Laing as the best British boxers never to win the world title. This should be revised.

Kirkland Laing never encountered the chance because he favoured the relentless pace of life's fast lane and all the social temptations that went with it, therefore squandering various golden opportunities. Herol Graham, on the other hand, fought for world honours and should therefore hold the paradoxical mantle as the most talented British boxer never to win a world title fight. While this particular distinction embodies negative undertones, it is nonetheless one of a number of distinguished features that define the remarkable career of this most naturally gifted of athletes.

7
Billy Schwer

IF you scan through the opening pages of Billy Schwer's book, entitled *MENTAL BOXING – The Science of Success*, you will notice three particular words which are repeated, and referred to, frequently throughout. They form the basis of the book and, as Schwer himself is rapidly proving, the backbone to recognising one's own success. DISCIPLINE, DEDICATION and DESIRE.

The former two-time British lightweight, Commonwealth and European lightweight and International Boxing Organisation light-welterweight champion is now an 'Inspirational and Motivational Speaker' and 'Performance Coach'. This new lease of life which he has found, has given him a renewed vigour and purpose, attributes which were found wanting in the immediate aftermath of his retirement after his final fight in July 2001. This new-found zest for life was vividly present in the way he came across when we met at a cafe in Soho's Poland Street. The cafe was characteristic of the vibrant area we were in. The former boxing champion seemed to fit in perfectly.

'It had taken me 20 years to get this belt [the IBO world title] so I was going to make it pay. So, my first defence was three months later against Sarmiento and I got knocked out. Upon reflection, there is nothing to take away from him at all but I just had a fight too soon. I went to hospital after the fight. There we are, going through central London in the back of this ambulance and I looked out of the window and it was then that I realised that my life, as I knew it, was over. That was it. My life had no purpose any more. My whole life, my whole being had been about being a winner. My whole life had been geared to that. My whole life fell apart. My first two years of my retirement were the worst two years of my life. I made some really bad choices and bad decisions, wrecked my marriage and went through the divorce. I went through the wilderness and didn't know what to do. I went and did a programme called The Landmark Forum which is the catalyst of what I'm doing now.'

It was as a young boy of five years that Schwer started to develop this mental attitude of not allowing others to defeat him or get the better of him. A mindset that would nourish the foundations for what would eventually become a successful professional boxing career that would tally 39 wins with six losses, all of which came against holders of various titles. It was a mentality that would strengthen his resolve to an almost tangible level. Watching Schwer fight in the ring was a show of confidence in motion. Darting in and out with impressive hand speed, head movement and accurate punches to his adversaries' head and body, the pace never seemed to slow even when he was up against either the odds or his opponent's superior ability. The confidence shone through.

'I was five years of age and I have two older sisters, Mandy and Lisa. We were in my mum and dad's front room, rolling around the floor and they're beating me up…again! One would sit on my chest and the other would pin my arms to the floor,' he said with expressive hand movements. If anyone is able to maintain a conversation without the use of the tongue, Billy Schwer is a natural candidate. 'I'd kick and scream and I couldn't fight them off. I would hyperventilate and turn blue. I just couldn't breathe. I thought I was going to die. They both had long blonde hair and as I was pinned to the floor, they used to wave it in my face and they'd sing to me, "Biiiiilly, don't be a heeeero!" I made a decision then, at five years of age, that no one was ever going to beat me, dominate me, hurt me or top me ever again. I made an unconscious decision about myself. I was weak. I couldn't fight my sisters off so I must be weak, right? I became really tough, to survive being weak in my mind. It's about getting people to look at the decisions they make about themselves. Are they true? Is it reality? Are they empowering themselves to live the life they want?' This toughened approach to life at such an early age led to the path that guided Schwer into the world of amateur boxing.

'My dad used to be a boxer. He was the Irish featherweight champion, boxed for England and Ireland and was a schoolboy champion. He came over to England when he was 14. He was a jockey and a stable-lad too so he became a very successful amateur boxer. I used to see the old black and white photos of him around the house so I felt something was going on. At the age of eight, my dad takes me down the gym. He said I kept on at him to take me down there. I was looking for a way to express myself. I was trying to cover up being weak. Boxing is such a perfect match for someone who is trying to prove they're not weak. That was one of my insecurities. I went down there and had my first fight when I was 11. I was crap at school, spending all my time looking out of the window and I was dyslexic too so I just didn't get it at all. I excelled at sport and I was good. In my third amateur fight, the other kid wins. I'm in absolute bits, bawling my eyes out. My dad's trying to console me. I made another unconscious decision about myself that I wasn't good enough. My belief was that I'd won the first two so I was a natural. I should have won that third fight. All these doubts I had about myself were perfect drivers to become a champion fighter. I'm prepared to go to the death to prove that I'm not weak and that I'm good enough. At 13 I won a schoolboy title. They got me to stand up in assembly as it was a really big thing. I remember everyone looking at me when I stood up and thinking, "I don't fit in. I'm different, I'm alone and I don't fit in."'

It is a sign of Schwer's mental strength, whether natural or self-developed, that regardless of these self-doubts and knocks to his confidence, he was able to go on to significant amateur success. In 1990 he reached the finals of the ABA Featherweight Championships at the Royal Albert Hall, losing out very closely to Patrick Gallagher in the lightweight category.

'I also boxed for young England against young Yugoslavia and Mickey Duff was in the room. I stopped the guy and Mickey Duff came up to me and my dad after and said, "If you ever want to turn pro, give us a call." At the time, he was the main man. He had control of the BBC. That was the only media showing boxing. There was no Sky. He was the guy I wanted to turn pro with. After losing to Gallagher in the ABA finals, which could have gone either way, I thought I may as well give it a shot at going as a pro. Mickey was the only guy I wanted to see so I went to his office in Wardour Street with my dad. I imagined myself becoming world champion and that was that.'

During that meeting, Schwer signed a three-year deal with Mickey Duff and his professional career began at York Hall, Bethnal Green, on 4 October 1990 with a first-round stoppage of Frenchman Pierre Conan. On the same fight bill was the Commonwealth cruiserweight champion Derek Angol in a non-title fight, and the European light-welterweight champion Pat Barrett, also in a non-title fight. They were both being primed for world title challenges. Schwer had his sights fixed in the same direction. Over the next 23 months, Schwer built up an impressive résumé with 16 more wins including 13 of them coming inside the distance. He fought an assortment of tough journeymen with the occasional easy-picking to bolster his record and, more importantly, his confidence. Benefitting from the expertise and high standing of Mickey Duff, he gained some invaluable exposure during this time, appearing on the undercard to main events that had substantial international significance. He fought in the build-up to Paul Hodkinson's European featherweight title defence against Guy Bellehigue and Gary Mason's heavyweight international ten-rounder against James Pritchard, both in 1990. The following year, he popped up on the supporting bill to Del Bryan's British welterweight title victory over Kirkland Laing, Lennox Lewis's second title win when he jabbed and boxed brilliantly to take the British heavyweight title off the aforementioned Gary Mason, Duke McKenzie's stunning win over the Texan Gaby Canizales for the WBO bantamweight title, the third instalment of the Jeff Harding–Dennis Andries light-heavyweight world title trilogy and then Frank Bruno's first comeback fight post-Tyson when he reduced the Netherlands' John Emmen into the human version of that famous locomotive, 'The Flying Dutchman'.

'I sparred Dennis Andries once!' Schwer said animatedly with a huge grin spread across his face. 'I was a kid sparring him. Can you imagine that?! He was very gentle with me thankfully. It was like boxing a bit of granite. It was a kid boxing a man. Brilliant!'

With 17 wins under his belt, Schwer was manoeuvred into position to challenge Carl Crook for the British and Commonwealth lightweight title at the Royal Albert Hall on 28 October 1992. Mickey Duff beat rival promoter Barry Hearn to win the purse bids for the fight and earned as good as home advantage for Schwer. His legion of fans travelled down from Luton with Crook and his army of followers having to make the trip down from Manchester. Claude Abrams of *Boxing News* predicted a successful defence for the Mancunian. The fighters had one opponent in common by the name of Patrick Kamy. Crook outpointed him while Schwer sent him packing within the first three minutes of their contest a few years after. This, ominously, suggested who the puncher of the two was and so it was to prove. In a fight featuring fluctuating fortunes, the pair put on a show that was not much short of thrilling. Apart from a small number of fans watching, who decided to instigate a fight of their own, those present were treated to one of the best British fights in recent memory. After a feeling-out session in the opener, Schwer took the ascendancy in the second and held it until Crook demonstrated his hit-and-move tactics in the middle rounds to even up the tally. Throwing in the occasional power shot too, Crook seemed to have found a way through. In the sixth, however, Schwer hit home with a crunching right hand that placed the fight firmly back in his control and that is where it stayed. Producing a brilliant display of power-punching, Schwer went on to lift the belts with a ninth-round stoppage after Crook had been floored three times, courtesy of a series of punches which landed with sickening accuracy.

'That was one of my favourite venues. That was a moment in time, a day I will never forget. We had the whole of Luton there. I remember walking out of the changing rooms which were underneath where the ring was and it was like being a gladiator. The place was like a cauldron. The noise was incredible. Because of the shape of the Albert Hall, it was like going into an amphitheatre. It was absolutely phenomenal. I boxed brilliantly. I was the new kid on the block but I would have won a world title that night. I had Dennie Mancini in my corner and I was absolutely flying. I had to keep looking at the cards because the whole fight just flew past. I could have boxed all night. Before the last round, the fans invaded the ring because they all knew it was about to be over and John Morris [then general secretary of the British Boxing Board of Control] was telling them all to get out! After the fight, I remember being carried off back to the changing rooms. My dad's friend took us there in a Rolls-Royce, I was unbeaten and I won the titles! What a great memory.'

With a third-round cut-eye stoppage over the former WBO lightweight champion, Mauricio Aceves, in December in a non-title fight, Schwer signed to fight Preston's Paul Burke in his first British and Commonwealth title defence on 24 February. Schwer had, ominously, been cut himself against Aceves and this served as a warning. Burke had just come off a points loss against Jean-Baptiste Mendy the previous November for the European title in Paris. He gave the Frenchman a good fight and showed capable all-round skills. Fighting out of Phil Martin's impressive stable based out of Manchester's infamous Moss Side district, Burke was a serious test. In the end, Schwer lost his titles in bloody fashion, sustaining cuts that brought about a premature end in the seventh round.

'There were a couple of cuts and he was a good fighter. It was a good fight too.' Schwer was gracious in defeat. His cutman, Dennie Mancini, was furious. Mancini claimed to have been able to stem the flow of blood flowing down the centre of Schwer's face and deemed the stoppage particularly galling as Burke had suffered a cut himself.

Boxing News stated at the time, 'The injuries which curtailed his brief spell as champion must now also cast serious doubt over the rest of his career.' Characteristically, Schwer is not one to let such issues disconcert him.

He returned in June to get a good ten-round workout under his belt against Farid Benredjeb, former two-time European featherweight title challenger, in Hemel Hempstead, registering a comfortable points win. The path was now unobstructed and led to the Watford Town Hall on 10 November where the rematch with Burke took place. Schwer worked methodically over the course of 12 hard rounds to regain the titles he'd lost previously, flooring Burke in the third, tenth and 11th rounds to secure his victory.

'I didn't really change my fight plan from the first time. I remember hitting him with a right in the fifth round, I put him down but broke my hand so I boxed for seven rounds with one hand really. I was in absolute agony but floored him twice more with left hands! I got smashed to bits and my nose was that big,' Schwer said, holding an open palm out a few inches in front of his face. He passed me a couple of photos he'd brought to show me of him after the fight back in his dressing room. His nose was noticeably misshapen and his right hand was sunk, deep inside a large bucket full of ice. The smile hadn't left his face. 'It tells a good story, that picture,' I said. 'Corr yeah, an occupational hazard!' he replied.

Three months later, Schwer stepped back into the ring to defend his newly regained titles against St Albans's Sean Murphy, the former two-time British featherweight champion and, in his previous fight, unsuccessful challenger for Steve Robinson's WBO featherweight title. Murphy gained weight to bypass the super-featherweight division to go head-first into a fight with Luton's favourite son. The fight ended in the third round, therefore giving Schwer the Lonsdale belt as he had now successfully defended his British title twice. It was to be Murphy's final professional contest. 'That was a good fight for me. He'd been in some wars but he was a featherweight really. That was the fight that got me the Lonsdale belt. I got to keep that belt. It's my pride and joy. It's beautiful.'

'I'd boxed at lightweight once before,' Murphy explained to me. 'I knocked out Ian Honeywood in a round but I was called at Christmas and was told I had a bout. I presumed I'd be moving up to super-featherweight. I was told I had Billy Schwer at lightweight! I never ducked anyone. I would have fought anyone. I told my wife before the fight that whether I win or lose the fight, I would retire. I went out there and had a toe-to-toe war with him. I should have boxed him!'

For Schwer, there was no resting on his laurels though as the following month, he travelled twice to York Hall to despatch John Roby and Edgar Castro in two and five rounds respectively. Attention within the Schwer camp now turned towards the world title and the belts on offer were owned by Miguel Angel Gonzalez (WBC), Orzubek Nazarov

(WBA), Rafael Ruelas (IBF) and Giovanni Parisi (WBO). The choice of Schwer's next opponent was used as a benchmark to see how he would cope with someone of a similar physical stature to the IBF champion, Ruelas. Challenging for Schwer's Commonwealth title, Howard Grant was the first unbeaten opponent of Schwer's career and travelled over from Canada with serious intent of gate-crashing the world scene. He had a very impressive amateur pedigree which included a silver medal in the 1996 world championships, a gold medal in the Commonwealth Games that same year and participating in the 1988 Seoul Olympic Games. As a professional, he had held the future IBF light-welterweight champion, Jake Rodriguez, to a draw. While the champion outweighed Grant by three-quarters of a pound, the challenger from Montreal looked bigger. He stood tall and was well-defined in physique. He was the ideal tune-up for the proposed Ruelas fight.

The fight took place on 11 May and was considered by Mickey Duff to be the finest performance of Schwer's career to date. Schwer, again, had to overcome the hurdle of fragile skin tissue around the eyes. Suffering cuts and bruises to both eyes, Schwer stuck to the task and ground Grant down for an impressive win in nine rounds. In relation to the planned title challenge to Ruelas, *Boxing News* stated in its fight review, 'The same concentration, composure and sharp, disciplined attacking should assure Schwer a fair chance against the Californian.'

'Mickey got me that fight because Howard was tall and gangly, similar to Ruelas. That fight was brutal. I remember I had three cuts. I'm in the ring and he's knocking the daylights out of me and I'm getting battered. My next fight is for the world title and I'm thinking, "Mickey, what are you doing getting me this animal!" I remember him whacking me around the body and I was thinking, "What the hell is going on here?" Dennie Mancini was doing his job in the corner with the three cuts and I remember having this thought during the fight, "If I get stopped at least it will be on cuts." I had that thought but I stuck with it and I ended up doing him in the ninth round. Tough, tough fight that was.'

The final hurdle before Schwer's first world title challenge had been jumped. An unusual step was taken by promoters Bob Arum and Barry Hearn to stage a promotion that October in Hong Kong, featuring Schwer's title challenge to Rafael Ruelas along with WBO title defences for Steve Collins and the organisation's heavyweight flag-bearer, Herbie Hide. Also scheduled to feature was a fascinating heavyweight contest between Frank Bruno and the former WBO champion and US Army Sergeant, 'Merciless' Ray Mercer. Financing the event was a company called Hemdale, headed by John Daly, who famously played a part in making the 'Rumble in the Jungle' happen in 1974. Promoted as 'High Noon in Hong Kong', the event hit obstacles from the off. Both promoters had been guaranteed $1.5m by Daly. The boxers' contracts were held by Bob Arum's Top Rank outfit. When Hearn wanted his guarantee to be honoured, Daly's bank wasn't forthcoming with the necessary funds and the promotion's cancellation was announced at the weigh-in the day before. Mickey Duff left no doubt in his book, *Twenty and Out*, as to whose head should have been on the chopping block.

'Daly said he had arranged the stadium, air fares and pre-fight promotional expenses but the purses for the fighters were a matter for Top Rank as they held the contracts. Arum was not prepared to put his company's money in to salvage the show. What kind of a promoter is that? I've been in this business 45 years and I've never cancelled a show because I was going to lose money. I would rather cut my throat.'

Keeping in shape, Schwer scored a sixth-round knockout on 9 November against Mexican Manuel Hernandez at Millwall. The Ruelas fight was rearranged for 28 January at the MGM Grand hotel on the Las Vegas strip. Under the auspices of Dan Goossen, Ruelas and his brother Gabriel had built up a formidable reputation, scoring a long list of spectacular knockouts against a varying pedigree of opponent over the years. Rafael had been IBF lightweight champion for just short of a year and was making his second defence against Schwer.

The fight started well for Schwer as he got down to business with his jab and scored a series of nifty, points-scoring uppercuts in close. Ruelas looked unsettled and generally riled by the effectiveness of his challenger's punching. What was noticed though, were Ruelas' overhand rights that regularly found their target. While they didn't appear to put Schwer off his fight plan, they reddened the areas around his eyes and the sands of time looked to be diminishing. In the third round, the first cut appeared over the left eye. The work of Dennie Mancini stemmed the cut but in the fifth, Schwer's face was a mask of blood. Referee Mills 'Let's get it on' Lane called over the ringside doctor to have a look at the injury at the end of the round. When it reopened at the start of the sixth, another check by the doctor was given. Sensing an element of desperation, Schwer responded ferociously, landing enough hooks from both hands to take the round on two judges' scorecards. In the seventh, Ruelas lowered his workrate and in the eighth, Schwer repeatedly made the Californian miss. During the interval however, Mickey Duff compassionately withdrew his fighter, his cuts too bad to allow him to continue.

'I had a 50-50 chance to win that fight. I went in there to win and really believed I could. It was amazing. I was a kid from Luton and I arrive in Vegas. I was walking down the Las Vegas strip and you look at the big hotels, the lights and the limousines. Standing outside the MGM Grand, I look up and 30 feet up is my name with big flashing lights. 'BILLY SCHWER – LUTON'. Amazing. We had a fair few fans over there. I had two huge cuts in that fight.

'I remember Mills Lane coming over to my corner at the end of the seventh and he said, "Kid, I'm gonna give you one more round!" Have you ever felt under that sort of pressure to perform? He was saying I had to go and knock him out. I didn't so they stopped the fight.' Mickey Duff turned to Dr Flip Homansky and simply said, 'Do what you have to do.'

'Mickey Duff fights for his fighters. Because of that, Mickey Duff will have a run-in with anyone! I haven't a bad word to say about him. I knew he was on my side and I've seen him kick off but he fights for his fighters. He's a businessman. He's a Jewish businessman. We are in a business. We're a commodity. Fighters are nutcases! Fighters aren't all there. Think about it, if you go in a ring you are not all there. You're nuts! But it was our lifeblood and we LOVED it! To get that opportunity to express yourself on the world stage was incredible. I loved it! It was such a rollercoaster, such a mixed bag of emotions.'

Schwer went on to outline the theory he has adopted to aim for success. The criteria needed to push oneself forward and realise their potential and the part one plays to make their dreams and hopes a reality. It plays a key part in his current role as a performance coach and motivational speaker.

'Win or lose, you choose. CHOOSE. Choose your future, choose your life. Confront and challenge your fears. CONFRONT. I had a fight in the National Schoolboy finals at 13 years of age. I walked into the Assembly Rooms in Derby and I was absolutely petrified. Didn't sleep, didn't eat and couldn't sit still. In the corner before the fight, I went to put the gloves on and I said to my dad, "I can't do it, I can't do it." He turned to me and said, "What do you mean you can't do it?" I went off behind these drapes and was physically sick. I came back, stepped into the ring absolutely petrified but stepped out a champion. At that stage I knew I could succeed. Confronted with adversity, you CAN succeed. FIGHT FOR WHAT YOU WANT. YOU'RE ONLY AS GOOD AS YOUR NEXT FIGHT. It is all about the future you are moving in to. The future that you are creating, generating and causing. I go and lecture this to corporations. It's not hard. It can't be. I made them up! You CAN succeed. What happens in the future is down to the decisions you make NOW.'

Schwer made a decision at this point to continue after the loss to Ruelas and made a successful defence of his Commonwealth title against Stephen Chungu at York Hall, scoring an 11th-round knockout, to get him back on the winning track. A non-title win against Bruno Rabanales and another Commonwealth title defence against Ditau Molefyane, which ended in the eighth round, followed.

His next defence was scheduled against David Tetteh for 25 November to top off a hectic year's schedule. Schwer lost his title by a 12th-round stoppage in a fight which lent weight to the argument that the deposed champion was in need of a break from the ring. Most viewers had Schwer ahead going into that fateful last round. The referee, Richie Davies, stopped the bout with Schwer under pressure against the ropes and later told Mickey Duff that his fighter had no chance of winning. 'That was a bad experience. I don't think they should've stopped that fight. That's my view. After that fight, I found myself out in the wilderness and had to get myself back up there. Everything sort of crashed a little bit.'

In 1996 Schwer recorded four wins to get himself a ranking with the European Boxing Union. 'I got ranked number one in Europe but we lost the purse bids to host a planned European title challenge here. We went to Spain to fight Oscar Garcia Cano for the title. What an experience that was.'

While Schwer was stepping into the lion's den by climbing through the ropes at the Pabellon Principe Felipe in Zaragoza, he was up against a European champion who, while enjoying the advantage of home support, was distinctly inexperienced compared to Schwer and appeared to lack the skills of the Luton challenger. In having just nine fights, all wins with six knockouts, his ring experience was incomparable to Schwer's. Claude Abrams predicted a win for Schwer but went for a distance fight, confident that the judges in a foreign land would not allow themselves to be swayed by home support. What transpired was a victory for Schwer that surpassed all expectations. In winning, he became the first British challenger to win a European championship from a Spaniard outside of Britain. Cano also did much better than many thought. At the time of the stoppage in the tenth round, all three judges, from Italy, France and Switzerland, had the champion ahead. Schwer had to survive many anxious moments but ultimately, it was his tenacity and perseverance which saw him through. Two huge right hands bowled Cano over in what turned out to be the final round. He rose and was instantly backed up by a couple more blows whereupon referee Bob Logist brought proceedings to a close. The path to another world title challenge seemed defined once more. After a non-title fight the following March, a near whitewash of Senegal-born French journeyman Jean Gomis over ten rounds, he defended his title with a seventh-round stoppage of a previous holder of the title, Carlos Fernandes and then the same result over a future WBO lightweight title challenger, Hungary's Zoltan Kalocsai, in January 1999.

Speeding up the world rankings, Schwer faced one more obstacle before a likely second world title opportunity. On 8 May 1999, he faced the Italian lightweight champion, Sandro 'Zorba' Casamonica from Lazio, back at the York Hall. At one minute and 27 seconds into the eighth round, the Italian turned his back and walked back to his corner, signalling his retirement from the fight. Casamonica would come to these shores again over three years later and face Jason Cook for this same belt, only to come up short again courtesy of a third-round left hook.

The British Boxing Board of Control's inspector for that fight was Richard Clark. He remembers the occasion well and was left with an everlasting impression of the compassionate and warm personality of the European champion.

'There are a lot of parallels between Billy Schwer and Henry Cooper. He was brought up the right way, Henry Cooper was, with Jim Wicks. I don't think Bill was rushed in either with Mickey Duff. The one parallel which I really like is that they were both such down-to-earth nice men in such a really, really hard, horrible, cut-throat business. Bill was always one who endeared himself to the public by the way he conducted himself. He was boxing for a company called National Promotions run by Mickey Duff, Terry Lawless and Jarvis Astaire. I remember going to York Hall to watch Bill box before I got involved with the board. It was a ten-round non-title fight. He must have got caught in traffic because we were in the changing room. Me and Terry Lawless's son, Steve, were there. Bill came in and it was the first time I had ever experienced a pro dressing room like it. Bill's attitude was like talking to a brick wall, not that there was any talking to a pro fighter on fight night anyway. You could tell his mindset wasn't on being nice, sociable or exchanging pleasantries. I'll never forget. It was the first time I'd ever seen Bill like that. He was very, very businesslike, very professional and very stoney-faced. His father was a lovely man. The whole team was a joy to be around and his father always wore a t-shirt with a picture of Bill on it. They used to sell shed-loads of tickets. It was almost like a London fighter really. He used to fill York Hall and Wembley. He wins his European title in Spain. Unbelievable that was. By the Casamonica fight, I was an inspector with the board. I had a mate called Bradley Horne at that time who had cancer and it was terminal. He loved his boxing and he came up that night. I told Mickey Duff about this fella and he clearly wasn't well. He was suffering.

'I asked Mickey, "Would it be alright if he came in the changing room and meets Bill?" and Mickey Duff said, "I don't care about the result. Win, lose or draw, you bring the lad through." Mickey Duff went up to this lad, put his arm around him, wished him well and signed his programme. Bradley went into the dressing room after the fight and there was Bill in his underwear with his European championship belt wrapped around his waist which he took out of his bag especially to have a photo with my pal. Bill signed that photo for Bradley when it came out. My pal died shortly after that. Everything seemed to be going well for Bill at this stage. He seemed to have the cuts problem under control. He used to have his shorts made by a company called Mr Power I think. He only wanted to have an inch gap between the thigh and the shorts! The impression it gave was that he either had these skin-tight shorts on or it made him look big. He looked like a very hard, solid lightweight. He looked good at the weight too. He was an aggressive, good, two-handed, authoritative puncher-boxer.'

The way was now clear for a second crack at world honours. In the opposing corner in Wembley on 29 November 1999, having travelled to these shores, was the World Boxing Council champion Stevie Johnston. He was enjoying his second tenure as a world champion, having avenged a prior, controversial decision loss to Cesar Bazan to initiate his second term in power. He was defending against Schwer in his ninth world title fight and had scored wins over such quality adversaries as James Page, Sharmba Mitchell, Howard Grant, Jean-Baptiste Mendy and Angel Manfredy. Johnston was a slick operator who was clever, experienced and was regarded as one of the best of his day. Unfortunately for Schwer, he came up against one of the best on one of his best days and, while performing gamely, was unable to match the champion's superior ability and lost a points decision by three identical scores of 118-110. Ironically, while Schwer suffered his, now customary, facial cuts, the champion also suffered facially with cuts to his right cheek, right eye and to the bridge of his nose. The preparation for the fight, however, was not ideal and while most people would state that Johnston would have been too much for Schwer on any given day, there is little doubt in Richard Clark's view that the fight would have been more uncomfortable for the champion had the build-up for the challenger been better.

Rod Douglas with trainer, Peter Morgan. Both pictures Rod Douglas

Rod Douglas stands over another brutalised opponent with his trainer, Peter Morgan, looking on.

Dr O'Callaghan gives George Groves a post-fight check after the Fulham boxer was knocked out in his rematch with Carl Froch. David O'Callaghan

Tony Conquest lands a crunching right hand to the side of Wadi Camacho's head in October 2013 at the O2 arena in Greenwich. Pictures Richard Clark

Tony Conquest stands with his manager, Richard Clark, and his trainer and former British and WBU light-welterweight champion, Jason Rowland.

Steve Goodwin (right) with Goodwin Promotions' matchmaker, Kevin Campion, son Josh, fellow promoter Eddie Hearn and his daughter Olivia. Pictures Kevin Campion and Steve Goodwin

Steve Goodwin stands with Miles Shinkwin and Joel McIntyre prior to their ten-round contest at Bethnal Green's York Hall in July 2014.

James Cook with (from l to r) Johnny Melfah, himself, Herol Graham and Michael Watson, prior to his British middleweight title fight with 'Bomber' Graham. Pictures James Cook

James Cook in his fighting pose.

Herol Graham goes on the attack against Mike McCallum in 1989.
Pictures Action Images

Vinny Pazienza looks for openings in Herol Graham's defence.

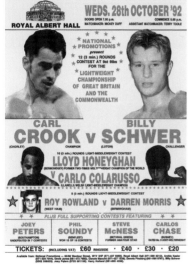

The promotional poster for Billy Schwer's British and Commonwealth title challenge against Carl Crook.
Pictures Action Images

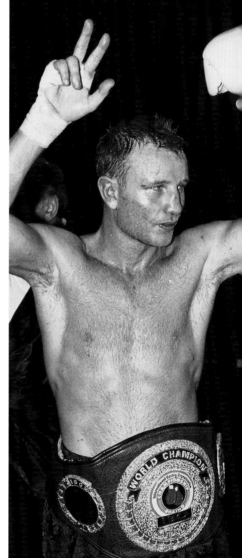

Billy Schwer, showing the wounds of battle, in celebratory mood after wresting the IBO light-welterweight title off Newton Villareal in April 2001.

(Above left) Wayne Alexander with trainer, Jimmy Tibbs.
(Above right) Wayne Alexander standing proud with his WBU light-middleweight belt.
(Left) Wayne Alexander walks away from the flattened Christian Bladt after landing one mighty right hand in the fifth round of their 2005 contest.
Pictures Wayne Alexander

(Above left) Colin McMillan lands a flush right cross on the jaw of St. Albans' Sean Murphy in their 1991 contest which McMillan won handily to win the Lonsdale belt outright. (Above right) Colin, as he is today, with old foes, Sean Murphy and Gary De'Roux. (Left) Colin McMillan with the author at a fundraising event – March 2014. Pictures Colin McMillan, Phil Sharkey and Ben Calder-Smith

Sammy Reeson dodges a straight left to land a right cross on Stewart Lithgo on the way to winning the British cruiserweight title at Battersea's Latchmere Leisure Centre in 1985. The win sealed his place in boxing history.

After the Lithgo fight, Reeson stands proud with the late Tony Lavelle and his eldest son, Scott.

The Reeson family. Sammy, his son Scott and his father, Nobby celebrate his British title victory. Pictures Sammy Reeson

(Above left) Derek Williams stopping the former world title challenger, David Bey, in 1991. (Above right) Derek Williams destroys the former British heavyweight champion, Trevor Hughroy Currie, in one round in 1989 to lift the vacant European title and to defend his Commonwealth belt. (Left) Derek Williams savours his win over Currie. Pictures Derek Williams

McDonnell strikes a fighting pose with arch-rival and former world champion, Barry McGuigan prior to their fight in May 1989. The win would set McDonnell up for the challenge against Azumah Nelson. Pictures Action Images

McDonnell throws the left against a crouching Azumah Nelson on fireworks night 1989. While ultimately losing, McDonnell produced a cracking display.

Horace Notice lands an overhand right to the head of Trevor Hughroy Currie in their rematch. Pictures Horace Notice

Infighting as Currie goes to the body and Notice lands to the head.

Mark Prince throws the jab with deadly accuracy against the veteran Lenzie Morgan in 1995. Pictures Mark Prince

Prince prepares to enter the ring to resume his professional career in October 2013 after a 14-year hiatus.

'My friend Bradley died on 10 November 1999 and a few weeks later,' Richard Clark stated, 'Bill was in the ring challenging for the world lightweight title against Johnston. At one point in that fight, Dennie Mancini folded a wad of lint and stuck it in the hole in the bridge of Billy's nose, a bit like the one Colin Jones had against Don Curry. His nose was split right in two. It was blatantly apparent that nothing was right in that fight though. Bill just didn't seem to catch fire. Everything that seemed so good in those European title defences was seen to be flat. You almost felt as though this fight happened too late.'

There was controversy after the contest when it came to light that Johnston had failed a drug test, tarnishing his dominant performance and therefore starting demands for the World Boxing Council to strip the champion of his title. 'I think the WBC should have ordered an immediate contest of their lightweight title between Bill Schwer and their number two contender. I also think that Johnston should have been stripped, undoubtedly because he retained that title on drugs,' Richard Clark said. Almost a year later, Schwer went in with Liverpool's Colin Dunne who was making the fifth defence of the World Boxing Union lightweight title. In a to and fro match which saw each fighter's fortunes shift time and again, Dunne came through on a split decision. Not to be deterred, Schwer was handed a chance to lift the IBO light-welterweight title from the hard-hitting champion from Colombia, Newton Villareal. The higher weight suited the challenger as making the lightweight limit was becoming increasingly trying. As his trainer, Jack Lindsay, said at the time when interviewed by *Boxing News*, 'No matter how hard he worked in the gym for Dunne, at the end of each session he was 10st 2lbs.'

In a gruelling, hard fight, Schwer emerged the winner after 12 tough rounds to finally lift a version of the world title. 'When I won the title and beat Newton Villareal, I ended up in hospital. I was there for a couple of days with concussion but I was ok. I was lying in hospital waiting for a brain scan. I was frightened. We organised an after-fight party in Luton and while in the car, I said I didn't feel right. We stopped the car and I threw up so we went straight to hospital and missed the party! When I came out of there I just wanted to see the money! I went for the Sarmiento fight a few months later and got knocked out. I was just in a hurry.'

This was Schwer's final fight. It was shortly after this that he had got involved with The Landmark Forum. After about ten years, he came up with the idea of 'mental boxing'. It has proved hugely beneficial to those people and groups he addresses to explain his self-defined secrets of success. Numerous testimonials support this and his influence through his power of speech has resulted in much positive feedback, stating how his work has changed the lives of many of those who gave up their time to listen. He goes into prisons to speak with the inmates. He likes the idea of these individuals creating their future and realising that dreams and aspirations can become a reality with the application of those three Ds.

Billy Schwer is someone who refuses to be discouraged from the task at hand or the plan for the future. As Richard Clark accurately stated in his summing-up of the boy from Luton, 'Consummate professional, a credit to the sport, somebody that could show any young fighter how to conduct themselves in or out of a boxing ring and I would say he is up there with some of the best role models this country has ever produced. He was actually an excellent fighter too; someone I was privileged enough to sit ringside and watch. I can't speak too highly of him.'

The 1974 hit 'Billy Don't Be A Hero' by Nottingham-based band Paper Lace, that Schwer was taunted with by his sisters all those years ago, was about a young Unionist soldier going off to battle in the American Civil War and refuting the pleas of his young fiancée, who begged him not to go. He never returned alive. At the end of the video, Billy's fiancée receives the letter informing her that Billy had died in battle. She screws it up and discards it to the wind. The similarities are apparent up to the moment of destiny. For, while the soldier meets his end, one has the distinct impression that his present-day's namesake has many more chapters to open.

8

Wayne Alexander

'MY dream, as a kid, was for people to say in years to come, "Wayne Alexander was a good boxer,"' he said as he handed me a freshly-squeezed mango juice and sat down in the cafe at East Croydon train station. 'It wasn't about money or fame. It was about people saying he was a bloody good boxer,' the former Southern Area, British, European and World Boxing Union (WBU) light-middleweight champion added. What subsequently took place was a boxing career that increasingly became a byword for crippling punching power; power which treated the viewer to knockouts of chilling, clinical precision. It was during the very early years, however, that the boxing bug burrowed.

Born in St George's hospital in Tooting, south-west London, in 1973, Alexander and his family moved to Croydon in 1981, where he has remained ever since. The high energy levels that would guide him into his chosen profession were apparent from an early age and he wasn't unaccustomed to the occasional scrape with other pupils at school and other members of his family.

'You know what? I was a very hyperactive kid. Getting into little fights at school and giving my sister a few scraps here and there. When I moved to Croydon I had a friend of mine who was boxing for Croydon Boxing Club in Thornton Heath. It's gone now but I heard my friend saying he did boxing and I asked him where it was because I wanted to try this boxing thing. I wanted to have a go. I went to the gym and I would say within ten minutes, it was like I found what I was looking for. It was my niche. I wasn't very good at school. I didn't think I was very good at much, even at ten or 11. I went to the gym and it was like I was at home. Within a couple of weeks I was the best guy in the gym.

Everyone looked up to me and I felt like I was special there. Outside the ring, I didn't feel I was worth much so in the gym I was the one people were talking about. That is where I expressed myself. That was my talent. John Niverson, my first trainer, people could see was spending more time with me. He was watching the other kids but he made me feel special. He was a great man and may he rest in peace. He told me I was going to be good and just to keep training. I had a few trainers there and they all said I was going to be a champion.'

With this talent starting to shine through and grab the attention of those nearest to him in the gym, the blessing of those nearest to him back home would also be sought.

'My dad followed me from day dot to the end of my career. My dad was like my best friend. My mum didn't like boxing. She didn't like it. She basically saw two guys hitting and hurting each other. She didn't really see the skill side to it. She didn't understand it. She knew I was good at it. She didn't say "don't do it" but in my whole career, my mum never came to see me fight once. You'll laugh, the first fight she ever watched of me in my whole years in boxing was the Paul Samuels fight on TV! She told me she almost had a heart attack! She was with my sister and her friend and it was the most exciting fight in years. When she watched it, the commentator was saying, "Oh, Wayne's hurt! He's knocked down!" The fight was so exciting, she nearly collapsed! She didn't watch a fight after that again! That was the only fight she watched in her whole life!'

Alexander is quick to mention the differences between the Croydon he grew up in and the Croydon which exists today. The Croydon which became one of the media focal points during the infamous London riots which ignited on 6 August 2011 is a far cry from that which existed during Alexander's youth. 'Croydon wasn't the Croydon of now. Obviously as a ten-year-old back in the 1980s, you weren't as advanced as the ten-year-olds of nowadays. I wasn't allowed to go round the block on my bike. Things were more innocent then. Croydon has changed, it's definitely changed. Me growing up in Croydon, I'm not going to say I am from the mean streets or from the ghetto because I wasn't. Croydon wasn't rough. I noticed that change when I was in my late teens but I had good parents. I was kept indoors. I wasn't allowed to roam the streets as some kids were. Mum and dad are still together now so I had a good grounding. To see a couple together now for more than ten years is unheard of isn't it?'

Apart from a cousin who was married to Bunny Johnson, the former British and Commonwealth heavyweight champion and British light-heavyweight champion, Wayne Alexander initiated the connection between his family and the noble art. He revisits the connection to Bunny Johnson with a smile. 'I wish he was my cousin so we had the same blood. As a kid, I was telling everybody he was my cousin but he was just married to a cousin of ours! No one else in my family ever boxed.'

Under the strict scrutiny of John Niverson, Alexander proceeded to have a very accomplished amateur career. In 1990, he won the London ABA class B welterweight championship to sit alongside the National Junior ABA title he also collected. 'That was special to me, my first national title. As a schoolboy, I wanted to become schoolboy champion. I done that and then wanted to win the national title. As a kid, that is like winning the Lonsdale belt or world title, to win the national title. I still remember it today. May 1990 at the York Hall. Naseem Hamed and Junior Witter were on the bill. I remember the crowd booing Hamed then. He was flash but he had no power then. Good on his feet but had NO power!'

In 1993, Alexander dropped a decision to the future British, Commonwealth and European middleweight champion Howard Eastman, but four years later he reached the final of the ABA light-middleweight championship where he squared off against Triumph ABC's Steve Bendall. Starting the contest confidently, Bendall speared Alexander with several southpaw jabs before unleashing a left hook in close which dumped Alexander on the seat of his pants for a brief count. Alexander fought back and got through with a series of hard lefts and a right to force his opponent to take a standing count. A stunning left hook followed to put Bendall down and when the follow-up combination hit home, Alexander was the new ABA champion. I spoke with Steve Bendall about this contest and he showed no hesitation in rating the Croydon boxer's punching power.

'He hit like a hammer! The hardest puncher I ever met throughout my amateur and pro career in over 150 fights. I dropped him which shocked me. I didn't want to get involved because he would be dangerous but he dropped me and the ref stopped it not long after. There was actually a picture in the paper after he'd hit me and I was obviously trying to hold myself up through natural instinct. You could see in the picture my eyes were gone!'

While winning the ABA title was a big accomplishment for Alexander, 1994 was also a year of big disappointment and frustration. He just missed out on realising one of his dreams of competing in the Commonwealth Games in Canada.

'My dream was to go to the Commonwealth Games. That was one of my biggest disappointments as an amateur. Even thinking about it today upsets me because even though it wasn't as big as the Olympics, I could have shown the world my skills in an international tournament. It would have been a great thing to do. The worst thing about it was after I won the ABAs in 94, I boxed in the Multi-Nations in Liverpool and I beat Joe Townsley from Scotland and I lost to Allan Bayne from Canada in the quarter-finals. Scotland picked Joe Townsley to represent them in the Commonwealth Games. He went on to get the bronze medal and the guy that beat me went on to get stopped. That just shows you how boxing is!'

The following year, Alexander climbed into the ring with Richard Williams, the future Commonwealth and IBO light-middleweight champion in the professional ranks. Having been crowned the South-East London champion for the third year running, Alexander climbed into the ring against Williams in the final of the London ABAs. What occurred in that ring has received endless plaudits and is recognised as one of the finest amateur contests you are likely to see. It could have passed as a professional bout of the highest quality.

In the first round, Williams adopted a brilliant jab which kept his fearsome opponent at bay and then followed up with accurate combinations. Alexander went looking for openings to unload his power into. He got through with occasional lefts and rights but the round belonged to Williams. After the fight was stopped briefly in the second round to clear a smear of blood from Williams's face, the fight went up the gears and Williams found himself being given a standing count after sustaining a heavy body attack with head shots sneaking through. Williams had visibly tired but upon resuming, the action swayed back and forth until the bell went, each fighter taking turns in shipping big shots. The third round produced another sharp turn in fortunes as Alexander found himself on the canvas twice from big barrages. Both men then traded freely to the finishing line. Hugging each other warmly at the end in recognition as to what they had both been through, Williams was awarded a close majority decision. It was a fight which Williams recollects with understandable pride.

'Before that fight,' Williams explained to me, 'I had knocked out a guy in the second round who Wayne had knocked out in one. No one expected me to win beforehand. There was a feeling of me going to the gallows. The day before, I was talking to a friend about Wayne's power but he was just a human being and I was confident going in. Let me tell you though, he was THE hardest puncher I faced amateur or pro. He hit me with those big shots in the first round and I felt them go through me. Even his jab was painful. I was peeing blood after that fight.'

'That was a great fight,' Alexander explained. 'I'd had about eight stoppage wins in the previous season to get there and I thought I was unbeatable. I went out all guns blazing in the first two rounds, had him out in the second round, ran out of steam and put down twice in the third round and lost. That was one of the most devastating days of my life. One judge had it a draw, one for Richard and one for me but when you have a draw you have to side with somebody so the judge sided with Richard. I was still picked for the world championships but unfortunately I broke my hand in sparring so I had to pull out of that. I decided that I had no money. Me and Danny Williams were on the same path so we chatted to an agent who introduced us to Frank Warren and we turned pro around the same time. I was very nervous going into my first pro fight. It was a different world. You were boxing grown men and it was separating the men from the boys. It was a fairly stiff first fight for me. I got through but I wasn't very impressed with that performance. I was over-eager and fought with nerves. After the fight, Harry Mullan said my defence was not very good. He said he wasn't impressed and I had to agree with him.'

Alexander stepped into the ring in Derby on 10 November 1995 for his pro debut against Liverpool's Andrew Jervis. He doubled up with lefts sufficiently to force a corner retirement at the end of the third round and christen the start of an eventful and eye-catching professional career.

For his next fight on 13 February of the following year, Frank Warren's matchmaker, the late and highly-respected Dean Powell, fixed Alexander up with Paul Murray, a welterweight from Birmingham, who brought with him the experience of taking part in over a hundred fights. He stopped the future British welterweight champion, Kostas Petrou in his professional debut and had been in with the likes of Chris Pyatt, Rocky Kelly, Neville Brown, David Starie, Dean Francis and Clinton Woods. 'Dean Powell made the match and I had a lot of faith in him. Murray had lost a lot of his fights and he wasn't a hard puncher. I was confident I could beat him. I boxed pretty decent in that fight. I put him down in the second with a body shot. I gave away about six pounds for that fight but I beat him clearly. I was quite impressed with that performance. After my first fight, Jimmy Tibbs said to me, "You gotta keep your chin down. You gotta calm down." Once I got the nerves out of the way in the first fight, I settled down well for the second. I was pleased with it.'

In Alexander's third paid fight three months later, his awesome punching power was again brutally on show. Facing another professional newcomer in Jim Webb, who had four wins to his name, he unleashed a short left uppercut in the second to send Webb crashing face first to the canvas. A follow-up combination almost froze him in mid-fall as he crashed again to bring about the ending. After the fight, promoter Frank Warren admitted in a call to *Boxing News* that Alexander, 'looks for real'. It was almost embryonic days in Alexander's professional career but his fearsome reputation was already doing the rounds and others were sitting up and taking notice. It was a brilliant performance.

Six more inside-schedule wins came before Alexander stepped in against Jimmy Vincent in Bristol in December 1998. Vincent was a solid, pressure fighter who never seemed sure how to take a backward step and so the Alexander fight proved. Vincent's style ultimately played into Alexander's hands. A flash knockdown in the opening round followed by another, courtesy of a huge right hand, at the bell to end the second and further punishment at the start of the third, brought the referee's intervention. It was a hugely impressive showing of discipline and power and having notched up his ninth stoppage in ten wins, the time had come for a step-up in opposition. 'That was to be a test for me and it was my best performance to date,' Alexander said. Sky Sports commentator Ian Darke said at the end of the fight that it was 'the most impressive performance from an up-and-coming British professional in the whole of the year'. 'That fight put me on the map. It made people say I could be a champion,' Alexander said.

Alexander's first title came in his next fight on 23 January 1999. What also came was a harsh lesson in how to maintain composure and handle someone who had blatant disregard for the rulebook. Admittedly, Ojay 'Me, Myself and I' Abrahams was a tough opponent who could give anyone a hard fight but he was noticeably edgy during the ring announcements for this bout and appeared impatient to get proceedings underway. The abundance of energy Abrahams possessed was subsequently too much to keep within the rules and it was expended through flagrant use of the head and, crucially, an uplift of the knee as he backed Alexander into a corner. Alexander looked on incredulously as the referee waved the fight off, awarding victory to the Croydon man by way of disqualification. The unsatisfactory ending to what could potentially have been a thrilling fight, paved the way for the inevitable rematch.

'Me and Ojay are friends now but he told me that in that first fight we had, he was shitting himself. I was like the big prospect coming up, fighting for the Southern Area title and I remember he said to me that

Dean Powell was telling him in the corner to look at me in the eyes. His legs were shaking. The bell went and within 30 seconds he started fouling. Using his head and elbows and then in the corner he put his knee up to knee me in the groin. The referee disqualified him. It was all down to nerves.'

Faced with such foul play, the course of a contest could conceivably denigrate into a farce and leave the referee with a long night trying to bring about some form of order. On this night, the referee thankfully had little tolerance with such antics. Wayne Alexander, as the victim, kept his composure and didn't reciprocate in kind. 'I was always very focused. I keep composure when anything like that happens. I didn't want to go down to his level. The referee could have given a stern warning and let it go on. I wanted to win the title legitimately and not on a disqualification but it never got to me.'

Four months later, in May 1999, the pair stepped once more into the ring at Crystal Palace to give the sort of mini-classic that was expected when they first met. In a five-knockdown thriller spread over a little under nine minutes of pulsating action, the pair put on the type of performance that left those present there that night in no doubt that they had witnessed something truly special. Put down soon after the start by a hard right cross, Alexander got up to detonate his bombs on Abrahams, decking him twice before the round was out. A sustained volley by Abrahams put Alexander down again in the second and referee Richie Davies finally waved the fight off after Alexander drilled Abrahams with a strong attack in the third round culminating in a crippling body shot which left 'Me, Myself and I' in a crumpled heap on the canvas. When the fight was waved off, Abrahams threw his arms around the referee in a gesture of near-gratitude.

'He was up for the rematch! The board of control gave him a suspension and fined him but he said to me, "Wayne, this is do or die. I ain't going to give in!" I thought it was going to be the same as the first fight. Come out and freeze! He came out and within 30 seconds, BANG! He hit me with the right hand and I was down. I looked across at Jimmy Tibbs and he was shouting, "Get up! Get up!" I was groggy and I thought, "You know what, I'm in a fight here!" I had groggy legs but the rest is history. The second knockdown he got me with was a heavy knockdown, I got up about seven or eight but I was on shaky legs. I never give up, it's my will to win. I would never quit in the ring and that was my most exciting fight to date.'

'When I got the call to referee the return,' Richie Davies explained to me, 'I knew that I would have to be on top of my game because of Abrahams's illegal use of the head and kneeing Alexander in the crown jewels. Abrahams behaved himself and the fight turned out to be a cracker. When I waved the fight over, Abrahams fell into my arms exhausted. I've met them both on many occasions since and they are both very nice gentlemen.'

A warm-up fight in August 1999, a predictably destructive knockout of George Richards, cleared the path for a challenge for the vacant British light-middleweight title at the Goresbrook Leisure Centre in Dagenham, east London, on 19 February 2000 against another renowned puncher, Paul Samuels. Samuels, like Alexander, had fists packed with dynamite as his ten knockout victims would clearly attest to. The expectation in this showdown was that one would snatch victory from the jaws of defeat and the other would quite literally snatch defeat from the jaws of victory by leaving his chin out while on the attack. Such was the sense of anticipation leading up to the contest that *Boxing News* headlined the preview, 'Don't blink or you'll REALLY miss it!' Throw in the crowd-pleasing factor that both combatants were vulnerable to a heavy wallop and you have a fight where there was really no need for promotion or hype. It created itself on past merit. Samuels held the IBF intercontinental light-middleweight title courtesy of a ninth-round stoppage of experienced American journeyman Eric Holland, but in his last fight prior to the Alexander fight, he was taken the distance by former Alexander knockout victim Ojay Abrahams. Recent form, therefore, favoured Alexander but with the type of brutal power each fighter had, the proverbial rule book had its own clash with the referee's scorecard to determine which would be more unnecessary on the night. What transpired lived up to expectation.

In a fight described by *Boxing News* the following week as 'The British Hagler–Hearns', the action simply swayed back and forth. Each fighter took it in turns to land short, concussive shots which landed squarely on the opposing chin. One would be on the verge of losing when he would spring back to land equally crunching shots. This tempo continued throughout the first two rounds leaving the crowd standing in awe. Something had to give as the pace being set would have to peter out. This it did, in round three when a savage assault by Alexander, topped with a huge right hand, sent Samuels careering out of the ring on to the apron.

'He was the hardest puncher I ever faced,' Alexander said of Samuels. 'He busted my eardrum and cut me. In the second or third round, he hit me with a couple of shots and I thought I was going to go. My desire just wouldn't let me go down. One more shot, I would've gone down.

That's how hurt I was. My will to win pulled me through. In a boxing ring, I'd rather die than lose. That's how much it meant to me. Losing a fight as a kid, I cried my eyes out.'

Winning the prestigious belt was the realisation of a long-sought-after dream for Alexander. 'Winning the British title and lifting the Lonsdale belt was my dream as a kid. I was growing up and watching the fighters in the 1980s winning that belt and it was my dream to win it too.' Returning to the gym with the aim of claiming that Lonsdale belt with just two successful title defences his immediate goal, he took a non-title fight at Wembley that August and blew away Paul Denton in one round. Two knockdowns from right crosses put paid to the Birmingham boxer but having lost his previous 11 fights and going on to lose the remaining 22 bouts of his career, Alexander simply went out and did what was expected. It gave Alexander 'The Great' a payday, kept his hand in the ring and allowed him to bide time while a British title defence was arranged.

The circumstances surrounding his next visit to the ring could not have been predicted by anyone and it was an opportunity that Alexander couldn't refuse. Six months after the Denton breeze, WBO light-middleweight champion Harry Simon was due to defend his title for the fourth time against Robert Allen of the USA. Allen had made two unsuccessful bids for Bernard Hopkins's IBF middleweight title but was coming off four straight wins leading into his challenge for the Namibian's WBO light-middleweight title. Shortly before the official weigh-in, the day before the fight, Allen had a grievance with the British Boxing Board of Control, claiming it ordered him to lose more weight than he was comfortable with. He subsequently claimed stomach cramps as the reason for his last-minute withdrawal. Frank Warren's show was now in danger of collapsing with the headliner all but gone and the search was on for a replacement.

Ranked number three by the World Boxing Organisation and in training for a pending British title defence against Yorkshire's James Lowther, Alexander answered the call to step in against the world champion. A straightforward victory was expected against Lowther, who was coming off two wins in his previous five outings, one of those losses being on points to former Alexander foe Jim Webb for the Irish middleweight title. The lure of a world title challenge was something which Alexander knew couldn't be turned down, at one day's notice or not. 'Twenty-four hours! I got the call from Ernie Fossey asking, "Do you want the fight?" I was walking down the road with a mate of mine and I rang Jimmy and asked him what he thought. I said how much I was being offered and he said, "Nah, ask for more!" I went back and asked for more. They asked Takaloo but he wanted a certain amount. They didn't pay Takaloo what he wanted so they came back to me and said, "All right Wayne, we'll give you what you want!" Because of my pedigree and because I was British champion, they couldn't say no because I saved the show. They were desperate for TV.'

Harry Simon was an accomplished tactician, durable and a thinker who was able to work out different styles and exploit his opponents' weaknesses in order to register the win. To date, this had worked perfectly as proven by his unblemished record of 20 wins. In his 17th fight, he had comfortably beaten the classy American Ronald 'Winky' Wright to claim the title and had made three defences, one of which was a third-round win over another British fighter, Kevin Lueshing. His second defence was a tenth-round retirement win over Argentine southpaw Enrique Areco on the Alexander–Samuels card the previous February. Simon was expected to record his fourth defence with relative ease against Alexander. Shortly before the Samuels war, Alexander said he couldn't see anyone at his weight taking him 12 rounds and that whoever he hit, 'would go'. 'I believed I could win. I didn't go in there just for the payday. I went in there thinking, "I've got the power to beat this guy. If I catch him, he'll go."'

With nothing to lose, Alexander stepped into the ring on the biggest night of his career and put in an effort so remarkable, commentator Ian Darke described it as 'a heroic effort'. Alexander came out in the opening round full of confidence and Simon realised at this early stage that his substituted opponent had not just come to take sterling notes but also to give a sterling effort. Simon's strong chin was put to the test immediately as Alexander got through with some big shots. Simon took them well and started to fire back in the second round, seeing Alexander was becoming more open to his punches. Simon was punching accurately but a thunderous right cross to the point of Simon's jaw wobbled him back against the ropes. Showing excellent recuperative powers, Simon stormed back in what was turning out to be a surprisingly competitive and exciting fight. The third and fourth rounds saw Simon, while still mindful of his adversary's power, move ahead with fast and accurate combinations. Alexander was slowly being worn down and a series of draining body shots finally put him down in the fifth round. A follow-up salvo of shots forced the referee's intervention but Alexander was able to walk out of that ring with his shaven head held high.

'It wasn't a bad performance,' Alexander said. 'I would say he was the best fighter I ever fought, amateur or pro. He should have been up there with De La Hoya and Vargas and mixing with the big boys. Harry said I was the hardest hitting guy he ever faced. I wasn't 100 per cent prepared but that fight had it all with speed and power. After three rounds I was up against it. It was a shame he never went on to become a great fighter. He had two bad car crashes where a couple of people died and he broke bones in his body. That took a long time out of his career. He also won the middleweight title though, so he was in the mix.'

After his admirable showing against Harry Simon, Alexander developed a new-found confidence knowing that he had what it took to engage competitively at the highest level. To ease back into winning ways, Viktor Fesechko was served up; not so much a sacrificial lamb, more a durable, stoic journeyman against whom Alexander could get some rounds under his belt. A veteran of 57 bouts to date, the Ukrainian had, only a week earlier, extended the reigning European light-middleweight champion Roman Karmazin the full six rounds in a time-killing non-title bout. Fesechko had proven himself as a matchmaker's dream with a résumé that included solid work-outs for the likes of Laurent Boudouani, Gary Jacobs, Howard Eastman and Hacine Cherifi. This is precisely what Alexander was given as, for just the second time in his career, he was taken the full distance against someone who was able to withstand the power of the Croydon puncher and force him to adopt an alternative strategy to overcome his experienced opponent.

'That was the first time I got into a fight knowing I was punishing my body. I was just coming off a bout of shingles. I'd seen Fesechko box the top welterweights and light-middleweights but, me believing in my power, I believed I would have stopped him. It was actually a very hard fight for me and after three rounds I had nothing left in me because of the shingles. People on the outside thought that I was finished but I was ill for that fight and I won it by just one point but that wasn't me that night. I didn't look impressive that night and if I was fit, I would at least have won it by four or five rounds. I'm not saying I would have stopped him but I would have won it convincingly.'

With Alexander's first planned defence of the coveted British title scuppered in favour of the more attractive proposition of challenging for Simon's world title, the focus in his camp once again redirected itself towards the goal of finally obtaining the Lonsdale belt for his own keeping. His first defence was arranged and in the opposing corner was the Scottish fighter who Alexander had beaten in the Multi-Nations tournament in Liverpool in 1994 and who, unlike Alexander, had taken part in the Commonwealth Games that year, Joe Townsley.

When the two fighters stepped into the ring on 17 November 2001 at the Bellahouston Sports Centre in Glasgow, the British champion didn't just want to reiterate his superiority over his former adversary, he wanted to brush his opponent to one side in his quest for further titles and do so in his opponent's backyard. They fought on the undercard to Scott Harrison's British and Commonwealth featherweight title defence against Wales's Steve Robinson, a fight the Scot won handily in the third round. It was also to be a double-header for Sky Sports with Lennox Lewis regaining the world heavyweight title for the second time against Hasim Rahman over in the Las Vegas desert.

'That fight there, I remember feeling really up for it, on form and in shape. I boxed live on Sky. It was the same night Rahman fought Lewis. It gave me a massive buzz. The pressure either makes or breaks you. I was sharp. Like Cus D'Amato said, fear is a man's best friend. I felt on top. Townsley had a decent career so I thought he may take me into the latter part of the fight but I took him out!'

After being incorrectly counted by referee Paul Thomas for a knockdown that was blatantly a slip in the first round, Alexander stormed back to floor Townsley twice in the opener before decking him for a third time in the second round with a left hook which convinced Thomas to bring matters to a close. It was a solid, powerful performance by the champion which reminded those within boxing circles that he had lost none of his menacing power or ability to end a bout with sudden brutality.

Winning his first British title defence earned him the chance to challenge for the European light-middleweight title. While the focus appeared to dim from the British title, the opportunity to go for European honours was too good to refuse and if this could be won, the chance of another world title shot may suddenly rise up over the horizon.

Paolo Pizzamiglio was the Italian light-middleweight champion and had failed in previous bids for the WBU and European light-middleweight titles. In January 2001, Pizzamiglio had ventured outside his native Italy for the first time in his career and had been stopped in eight rounds in Paris by former world title challenger, Mamadou Thiam. For his fight against Alexander for the title vacated by Thiam, Pizzamiglio once again travelled away from home to make the lonely walk to the ring at Bethnal Green's fiercely patriotic York Hall on 19 January 2002. The fighters' backgrounds suggested that Alexander should be able to lift the European crown without too much trouble. Pizzamiglio, on the other hand, appeared to be brought in to make up the numbers. He was coming off two six-round points wins since the loss to Thiam. One was against a professional debutant and the other was against Francesco Cioffi who managed to register just nine wins from 39 fights.

The fight itself again highlighted the numbing power of the British champion and after repeatedly nailing the Italian with hard, single shots throughout the first two rounds, a straight right cross landed with such force during the third round that Pizzamiglio was propelled into the ropes before rebounding on to the canvas. The shot was perfect. Upon rising, Pizzamiglio was panned by an onrushing Alexander and the fight was stopped. It was to be Pizzamiglio's final fight.

'He was a good fighter. He had defended his Italian title a few times and was a good, hard European fighter. The stoppage against Thiam was debatable and the EBU ordered a rematch. Thiam gave up the belt instead of facing Paolo again. It was a great night for British boxing as Johnny Tapia was making his British debut on the same bill. Johnny Tapia was a guy I watched in the early nineties so having him on the undercard was special. The place was rammed.'

After a repeat, but significantly more comfortable, win over Viktor Fesechko in January the following year, Alexander went up against Brixton's Delroy Mellis, who was coming off six straight losses. With the Fesechko rematch being Alexander's only fight in almost two years, he was keen to take a relatively safe opponent and Mellis was deemed to fit that mould nicely.

'I'll be honest and say that at that period of time, I was slacking in training and wasn't living the right life. I started to pile on a bit too much weight. I was nearly 14st about six weeks before that fight. I told Frank [Warren] I would knuckle down. I was still highly ranked by the WBO and so I would take that fight and then get another title shot. I was offered Delroy Mellis and I felt I would stop him. I trained for six weeks and ate like a rabbit. I fed on water and vegetables and I just changed my weight. I lost the weight but I felt that if I got some good food down me I would stop this guy. I won the first five and then I was sluggish and slow. I was then firing on empty from about round five onwards. He put me down in the last round but I didn't even see it. All I can remember is the ref saying, "…eight…nine…" He stopped it but I was gone! I remember going into the changing room and I cried my eyes out like a baby. I sat down and cried. That was the first time I sat down and cried since I was a kid.'

Having reached the heights of British and European title success and putting in a monumental effort at next to no notice in a challenge for one of the world titles, the loss to Mellis hit hard and it hurt badly.

Believing he should be able to negotiate his way past foes of Mellis's calibre, Alexander started to feel doubts as to whether he was fit to continue with his chosen profession. 'I doubted myself. I thought this may be the end. You can't live by burning the candle at both ends. I knew where I went wrong.'

If Alexander's career nose-dived against Mellis, it almost hit an irreversible decline in his next fight against Howard Clarke of the West Midlands. Like Alexander against Harry Simon, Clarke also found himself with the chance of pulling off a big upset. When his record stood at 25 wins, ten losses and two draws, he found himself called up to challenge California's rising star and IBF light-middleweight champion Fernando Vargas for his version of the world title in the famous setting of New York's Madison Square Garden on the undercard of the first Lennox Lewis–Evander Holyfield battle on 13 March 1999. Fighting as best he could, Clarke was sunk in four rounds but he'd had a taste of the high life. It was not something he could build on and of his subsequent 70 professional fights, he lost another 68 times with one draw and just one win. It did not come against Alexander, though Clarke did manage to send him to the floor in the first round with a textbook left deep into Alexander's side. 'Howard Clarke was a good operator. When I fought him, he put me down with a body shot in the first round. I got up and I remember hitting him with a left hook and his legs started quivering. The bell went and come the next round, his legs were still shaking. I always remember his legs wavering! I stopped him eventually!'

The end came in the second round. Alexander had Clarke backing up in a corner when he got through with a series of hard shots. In his eagerness to plough forward, he slipped but regained his footing to batter Clarke around the ring before a flush left hook prompted the referee's intervention.

The former two-time WBU light-middleweight champion, Mehrdud Takaloo, had burst on to the scene with a performance against the unbeaten Mancunian, Anthony Farnell, in July 2001 that would have been more associated with Wayne Alexander on one of his best nights. Takaloo had lost a couple of times and was coming off two points wins in his previous three outings against Howard Clarke and James Lowther. Clarke was subsequently destroyed by Alexander and Lowther was expected to be taken out in style by Alexander until the match fell through to make way for Alexander's world title challenge. Anthony Farnell had yet to taste defeat in 26 contests. One swift, blistering uppercut in the first round from the Margate Rock put paid to his unbeaten record as well as any immediate ambition of escalating further up the rankings. A further barrage from Takaloo and the fight was stopped. The result was brilliant and it instigated a run of form which led to his two reigns as WBU light-middleweight champion. Against Alexander, he was contesting the same governing body's vacant title which was stripped off him after he lost a non-title fight to Eugenio Monteiro on points over eight rounds after having been floored in the first.

While Alexander and Takaloo didn't despise each other, there was genuine needle between them which stemmed from a sparring session they shared years before. With conflicting versions of what happened during this sparring, the need was present that night of Friday 10 September 2004 at York Hall to clear up any arguments about one's superiority over the other. The showdown was originally set for earlier in the year but a knee injury sustained by Alexander forced the postponement of the fight. This, along with the conflicting versions of what happened in sparring, led to the animosity within Takaloo to build up. Takaloo claims to have knocked Alexander out in sparring whereas Alexander, though admitting he was floored, claims that his trainer Jimmy Tibbs had to curtail the session after he roared back to gain the upper hand.

'I came into the gym one day around 1997 in the Peacock Gym and Jimmy said to me, "Spar with Takaloo." Whenever me and Takaloo sparred it was like a world title fight. He'd had one or two fights and I'd had about eight or nine so I was the one who was the bigger prospect. I put the gloves on, warmed up, bell started and the next minute, bang! Takaloo just jumped on me and put me down with a right hand. I looked over at Jimmy and he was just there shaking his head! I got up, carried on sparring for four or five rounds and, lo and behold, Takaloo was telling the whole world that I was knocked out and carried out on a stretcher! He fails to realise that about two days later we sparred again when I was up for it and I gave him a hiding. Jimmy said to me around round two, "STOP, STOP, STOP SPARRING!"

'He was active and he was seen more than me so people were like, "What are you doing?" After I beat Pizzamiglio I did go downhill again with my training and not living the right life but this fight was so personal to me, I always said I'd have rather died than get beat by Takaloo. I was still getting distracted though so I left Jimmy sensitively saying I wanted to go a different route. I wanted a change of scenery and environment. Me and my partner was rowing and I wanted to get away. I went and told Frank Warren and he said I should go to Belfast.

I always remember flying over Belfast in the plane thinking, "I'm not going to stay here for long!" I tell you what, that was one of the best ten weeks of my life. I made new friends, worked with John Green who was a brilliant trainer and Mickey Hughes looked after me. They took me in like part of the family. I was treated brilliantly in Belfast. That was my camp with Eammon Magee and Jim Rock too. I was there for a couple of months at a time from 2004 to 2006. Since my sparring with Takaloo, he'd been saying what he was going to do to me so that's why it was personal to me. I knew in my heart that, me on my day, I could beat Takaloo.'

When they collided for real that September night in Bethnal Green, the fight started cautiously with both fighters exchanging quick left jabs. Alexander threw big, single shots in the hope one would hit the Margate Rock's chin. With a good defence and slippery defensive skills, Takaloo eased his way smoothly out of the line of fire. Most notably, one big right hand got through to Alexander's chin but was taken well and paid back with a stiff left to Takaloo's body. The second road opened and, ominously, Alexander's left hand was busier and getting nearer the target. A flurry of punches from Alexander drove Takaloo into the ropes but for his insolence, Alexander had to take a hard left hook to the chin. This was immediately responded to by a left hook of such leverage and power that Takaloo's head twisted violently around on his neck. All the resistance in Takaloo's neck muscles had gone as his head swivelled and his body fell to the canvas like the proverbial puppet with its strings cut. His head slammed against the canvas and with his eyes completely glazed over, referee Mickey Vann, conscious of the possible consequences, instantly went over and rolled Takaloo over on to his side to initiate the recovery position. It was an act borne out of sheer professionalism and experience and has stayed vividly in my mind since. At the moment of impact, Alexander simply turned and walked away as if it was always in the script.

'That is my finest hour. You mention my name, you gotta mention Takaloo! That was my career!' Alexander said to me, still relishing that moment of victory. 'I didn't think I would knock him out so quickly. I thought I'd get him in four or five rounds. He really hurt me with a left to the body and in any other fight I may have gone down. He made the bad mistake of opening up and leaving himself open. Jimmy Tibbs always taught me that you roll with the left hook. I see Takaloo coming on to it. It wasn't a lucky shot. I saw him coming on to it. It was the most perfect shot I ever threw in my entire life, my whole career! I was always a better fighter than a gym fighter. Takaloo was a very good gym fighter. It's what happens on the night. It's do-or-die. I've walked down the streets since and I've seen people shout out to me "Takalooooo!" People I didn't even know. "Takalooooo!"'

The win, and its manner, seemed to propel Alexander back into the public eye and having picked up the vacant World Boxing Union light-middleweight title in the process, Alexander could look ahead to a number of good paydays. 'Takaloo was the man to beat and I had beaten him. At the time Daniel Santos was the champion. Frank Warren got me a rematch with Delroy Mellis and I beat him convincingly. I trained for that fight in Belfast. I was running in the mountains in County Armagh and doing 25 miles a week for that fight. I won eight of the ten rounds.'

Six months later, Alexander travelled to Manchester and stepped in with the former European welterweight champion Christian Bladt of Denmark. Again, Alexander's power was on full show and in the fifth round a single right cross detonated on Bladt's jaw and he dropped face-first to the floor where he stayed for the count. 'I put him down in the first round but my eye got shut in the second so I was fighting with one eye for a couple of rounds. I put him down with one of the best right hands I've thrown. I threw the jab and slipped inside to throw the right and it worked perfectly. He landed on his face with a big thud!' Alexander laughed aloud. 'It was a great night too as Hatton beat Kostya Tszyu on the bill.'

Nine months later, in March 2006, Alexander returned to the Manchester Evening News Arena in Manchester to defend his WBU title for the first time. In the opposing corner was the unbeaten Thomas McDonagh, holder of the spurious WBU international title. With just five inside-schedule wins from his previous 29 fights, McDonagh was not expected to stall the power-surging relentlessness of the champion. The match went the full 12 rounds to the surprise of many, Alexander included.

'He was very awkward. I thought I would stop him. I hate to use the word "runner" but he fought quite negative. I showed the world that I could go 12 rounds because a lot of people said I wasn't a 12-round fighter. I trained hard. The first six or seven rounds were even. Come rounds eight and nine I came on when McDonagh thought I would flag and I won the last three rounds quite big. I was the first guy to beat him so it was a good win.'

That devil which had plagued Alexander at various intervals throughout his career reared its head again after this fight and its effects became apparent in his next and, fatefully, final fight. 'Again, after the McDonagh fight I lapsed in training. Perhaps in hindsight now, my mum would say, "You know Wayne, you've probably had enough." I wasn't the best trainer anyway. Before the McDonagh fight I wasn't training or living right. Frank offered me this fight with Vigne and he said if I won it he would get me the fight with Santos for the WBO title. I trained hard for the fight and I haven't said this before to many people but on the day of the fight I half-froze. I remember I froze and I just wasn't up for it. I always thrived on fights where there was a fear of me losing but this guy I didn't think he could beat me at all. I went in the fight figuring I could beat this guy but I don't know, I just didn't feel right.'

A left hook from Vigne hit home and Alexander went down for a count. He was caught cold but he rose in time and instantly started firing back. Concentrating on tagging the Frenchman, Alexander left himself open and Vigne capitalised with a right cross followed up by another big left hook and the referee stepped in to save Alexander from further punishment. With retirement as a viable option, Alexander looked around for other opportunities.

'It was in 2007 when they had the England v America series. I was offered a fight with "K9" Bundrage. I still wasn't training right though. I got an injury to my hands so I pulled out.'

Instead of facing Alexander, Cornelius 'K9' Bundrage went on to stop Colin McNeil in seven rounds. Bundrage would later claim the IBF light-middleweight title in 2010.

'I never announced my retirement until 2008. In 2007, I was in limbo and in 2008, I remember waking up one day and thinking, "You know what Wayne? Give up, you don't want it no more." It was kind of hard. I never had a trade to fall back on so I was basically in limbo and thinking what to do.'

If 2007 and 2008 passed by with little happening, 2009 gave Alexander an opportunity to get involved in something new. 'In 2009, I was asked by a guy called Darren Champ to work in the Fight Factory in Purley to train white-collar and unlicensed fighters. I put them in the ring to fight which I enjoyed. To be involved in boxing outside the ropes was great. In about 2010 I joined the Croydon Boxing Academy for about a year training more white-collar and unlicensed guys. After that, I started working with Ross Minter who said he'd love me to train some fighters. I work at a gym called the Like2Fight gym in Merstham.'

Alexander kept himself busy during this time and working with the son of the former world middleweight champion, Alan Minter, who reigned for six months during 1980 before running into the slashing fists of Marvin Hagler, seemed to have rekindled some of the old enthusiasm. He had been through a period of soul-searching. Travelling through that mental wilderness that so many retired fighters go through upon hanging up their gloves, Alexander saw a chance to unwrap the sparring pads. He found direction and purpose in passing on his knowledge and experience to young fighters.

In 2011, Alexander's mind started looking elsewhere for other challenges. 'In between 2011 and now, I went to college and got my SIA [Security Industry Authority] licence for the CCTV. Hopefully I'll get my CP badge and do some close protection. I just want to be happy and content. I'd like to have my own gym one day. Somewhere I can say is mine and work for myself.'

Having not fought since 2006 after a highly accomplished amateur and professional boxing career, reflecting back on his achievements was something I expected Alexander to do with a sense of satisfaction and fulfilment.

'I've realised maybe that I took boxing a bit for granted. I could have put more effort into it and could have done more. I definitely have regrets. It's every boxer's cliché but I should've done better. I never lost any of my titles in the ring but the Lonsdale belt I never won outright. That still hurts. A fight with Anthony Farnell wasn't made, Ryan Rhodes pulled out of a fight with me, Howard Clarke for the title didn't happen because I injured myself and Lee Blundell was disallowed to fight for the British title by the Board. I could have had three defences there definitely.'

With the likes of Oscar De La Hoya, Javier Castillejo, Santiago Samaniego and Ronald 'Winky' Wright ruling the light-middleweight roost while Alexander was European champion, a world title challenge would have been a tough assignment at best but not one, Alexander will tell you, that would have been beyond his capabilities to succeed in.

'I believe, again in hindsight, if I was ticking over between fights, which I never done because I was a lazy trainer, and given eight weeks to fight, I'd have had at least a 50-50 chance of beating the likes of Castillejo, Fernando Vargas and Santos. I was ranked once at number four by the WBC. De La Hoya was the champion and I was honoured. I was showing the rankings to my friends. I could have fought De La Hoya!' Alexander laughs deeply at the thought of the two of them sharing a ring for the world title.

'I regret not being involved in the major fights. Jimmy Tibbs always told me your career will go by like a flash and it did. It was true and I wish I'd put more into it. People say, "Wayne, you done well," but I know I could have done better. I've got to be happy with what I've done though. I won British and European titles.'

One could be forgiven for thinking the modesty and self-criticism shown by Wayne Alexander, when reflecting back on his career, were the traits of a severe under-achiever. Indeed, Alexander will openly adhere himself to such a critical self-assessment. I, however, along with many other followers of the sport, look at the amateur contest with Richard Williams, the genuine barrel-smoking 'Hagler–Hearns'-type wars with Ojay Abrahams and Paul Samuels, the courage in his world title challenge against Harry Simon and the clinical destructions of Joe Townsley, Paolo Pizzamiglio, Mehrdud Takaloo and Christian Bladt, and see a thunderous-punching crowd-pleaser who helped lead British boxing into the 21st century.

9

Colin McMillan

BOXING has always been a constant for me. My first experience
of the sport was when I was aged eight. My eldest brother took
me to the ABC cinema on central London's Kings Road to watch
the third instalment of the Rocky Balboa story. Waiting for the bus
home afterwards, I was shadow-boxing with a lamppost and planting
my dynamite-laden little hands into my brother's palms. I was hooked.
Four years later, I saw the Larry Holmes–Michael Spinks rematch on
TV with both of my brothers and I sat there watching and wondering,
at just 12 years of age, what it was about the sport that had my attention.
I continued to watch the occasional fight but it was only with the Mike
Tyson–James 'Bonecrusher' Smith WBC and WBA heavyweight
unification title clinch in March 1987 that it became a serious hobby
of mine.

The irony of a 12-round cure for insomnia igniting the eternal
flame that fuelled my boxing obsession was not lost on me. Some of
my years at boarding school were hard. Boxing was my comfort blanket
and my source of escapism. It seemed only fitting, therefore, that on
22 May 1991, less than a week before I left the school which I never
felt particularly happy in, I was sitting in my room watching a British
featherweight title fight which kicked off a year during which Britain
could boast one of its brightest stars and etch into my memory a string
of performances that bordered on near-perfection. That performance
in May 1991 is as vivid now as it was back then, over 22 years ago. When
Colin 'Sweet C' McMillan told me he had picked up an ankle injury
shortly before stepping into the ring that night, it enhanced my view
that, back in 1991, Britain had a genuine star emerging to challenge the
featherweight division's front-runners.

As his book, *Fight The Power*, illustrates, Colin McMillan had his targets in clear focus and his resolve developed into a formidable foe for those who wished to attempt exploiting him, selling him cheap or putting the sport's businessmen and back-room negotiators before him when handing out the financial fruits of labour. In detailing his encounter with the American promoter Don King, whom McMillan and his friend and confidante, the late Jonathan Rendall, went to visit after his win over Sean Murphy, McMillan came away from the meeting having had his ears assaulted with a relentless barrage of propagandist spiel. It amounted to an impressive display of showmanship but as McMillan wrote in his book, 'There had been no mention of how much money we would earn, how long the contract would be for or even who I would fight.'

'Before I turned pro,' McMillan said to me as we drank coffee in Rowan's cafe on Barkingside High Street, 'I spoke to as many fighters and ex-champions as I could to try and find out their life stories and their experiences. They all had stories to tell about how they had been misused, abused and sometimes taken liberty of. I wanted to do as much as I could to control my destiny and not make those same decisions.'

Brought up by parents of Caribbean origin, the importance of a good education and the strong arm of parental discipline were always very prevalent in McMillan's upbringing.

'Both my parents were very strong on the importance of education. They would have liked me to make sure I had a good education and go to university to follow that path. When I was young, I was always quite sports orientated. Table tennis, football, cricket, basketball; you name it, I'd do it. I used to love sports. I was just trying to combine the two things of the sports I enjoyed and the education that my parents were strict on.'

Born in Hackney in 1966, the McMillan family moved to Stratford, east London shortly after. At the age of 13, the family moved to Chadwell Heath. This produced the challenge for the future world featherweight champion to integrate within a new community.

'This was a different set-up. Stratford at the time was very multicultural so when I moved to Chadwell Heath it was a completely different thing. There were only about five black kids in the whole year. As a youngster I was quite easy-going but you did see a few instances where you'd see people treated slightly differently. On the whole, I adjusted quite well and carried on with my childhood.'

In boxing terms, it will come as little surprise to those who saw Colin McMillan fight at his peak, that his inspiration for focusing on boxing as a potential career move came from a certain former world heavyweight champion who hailed from the streets of Louisville, Kentucky. Indeed, as McMillan's boxing career progressed, there were those who started to draw parallels between the styles of the two. Another former great, a certain five-weight former world champion from Potomac, Maryland, was also mentioned as someone who clearly inspired the fighting style of the young featherweight protégé.

'The main inspiration I had would have been Muhammad Ali. He was a great figure and he inspired so many people. Everyone got involved with the Ali bandwagon and I got the taste of boxing through that. He was like an inspiration and as I was very sports-minded I thought I may try that one day. Later on, "Sugar" Ray Leonard came along and he was very similar. They were the two guys who really influenced me and I thought I'd really like to try that. I loved the way they both fought. It was graceful and it was hit-and-not-be-hit. Both "Sugar" Ray and Muhammad Ali, to me, were like art. Skilful, graceful and all that dancing too got me along that route.'

As I, and undoubtedly others who have spoken with McMillan, can vouch for, the former boxer does not exude aggression or any level of bitterness or hostility in any form. Quietly spoken with a highly likeable manner, the role of former professional world boxing champion would not be your immediate choice when guessing what his career had been. It is therefore of little shock that his parents required a level of reassurance when realising what their son had chosen to take up.

'I think they were quite concerned to begin with. One of the young lads who used to live in Chadwell Heath, he used to go to the local amateur boxing club in Barking and he was quite good. We were just sitting around chatting one evening and we spoke about me going down to the local gym. There were a few of us who went down there. One by one they stopped going until it was just myself and this other guy. I was never a really aggressive guy so when I started they felt I would take a few hidings and then would call it a day. Initially they were very surprised but they started coming to a couple of fights and saw that I was ok and after that they were backing me. They were concerned as all parents would be but they were supportive at the same time.'

McMillan's pedigree as a boxer shone through during his amateur career and one particular confidante McMillan had who sang his praises at an early stage was a fellow Barking ABC regular, Danny Benn. The elder brother of the more famous Nigel Benn, he repeatedly gave McMillan his vote of confidence claiming that 'Sweet C' would one day become a world champion. By the age of 17, McMillan had seven O Level passes in core subjects. This was of obvious pleasure and satisfaction to his parents. To McMillan, what also mattered was the fact that he was now eligible to compete as a senior.

On 22 February 1985, just two days after his 19th birthday, McMillan topped off an excellent run of form when clearly outscoring Newham's Peter Bell to win his first London ABA North-East divisional title. Following this up with a majority decision win over Fitzroy Lodge's John Good in the London ABA final, McMillan found himself in the British ABA semi-finals against future two-time British super-featherweight champion and IBF super-featherweight title challenger Floyd Havard. Fighting out of Penyrheol in Wales, Havard stamped his southpaw authority early on and never gave the Barking fighter the chance to establish a hold in the contest. A standing count in the third round ensured the Welshman a clear victory on the judges' scorecards.

McMillan repeated the London ABA North-East title triumph the following February when he stopped fellow east-Londoner Roy Deeble in the first round on a cut eye and then retained his full London title with a unanimous decision over Joe Stephens. His stylish manner and fast hand speed was starting to take effect and determined opponents like Stephens were ideal tests for the Barking fighter. Stephens forced a standing count as the fight intensified to remind McMillan that an increase in quality brings with it an increase in risk. He was awarded another crack at the National ABAs but fell short once again, this time at the quarter-final stage to Paul 'Hoko' Hodkinson, the future WBC featherweight champion and, fatefully, a boxer whom McMillan would never get to meet in the ring again.

After winning the London North-East ABA titles in 1987 and 1988 by defeating West Ham's Mark Biggs on points and Repton's Marlon Jones via first-round stoppage, he won the London ABA titles in both these years too. In 1987, he defeated north London's Alan McKay on a second-round stoppage in the semi-finals before winning a back and forth war with Penge's Tony Davis to grab the title and in the following year, McMillan repeated the win over Alan McKay, losing the opening round to come back and outscore his future nemesis for his fourth consecutive London title. He participated in the national ABAs during these years and reached the finals on both occasions only to see his efforts fall short on the judges' cards when he saw himself as the comfortable winner.

His amateur career was rich in accomplishment and McMillan has fond memories of these times. Those two final attempts at wresting the national ABA titles, however, leave a slightly bitter taste in his mouth knowing that his conqueror in the 1988 finals jetted off to Seoul to compete in the Olympic Games.

'They [the London ABAs] were great. Four-time London champion! Back then, boxing seemed bigger as it was on terrestrial TV. Some of those fights at the Albert Hall were on ITV. It was great to be involved in that. I fought a couple of guys who were pretty good and it was exciting as it was a springboard for me to hopefully go on to national success. Both those times in 1987 and 88 I felt like I won. The first one against Peter English, we were both England internationals, I definitely felt I beat him based on the punches scored and the technique but he was coming forward and throwing a lot of shots. Sometimes in the amateur game, over three rounds, the way people fought me was to try to outwork me and throw lots of shots and they get scored for that. The pace was definitely faster in the amateurs.

'I was always a more pro-orientated fighter because I used to take my time, have a look, think and plan. If you get somebody who is, technically, not as good, all they want to do is outwork you for three minutes and have no regards for defence. They just want to come forward. For the English fight, I was sure I had won but they gave it to him which was disappointing. The following year [against David Anderson], we were both in the Olympic squad and obviously I wanted to go the Games and follow my dreams in the footsteps of Ali and Leonard. I put him down in the first round but, again, he had that high workrate of throwing loads of shots and it went in his favour. After this we both went to a multi-nations tournament and Dave won the gold medal so he deserved to go to the Olympics but for me, it was back to square one.'

David Anderson subsequently competed in the Seoul Olympic Games and performed admirably to reach the third round before coming up against Holland's future professional European and undefeated WBO super-featherweight champion, Regilio Tuur. Tuur stopped the Brit in the second round before losing in his next bout to Romania's Daniel Dumitrescu.

With this extensive amateur career behind him, just falling short of the Olympics seemed to be the right time for McMillan to look further afield towards the professionals.

'I started off quite late when I was 15 and a lot of guys start a lot younger but I felt if you start too young, you can get burnt out. For me, I served my apprenticeship in the amateurs and the natural progression was to turn pro. My whole style was pro-orientated and the guys I looked to were like Leonard, Ali, Hearns, Hagler, Benitez and Curry.

'I was looking forward to the pros. Obviously it's a new chapter in your life. Unfortunately, where I wasn't an ABA champion or go to the Olympics, I didn't have that springboard initially. You can get a decent contract and things look rosy but without that behind you it is a lot harder. Originally I fought on a few shows with the World Sports Corporation with Ambrose Mendy and my first manager was Terry Marsh. Without the amateur success with the ABAs and the gold medal, the likes of Barry Hearn and Mike Barrett wouldn't offer me anything so I spoke to Terry Marsh and we sat down. He was another very intelligent fighter and he talked about having more control over your career. He asked me to come on board so he could manage me and I was linked with the World Sports Corporation.'

This urge to be self-controlled and play the leading role in acting out his own destiny was reinforced years later when McMillan himself turned his blurring hands to the part of manager. In a September 1999 interview with Alan Hubbard of the *Independent* newspaper, he stated, 'Fighters come and go but managers and promoters seem to go on forever. Looking after the fighter should be the number one priority but that is not always the case.'

This is clearly a subject that McMillan takes very much to heart and his facial expression was one of utmost sincerity and concern for those fighters who are either prostituted out to the ring to fatten the accounts of those with the whip or those who don't benefit from the level of acumen and wisdom that has made the former featherweight champion a respected businessman and flag-bearer for the sport.

'Terry Marsh and I talked a lot together leading up to the first fight against Mike Chapman. I was looking forward to it because I had a good little fan base.'

McMillan's professional career got off to an encouraging start with two six-round points wins at the tail-end of 1988 against Chapman and Alric Johnson. While a fellow novice like McMillan at this stage of his career, participating in just his fourth paid fight, Alric Johnson went on to face top quality fighters such as Kevin Kelley, Derrick Gainer, Steve Robinson, Ivan Robinson and Nate Campbell. On this night, McMillan inflicted his first defeat. The next time he ducked between the ropes, however, the Barking express temporarily came to an unexpected and shuddering halt. On 31 January, McMillan's former ABA adversary Alan McKay stood in the opposing corner. Getting off to a good start, McKay soon found himself on the receiving end of McMillan's stinging left jabs. In the third round both fighters were separated from a clinch when blood was noticed seeping from a bad cut over McMillan's right eyebrow. The contest was immediately called off and so putting a surprise blemish on his as yet unbeaten record.

'It was a setback because most fighters have that mutual respect but he was the one guy who I really didn't like. I beat him twice in the amateurs but we just didn't gel so losing to him was a bit of a disappointment. People go on about an unbeaten record but when you get a loss on your record and you speak to other managers, they see you as just a beaten fighter even though it was just a cut eye. I didn't really see it as a loss. It was a clash of heads.'

His first fight back was mooted to be against Newcastle's John Davison on the undercard of the Michael Watson–Nigel Benn domestic war in Finsbury Park on 21 May. Davison would go on to spend 1990 smashing his way to a hat-trick of fifth-round stoppage wins over a series of oriental fighters to claim the WBC international featherweight title and would later claim the British featherweight crown. The fight with McMillan never came off though.

'I'd been out for quite a while and the fight didn't make too much sense at that time,' McMillan recalled. 'At that time I was just coming off the injury against McKay and Davison was an up and coming fighter. A bit further down the line, that fight could have happened but it wouldn't have been sensible then.'

The wins returned after this and for the next 18 months until July 1990, McMillan notched up a further seven wins against respectable, tough opposition. During this time, McMillan parted ways with Terry Marsh and went on to sign up with Frank Warren.

'We parted company amicably. He was talking at the time of making films and making a comeback and then we parted.'

The irony of this would take a sinister turn when McMillan faced a fighter named Sylvester Osuji in Barking in November 1989. Osuji was a fighter who had learnt his skills in the gyms in New York and whom Jonathan Rendall, in his book entitled *This Bloody Mary Is the Last Thing I Own*, described as being 'slick and fast like Donald Curry'. Other respected journalists had warned the team to steer well clear of Osuji but what materialised was a clinical exhibition from McMillan as he registered a fourth-round stoppage victory. Shortly before McMillan stepped into the ring, Frank Warren arrived at the venue and was shot by a masked gunman who immediately fled the scene. Subsequently, Terry Marsh was arrested and charged with the attempted murder of the promoter.

To improve his experience within the sport, McMillan travelled to the USA in the summer of 1990 and picked up two easy wins over Tyrone

Miller and Malcolm Rougeaux. While neither Miller nor Rougeaux were picked to particularly overstretch McMillan's capabilities, the opportunity to showcase his skills on the other side of 'the water' was capitalised upon nonetheless.

Guiding him during his American conquest was the experienced trainer and former North Carolina Golden Gloves champion, Beau Williford. Williford, who would go on to train Peter McNeeley for the unenviable task of being thumped by a comebacking and 'I've a score-to-settle' Mike Tyson in the former world champion's first post-prison fight in August 1995, had only glowing comments to make about the rising star.

'I first met Colin when, hey I'm not even sure he had a pro fight yet. I was training Glenn McCrory in Newcastle. I had a fighter with me, Chad Broussard and Colin came up to work with him to get some experience,' Williford explained. 'Jonathan Rendall contacted me and brought an amateur middleweight over here with Colin. They were both great guys. Everybody in the gym teased Colin about his hair. He had those three locks at the front!' Williford chuckled warmly as the image rushed back to the forefront of his memory.

'They all liked Colin to start with and when he started boxing they liked him even better. We all thought he was a beautiful boxer. He weren't scared. He sure didn't hang his chin out to dry but if you hit it, he'd hit you back! Listen, I had a guy called Kenny Vice and if he thought someone couldn't fight, he'd say, "This guy's a piece of shit!" He came to me and said about Colin, "This mother****er can FIGHT!"'

With regards to McMillan's two showings in July 1990 against Miller and Rougeaux, there was never much doubt as to what their roles were when facing 'Sweet C'. The man with the three locks was there to be showcased and the script would be returned with no unplanned changes made.

'He knocked out one in one round and the other in two,' Williford said. 'Whoever he knocked out in the second, he probably could have knocked out in the first! He just took care of business. If he hadn't been injured against Palacios, I really believe he'd have carried on for years. I really believe that. Colin was not only a great boxer, but also a fine young man.'

McMillan gave me his version of his experience stateside and, not surprisingly, it was a lot more modest and subtle than the robust quotes given by Kenny Vice.

'That was a great experience for me. Jonathan [Rendall] and I went over there and we met up with a guy called Beau Williford. It was great to see how things worked in America. We were down south in Louisiana so it wasn't Vegas or New York but it was a great experience. At that time people had the mentality that English fighters couldn't fight so it was good to go over there and see what it was like.'

I couldn't help but have a quiet chuckle at this. It seemed to me that McMillan saying 'it was good to go and see what it was like' was his way of saying he was going to prove them wrong and give some impressive showings to prove he was one Union Jack bearer who could resist the all-too-common pattern of adopting the horizontal position. It was akin to other such fighters promising to 'bring the pain', 'put the hurt on' and simply 'destroy' their adversaries. However, while it is easy to assume his demeanour outside the ring is on a par with his presence inside it, what was becoming increasingly apparent was that McMillan could be as vicious after the first bell as he could be vivacious after the last.

Over the next ten months he registered a further five wins including a points win over Mark Holt, the Midlands Area featherweight champion, and a points win over the experienced Russell Davison. The Davison fight took place on the undercard of the British featherweight title war between the reigning champion Sean Murphy and the challenger Gary De'Roux. Set at a breathtaking pace, De'Roux ground down the champion from St Albans in the fifth round in one of the fights of the year. De'Roux's grit, determination and courage were exemplary that night on 5 March at the London Arena. With one more win over the American Willie Richardson the following month, McMillan cleared the path for a title challenge against the new champion from Peterborough. The date was set for 22 May, back at the London Arena.

The champion was dismissive of his challenger's chances, believing his more rugged, aggressive style would overcome the more established craftsmanship of McMillan, take him out of his stride and eventually 'take him out of there' at some point during the 12-rounder. McMillan, in his normal non-provocative manner, smiled through it. The confidence he had in his own ability was blatant.

The fight was the closest thing you could get to a one-horse race without the promoter, Steve Goodwin, pitching in with a purchase offer to add to his Diamond Racing syndicate. This is of no criticism to Gary De'Roux. He showed the same level of commitment, courage and tenacity he exhibited against Sean Murphy, only this time he was in with a fighter who many believed would go on to record many more startling performances and head into the sought-after realms of boxing immortality. Yes, McMillan was THAT good. His style was all wrong for De'Roux while the defending champion played into the challenger's hands. His onrushing offensive was coolly picked off by McMillan, the left jab carving a niche around De'Roux's eyes.

'I'd just won my title against Sean Murphy in quite spectacular style,' De'Roux told me when I reached him over the phone. 'I was full of it leading up to the fight with Colin. I'd been warned he was quite a tricky, skilful fighter and was a bit of a stinger. I had some disdain for him to be honest and I thought his chance had come too early. I was at my best for Colin and I did everything right preparing for it but when we came out for the first round he smacked me in the face. The kid was just so fast and he was putting his shots together really well.'

In the second round, the viewers had all the evidence they needed that entitled them to get genuinely excited about McMillan's future. Swaying back on the ropes with his guard fending off the oncoming punches, McMillan sprung into life and rattled off a volley of blows so fast, De'Roux probably felt the impact of the first punch after the last one had landed. While it would have been ludicrous to have compared them stature-wise, I couldn't help but think back to THAT volley 'Sugar' Ray Leonard raked Hagler's head with when coming off the ropes in the ninth round of their 1987 brawl in Las Vegas. De'Roux was totally bemused and after almost seven completed rounds, the fight was waved off with De'Roux looking completely bemused as he was led back to his corner by the referee Roy Francis. 'Into a new era', 'the best we've had since Howard Winstone', 'the first of many title wins'; the headlines and praise were incessant. *Boxing News* described the showing as 'a display which bordered on perfection'.

'For that fight, I had an injury from playing football,' McMillan said. 'I got a knock on my ankle and leading up to the fight my leg wasn't 100 per cent. I was a little bit worried because he was someone I respected because people were saying he was a banger. He was one who people said to stay away from. Particularly after Sean Murphy, he looked dangerous but I was confident. One thing I learnt in life is that when you see people fighting and you think "wow, that was a tough fight" or "he looked good", you realise that he's not fighting YOU. I always had speed and when you have that everything changes. When you see these people fighting, they can't do the same thing to you that they can to others. I was always confident but I knew it would be a tough fight. At the press conference before, I could tell he was confident so I had to beat him physically AND mentally. He was strong. I felt his strength in there but he was a little bit reckless. I just kept chipping away.'

While McMillan witnessed his challenger's confidence before they stepped in the ring, he gave a virtuoso performance of the highest calibre to shoot the Peterborough man down in clinical fashion. De'Roux harbours no bitterness towards McMillan and, even now, almost a quarter of a century on, he has nothing but the utmost respect for the east London boxer.

'He had come 100 per cent prepared for me, he'd done all his homework and his tactics came to fruition. People were saying that Colin don't hit hard but velocity and speed kills in boxing and with me coming forward, it just doubled the force!' De'Roux said. 'Colin was an absolute revelation that night and I doubt I landed one and a half decent punches on him throughout the whole seven rounds! I knew he was going to go on to bigger things, without a doubt. He inspired me and I'm proud to call Colin a good friend.'

Six weeks later McMillan stepped into the ring in Reading and took apart the Louisiana import Herbie Bivalacqua in three rounds and then stepped in against former British super-featherweight champion Kevin Pritchard in his first title defence on 4 September at Bethnal Green's York Hall. A year earlier, Pritchard had deposed the defending British super-featherweight champion Hugh Forde with a fourth-round knockout in a startling upset. Winning just three of his previous 14 fights, Pritchard went in against someone tall and rangy who was deemed to be on the verge of breaking into the world rankings. Pritchard upset the odds by taking him out in impressive fashion. Since that huge win though, Pritchard had lost his title to the stylish Robert Dickie and had then been served up at feeding time to the future European and WBO super-featherweight champion, Denmark's Jimmi Bredahl. The McMillan fight was his last chance at glory. It turned out to be his last fight. With another classy performance with some hard body-punching to add to his already impressive résumé of weapons, McMillan kept his title with a seventh-round win. Pritchard announced his retirement the following day while McMillan could look forward to his second defence against former champion Sean Murphy.

Scheduled for 29 October, a win over Murphy would enter McMillan into the record books as having won the Lonsdale belt outright in the fastest time, beating the previous record held by Lancashire's lightweight champion Carl Crook, of 161 days, by one day. The Lonsdale belt was on the line for Murphy too, having registered two British title wins over John Doherty and Johnny B. Good in 1990.

In a fight of almost total dominance, McMillan walked away with the decision after 12 rounds. The result never seemed in doubt as Murphy was constantly playing catch-up with the elusive McMillan and was unable to find the punches to stem the champion's momentum.

'It was great. It is one of the premier belts in the world and to keep one for your own so early in your career was great,' McMillan said to me with a shining glint in his eye.

St Albans's Sean Murphy was under no illusion as to who the better man was on the night and has remained friends with his conqueror to the present day.

'I used to spar with Colin a little bit as we were both managed by Frank Warren and I was always half a stone heavier. I used to walk around about nine and a half stone so I was always stronger than him,' Murphy told me, keen to express his hunch that he could come out of their title fight as the victor.

'Going into our fight, I was pretty confident. I planned to take him into the corners and work inside but I got my weight wrong. I came in about 8st 12lb and I felt weak in there. It was the most frustrating fight I've ever had.' Indeed, watching the fight, it was all too apparent that McMillan had far too many weapons in his armoury to choose from to nullify Murphy's strength.

'It was his movement. Because Colin knew me from our sparring, he knew I was stronger so he didn't want to stand there and trade with me. He outboxed me for like, 11 of the 12 rounds! It was in one round around the eighth when I got him in a clinch and I thought for one second I'm gonna bite him it was so frustrating! He was a tremendous boxer, brilliant mover. It may sound strange but I've won fights that were harder, if that makes sense because he wasn't hurting me. He was like a little annoying fly, bop, bop, bop and he was gone! I was thinking, "Plant your feet and have a f*****g fight!" He was a stylist though, very much like "Sugar" Ray Leonard. Silky skills, great boxing. He looked smooth didn't he?!'

The late Jonathan Rendall, a close friend and advisor of McMillan, said at this stage of the fighter's career that his punching was similar to that of Thomas Hearns, the legendary multi-time world champion from the famous Kronk gym in Detroit.

The comparisons were not made necessarily with their punching power in mind. One would after all be heavily challenged to find a fighter of Hearns's physical stature who possessed the same level of ferocious power his fists had. No, the comparison was made more with the effect of their punches in mind. The punches that landed from unexpected angles that took your opponent by surprise were the damaging ones and he claimed McMillan was a master at doing this. Rendall, and Hearns' long-time trainer, the late Emanuel Steward, said the same about the 'Hit Man'.

'Yeah, when you see the punch coming, you can brace yourself for it, you can roll with it,' McMillan said. The ones that hurt you and knock you out are the ones you don't see coming. I've always believed in chipping away and eventually the building will fall down. People say I don't punch, but after a period of time when you're chipping away, your opponent will feel it.'

Now that McMillan was on the rise through the rankings and becoming more noticeable to the boxing public, the level of opposition was inevitably going to increase. He had won the Lonsdale belt in record time by dominating the domestic scene and the stage was now set for him to move up to the next boxing rung and announce his intention to dominate further afield. He had shown a masterful array of offensive skills and his quiver of defensive arrows was growing too. He could take a punch having been in with big punchers like De'Roux and Pritchard, had good head movement and fleeting footwork. All this enabled him to stay out of harm's way. Now he was ready to test his polished armoury against a better level of opposition. Next up was Percey Oblittey Commey from Ghana for the vacant Commonwealth featherweight championship.

With the film title *Out of Africa* in mind, Commey left his home continent, as the African featherweight champion ventured to the iconic Royal Albert Hall to face McMillan in a bid to be crowned the Commonwealth champion for a second time. He had previously won it in 1989 before losing it in his first defence the following year. Coming from a country with a rich boxing history, he was hoping to emulate the paths of its former greats. Ghana had unleashed the likes of Azumah Nelson (whom Commey had served as a sparring partner), Roy Ankrah, Nana Yaw Konadu and Ike Quartey on the world's best at various times in the sport's history, sometimes with devastating results. Commey was aiming to follow suit. Against McMillan, he backed up his intentions. An awkward, gangling fighter with impressive skills, Commey showed McMillan how it would be as the level of opponent was increased.

Yes, McMillan did record, ultimately, a fairly comfortable points win but he was neither allowed the free rein he commanded in the De'Roux fight nor was it a replay of the Sean Murphy whitewash. He was given a genuinely tough test while willing himself up a very steep learning curve. He never seemed on the verge of losing but the going got progressively tougher. Faced with a series of spearing left jabs with some long right hands thrown throughout the contest, McMillan was given an invaluable lesson. While it was hard going, the fact remained that he still managed to adapt himself to the threat in front of him and apply his skills to get inside often enough to pick up the points when needed.

'I looked at him and thought I was going to break him in half. He didn't look anything at all. Very tall, very gangly and he knew what he was doing. He gave me a tough fight. He was very game and awkward. It wasn't pretty to watch. I normally like to dictate fights but I got cut. There are going to be times when you can't always look good and you just go in there to get the win and move on to the next one. He was a tough guy!'

Having proved himself capable of more than holding his own with a fighter of Commey's calibre and showing his ability to overcome an element of adversity in the form of cuts sustained against the Ghanaian as well as having to endure numerous long-range right hands, McMillan's radar turned towards the world stage and Frank Warren started scanning the list of current world champions. The choice of career path was one which led him towards the reigning WBO featherweight champion Maurizio Stecca, from Italy. Negotiations started and the move was taken to have a double-header featuring McMillan and Stecca in separate bouts on a show at the Goresbrook Leisure Centre in Dagenham on 25 March. McMillan scored a sixth-round knockout over Tomas Valdez while Stecca also posted a sixth-round win, over Roy Muniz. It was great for publicity and whipped the boxing fraternity up into a high state of anticipation to see if McMillan could join the ranks of past great British featherweights such as Owen Moran, Jim Driscoll, Nel Tarleton and Howard Winstone.

There could have been no argument with the choice of Maurizio Stecca as the opponent for McMillan's world title challenge. He had a solid background which encompassed an Olympic gold medal in Los Angeles in 1984 and two reigns as WBO featherweight champion. Months after Los Angeles, he went 34 fights unbeaten before winning the vacant WBO title with a win over Pedro Nolasco of the Dominican Republic. Nolasco was after revenge as it was he who won the silver medal in the bantamweights 1984 having been defeated by Stecca in the semi-finals. Stecca's first tenure as world champion ended when he was defeated in his second defence by the excellent Louie Espinoza. Just over a year later, he regained it and was now making his third straight defence against McMillan.

The other world champions at this time were Young Kyun-Park with the WBA, Liverpool's Paul Hodkinson with the WBC and Mexico's Manuel Medina with the IBF. These were all tough fighters and as promoter Frank Warren accurately stated in the days leading up to the big event, 'You would have a hard job putting Stecca fourth out of all the champions.' Stecca was hugely respected and had he pulled off the win, McMillan would have undoubtedly been able to return to Commonwealth and European level to work his way up again. He had already proven his calibre and laid bare his potential for all to see.

Boxing News's front page of its preview issue was understandably taken badly by some readers and, above all, McMillan himself. 'FIGHTER OR PHONEY?' ran the headline. It punched the knowledgeable fight fan square in the face with its abrasiveness and planted the question in the reader's mind as to how much of a 'phoney' McMillan would prove himself to be if he did happen to fall short against an established and quality performer such as Stecca. Frank Warren's pre-fight summing-up of Stecca would appear to support this. It was deemed offensive to both champion and challenger. Win or lose, McMillan had already proven himself a 'FIGHTER'.

'I took exception to that headline. If I had lost to him it still wouldn't have made me a phoney. I think I know what Harry [Mullan, the magazine's then-editor] was trying to say because at the time great things were expected of me but I still wouldn't have been a phoney.'

On 16 May 1992, just a few days short of a year since his championship trail started against De'Roux, McMillan walked towards the ring at Alexandra Palace in north London's Muswell Hill to knock on the door of boxing history. Watching the fight live on television, I remember sensing the atmosphere coming through the TV screen. A sense of anticipation hovered in the air in readiness to explode in a frenzy of celebration. I was at school coming to the end of my exams and my friends were out enjoying the beginning of the end-of-term parties. I parried off the dismissive looks of disdain from them as I told them I'd rather watch a boxing fight on TV than go out and be sociable. A few hours later, my friends returned looking the worse for wear. So did Maurizio Stecca.

It all came together. McMillan's performance was a vintage display of boxing. It was the sort of display that elder boxing fanatics, the kind that would constantly hark back to past generations and mock the current crop of mere pretenders and their chances of surviving with past champions, would watch and slowly raise their hands in admission that the modern generation of pugilist really wasn't that bad at all. Using his potent left jab to transform Stecca's face into a bloody, bruised mask of defiance, McMillan dropped in frequent follow-up right hands. When the Italian went on the offensive, all he found was a target as easy to hit as a peak Willie Pep or Wilfred Benitez. McMillan was simply too fast, too fluid in his movement and possessed the reflexes to nullify virtually everything the defending champion had to offer. In the final round, McMillan literally toyed with his opponent. There were flashes of 'Sugar' Ray Leonard in the way he dangled his arms and had he stepped up the tempo, it was highly likely the referee would have stepped in to bring about the stoppage.

Two years later, I watched 'Prince' Naseem Hamed systematically destroy another Italian, Vincenzo Belcastro, for the European bantamweight title, giving him a 12-round beating which became painful to watch and increasingly one-sided in equal measure. I went back to the last round of McMillan–Stecca and saw the stark parallels.

While awaiting the scorecards, commentator Reg Gutteridge informed the viewer that he had taken a peak at one of the judge's scorecards which had McMillan a clear winner. 'Well,' the late Mr Gutteridge said, 'we're a third the way there!' This didn't spoil anything, for the fight was such a masterclass that the crowd could have left as soon as the final bell went, safe in the knowledge that Britain had a new world champion. However, there were sure to be temporary palpitations suffered by those in McMillan's corner when the MC announced the result as a majority decision, only to go and read one of the scorecards as being 116-114 in favour of Stecca and the other two widely in favour of the Barking man. This would have officially made a split decision but under further scrutiny it was confirmed as 116-114 in favour of the new champion, hence making it a unanimous decision. McMillan can therefore assume the unofficial mantle of having been awarded every possible winning combination on the judges' scorecards with just one performance.

'I was quite happy. I just felt I was on top of my game. It was my time and preparation-wise everything was going to plan, I was in great condition and during the fight I just felt I was one step ahead of him all the time. Whatever he wanted to do, I seemed one step ahead.'

With McMillan as the new WBO featherweight champion and Liverpool's Paul Hodkinson as the WBC champion, Britain now owned half of the featherweight belts. The fight between the two was a natural and would give McMillan the chance to avenge that earlier amateur loss to him in that 1986 ABA quarter-final. As styles go, this potential domestic blockbuster had the makings of a mini classic. Hodkinson's solid forward offence against the polished, more graceful skills of McMillan. Hodkinson had won the WBC title the previous November in a rematch against the veteran Mexican Marcos Villasana and had impressively taken out former Barry McGuigan conqueror, Steve Cruz, three weeks before McMillan had beaten Stecca. Before this mouth-watering clash could occur, plans were afoot for the pair of them to defend their titles in the summer to set up the inevitable showdown.

'I always said at the time that my aim was to be the undisputed champion, to unify the various belts. We had Paul Hodkinson who beat me in the amateurs and that would have been a great fight. Revenge! London–Liverpool, North and South, fighter–brawler! So many different connotations which made it a great fight and that's what we were working towards.'

That September, Hodkinson travelled to France to face the Frenchman Fabrice Benichou in his second WBC title defence. He registered a tenth-round stoppage win and then sat back to await McMillan to come through his first title defence unscathed.

On 26 September, McMillan stepped into the ring at Kensington's Olympia to face off against Colombia's national super-featherweight champion Ruben Dario Palacios. It was a clever piece of matchmaking. In his only other trip to these shores, in May 1986, he was stopped in the seventh round by another promising British fighter who was unbeaten in 16 fights by the name of Jim McDonnell. Palacios was a 'name' opponent and a hard-punching three-time world title challenger who could be counted on to give his all, a characteristic common of those who emerge from South America's gyms. However, it was deemed a safe contest for the champion. Indeed, *Boxing News*'s Bob Mee, who wrote up the preview, saw the fight as 'little more than a showpiece for the champion's skills to be laid out for all to admire'. Few people disagreed.

What played out was a nightmare that no one, least of all McMillan (and probably Palacios himself), saw coming. In what was, from the outset, a poor day at the office for McMillan, he found himself against a fighter who swaggered into the last-chance-saloon, slammed the last few coins of ambition he had left on the bar and got a barrel of vintage for his efforts.

For most of the contest, McMillan looked out of sorts. He started brightly enough but upon sustaining a cut to his head in the second round and facing an onrushing Colombian avalanche, he seemed to be taken out of his stride and roughed up on the inside by Palacios's rough tactics and roundhouse swings. McMillan looked the neater technician during the contest but was made to look distinctly uncomfortable. As Palacios continued his work on the inside, the champion looked to become increasingly frustrated and at times stayed on the ropes long enough to allow his adversary to unload some big combinations. It was therefore ironic that as McMillan started to find his rhythm in the seventh and the start of the eighth, the fight-ending incident occurred that would have long-lasting effects on the champion's career. After missing with a left hook, McMillan was crowded on the inside by Palacios who shoved his shoulder upwards, wrenching the champion's left shoulder out of its socket. It was several seconds before anyone knew what had happened. In obvious pain, McMillan was backpedalling until the towel came in. After deliberation among the officials, Ruben Palacios was crowned the new WBO featherweight champion on a technical knockout with McMillan unable to continue.

'It was a freak accident. I had no trouble with the shoulder before. We appealed to the WBO because their regulations said that if a fight is stopped due to accidental injury, it should go to the scorecards and whoever was ahead on points would be called the winner. They didn't follow that and now I had a loss on my record. It was a tough fight and he caught me a couple of times. It was a tough, tough fight and it was kind of wild in there. He caught me but I weathered the storm and I was coming on top so I knew I would have won that fight.'

For Palacios, it was a heartwarming episode. He had won the world title in his fourth attempt, having failed once for the IBF super-bantamweight title in 1985 and twice in 1990 for the WBA title against fellow Colombian Luis Mendoza. The McMillan victory was, however, to be his last contest. Tragedy was soon to strike as he was to face his most fearsome opponent. Upon returning to England in April 1993 to defend his title against John Davison, he was diagnosed with the HIV virus and his retirement from boxing was inevitable. He was later charged with drug trafficking for which he spent four years sat in a prison cell. In November 2003, he passed away at the age of just 40, succumbing to AIDS.

It was entirely possible that McMillan would have ground out a gritty points win had the injury not occurred but there was no doubt that it was a gruelling fight, the sort that tends to take something out of a fighter and accelerate the natural wear and tear. He was ahead on all three judge's scorecards, two of them comfortably. There was, however, the realisation that the injury would undoubtedly have the now ex-champion out of the ring for some time. The combination of the injury and the manner of McMillan's performance led some to speculate whether or not he could reach the highs of the Stecca performance again.

As part of McMillan's recovery process, he flew over to Miami to get in some training at the legendary Angelo Dundee's gym. The trainer of such icons as Muhammad Ali and 'Sugar' Ray Leonard, Dundee welcomed him in and summed up his training by describing the featherweight as 'a natural'. He sparred a few rounds with the European flyweight champion from Italy, Luigi Camputaro, but after four rounds of moving around the ring, McMillan felt his shoulder slip out of its socket. The physical motion of him jumping down off the ring apron to seek medical attention was all that was needed for the ball to fall back into place. McMillan returned to England to have an operation but his self-prognosis was not encouraging.

'When I started using it in training again, it started playing up. I had to have an operation and I had a metal pin put in it. When I was sparring Johnny Armour, I felt it go again and I knew it wasn't right. At the time I thought it would fix itself in a couple of months but later on I knew it wouldn't be the same again.'

Johnny Armour, the former Commonwealth and European bantamweight champion, has his recollections of the sparring and one would presume McMillan was near to his best from the appraisal given. 'It was a great honour to spar Colin,' Armour said. 'A great boxer, had very fast hands and he reminded me of "Sugar" Ray Leonard.'

The treatment and physiotherapy continued to nurture McMillan's left shoulder back to strength to enable him to continue with his boxing career. With Palacios now retired, a last-minute substitute for the Colombian came in the form of Cardiff's Steve Robinson, who went on to record a convincing points win over John Davison for the vacant title and hence parallels were drawn between the manner of his sudden elevation to fame and a certain Walt Disney character's surprising, yet fateful encounter with everlasting happiness.

With McMillan sensing that his shoulder may not regain full strength again after Palacios's upward barge into his armpit, he made the decision to head straight back into a challenge for his old title after one year out. Seeing the sands of time for his career filtering through the hour glass, he chose to go for broke and achieve what he could in the shortest space of time. On 23 October 1993, he stepped in against Steve Robinson in the champion's home territory of Cardiff's National Ice Rink. Stopping former McMillan opponent Sean Murphy in his sole defence of the title, Robinson was riding high on the crest of the world championship wave and his confidence was rocketing. His achievement in winning the title was astonishing. Prior to beating Davison, he had lost nine of 23 contests and was categorised as not much more than a solid, capable journeyman. McMillan's and Robinson's fortunes inside the ring had taken sudden changes of direction in the preceding year or so. Was it perhaps too soon or too much to ask for McMillan to return straight into such a challenge?

'When I had the original injury, I let it try and heal naturally and I saw a physio to try and sort everything out. It wasn't working that way. I had a subluxacation [where the ball slips in and out of the socket] so I realised I had to have an operation so I had the pin put in. During training, it popped out and I couldn't afford financially to have a couple of warm-ups and for the shoulder to go again. I needed to go for it but I still thought that even one-handed, I could still beat Steve Robinson. I was that confident in my ability that even less than 100 per cent, I could win.'

Sustaining a badly swollen right hand in the early rounds, a cut to his left eye and occasional twinges in his damaged shoulder, McMillan found himself bulled into the ropes by Robinson's forward-marching offensive. Although McMillan found room to pump out his classic jab at times, the champion seemed to set a pace that he couldn't match. He found himself outworked at various stages of the fight, being worked over by Robinson's eye-catching flurries. Enough of these got through to ensure he kept his title with a 12-round unanimous points decision. The Cinderella story of Wales's latest boxing star rolled to the next chapter. McMillan, meanwhile, was full of praise for his latest conqueror.

'He done really well. We were due to fight on the George Foreman bill at London Arena in September 1990 but they pulled him out and they brought another guy in for me. Robinson took the opportunity though and he has done really well.'

Shortly after the Robinson loss, McMillan was back in the States for more surgery with a keyhole specialist. Noticing that a piece of bone inserted to stabilise the shoulder in an earlier operation had come away, McMillan spent a considerable sum for the operation to be carried out. Returning to Britain, he decide to, while not retire from the sport, take some time out and indulge in some other interests. He dabbled with a burglar alarm company and a computer repair outlet, neither of which, for various reasons, took off. It was at this time that the Professional Boxers' Association was formed in alliance with another former world featherweight champion, Barry McGuigan.

The association set about forming a strict set of guidelines to promote and safeguard the welfare of boxers and a management committee was established which was endorsed by the likes of Chris Eubank, Nicky Piper, Lloyd Honeyghan and Lennox Lewis. From the list of preventative measures submitted by the PBA, the British Boxing Board of Control had adopted a number of them and they were instrumental in contributing to the full recovery made by the European super-bantamweight champion Spencer Oliver when he suffered life-threatening injuries in a title defence against Sergei Devakov in 1998.

'Barry had the idea for the PBA and it was something which I liked to do and being in tune with trying to look after fighters, not just after they retire but also during their careers. To look at their contracts and to make it better for them in all aspects of their careers. Financially, contractually, health-wise and to help them plan for their future. There was the Professional Footballers' Association and we wanted to find out if we could replicate some of their stuff. It was always going to be difficult though because the nature of boxing is different to every other sport. It is an individual sport. The guys who have the money don't need the help. It's the other guys who need the help. The PBA also tried to look at training programmes so fighters could make adjustments after boxing. It would be good to see more help for the fighters after their careers have ended.'

After an unsuccessful bid to gain a manager's licence for the budding light-middleweight star, Adrian Dodson, McMillan crossed paths with a physiotherapist, Kevin Lidlow, who helped bring his shoulder back up to strength. Offers to resume his boxing career started to creep back and it was with Frank Warren that he decided to continue his profession. Since his withdrawal from the boxing world, a bright new star from Sheffield had lit up the domestic scene. 'Prince' Naseem Hamed had emerged as Britain's most colourful, flamboyant and gifted young prodigy. He had crashed on to the sport's headlines at a time when Chris Eubank was left to lick his wounds after losing his world title to Ireland's Steve Collins, Herol Graham was no longer on the scene and Lennox Lewis had been knocked out in a shocking upset by a marauding 'Atomic Bull' in the autumn of 1994. Hamed was campaigning at bantamweight but being a fast-developing young gun with frightening power and foot, upper-body and head movement, a natural move to featherweight looked a certainty. Keanu Reeves in *The Matrix* was agonisingly flat-footed and rigid in comparison. A possible future clash with the 'Prince' could not be written off but Steve Robinson remained the initial target.

His comeback kicked off on the undercard to Steve Robinson's sixth consecutive WBO featherweight title defence against Domingo Damigella. Since defeating McMillan, the 'Cinderella Man' had swept through the rest of the current crop of British featherweights, stopping McMillan's ex-nemesis Paul Hodkinson in the 12th and last round, and he had knocked out the former three-weight world champion Duke McKenzie in nine rounds. Sandwiched between these was a solid, workmanlike decision win over the Dominican Republic's Freddy Cruz.

Ominously, three fights later Cruz would be demolished in six rounds by Naseem Hamed himself.

Facing McMillan in his first fight back was Sunderland's Harry Escott. Chosen to help McMillan ease his way back into the limelight, Escott fit the bill perfectly. After eight much-needed rounds, McMillan won a comfortable points win and three weeks later, on the undercard to the scintillating but ultimately devastating Nigel Benn–Gerald McClellan fight at the London Arena, he trounced Mark Hargreaves to a fourth-round stoppage victory. In May and July that same year he notched up eight-round points wins over Peter Judson and Dean Phillips respectively. The Phillips victory was slightly hollow as McMillan had to climb off the floor briefly to register the win.

At this time, it was apparent to McMillan that a potential showdown with Naseem Hamed could be on the cards as the 'Prince' had called out Steve Robinson after the Welshman's win over Damigella. Hamed was moving up to featherweight and it was obvious to everyone where the big money lay. Switching promoters from Frank Warren to Frank Maloney was a decision made by McMillan with this in mind. In his first fight under Maloney's banner, he scored his most impressive win in his latest comeback by hammering Justin Murphy to defeat inside of four rounds. The left jab was working well again and he seemed to recapture a good portion of the attributes he showed a few years earlier. McMillan donated his purse to the Professional Boxers' Association and to the King George Hospital in Chadwell Heath, Essex.

'Originally, after I lost to Robinson, I went away to America and had another operation and then I spoke with Frank Warren to get me a couple of fights and then get another world championship fight. That was the objective. At that time Naseem was coming through and he was doing really well so I was hoping to get that fight. For whatever reason, Frank Warren didn't see that fight happening in the immediate future so we parted company and I tried to do my own thing, to try and get back into title contention.'

Having comfortably trekked up the side of the mountain, picking up the British and Commonwealth featherweight titles on the way and then planting the Union Jack into the peak after outclassing Stecca, McMillan lost, first as champion and then as challenger, consecutive bouts for the world crown. While he hadn't exactly tumbled back down to the bottom, the comeback involved a return to facing opponents at domestic journeyman level.

'Yeah, it is quite hard when you're at one level with the world championship with all the associated things around it and then having to get yourself mentally psyched up for the British championship. It is kind of hard.'

On 21 March 1996, McMillan stepped into the ring against perennial loser but tough journeyman Peter Buckley and recorded a third-round stoppage. It was the last hurdle before he received the chance to reclaim the British featherweight title from the current titleist, Jonjo Irwin. The champion from Doncaster was making the second defence of the title he took from Mike Deveney the previous September. After 12 thoroughly compelling, intense rounds, McMillan emerged the winner and stopped the defending champion from winning the Lonsdale belt outright, a feat Irwin would go on to accomplish at a later date. Such was the intensity of battle that night that McMillan went to the Royal London Hospital for precautionary checks having complained of exhaustion.

'It was a typical route back and after the Irwin fight things started coming together again. I was promoted by Panix Promotions and they thought a fight for the world championship wasn't too far away. They expected a fight with Naz and we were quite close. The fight was on the horizon and was getting a bit of interest.'

In September 1996, McMillan stepped in with tough Zimbabwe fighter, Trust Ndlovu. Fighting outside his native country for the first time, Ndlovu was overwhelmed after seven rounds and McMillan could look forward to a January defence of his British title against the unbeaten and promising contender, Paul Ingle. The 'Yorkshire Hunter' from Scarborough sported a fine record of 14 wins with nine coming inside the distance. In what turned out to be a changing of the guard, Ingle swarmed over McMillan and gradually wore him down. McMillan suffered cuts to his cheek, nose, eyebrow and lip and during round eight, a final barrage of withering blows left the former world champion defenceless on the ropes when referee John Coyle dived in to end the fight and, ultimately, McMillan's boxing career. Ingle would go on to win both the Commonwealth and European titles before facing Naseem Hamed for the world title. Ingle performed admirably against the Sheffield fighter before succumbing in the 11th round. He later won the IBF world title but had to retire when beaten in his second defence, after an operation to remove a blood clot from his brain was carried out. Thankfully he made a good recovery.

'I didn't underestimate him but the fight with Naz was round the corner and I looked at Paul Ingle and I thought I was better than him, stronger than him, faster than him so I didn't give him the respect he deserved. Physically I was in shape but mentally, I don't think I was prepared because he brought a lot of energy. When I went to the press conference and the weigh-in, I saw how hyped up he was and I saw the eye of the tiger. He was fighting for the title and I could see he was ready.'

It can sometimes be immediately apparent to a fighter that he can no longer perform to the level that he has grown accustomed to. For others it takes time and a lot of reflection to come to the conclusion that his skills have eroded to the point where the body will obstinately refuse to obey the commands given by the mind. The trigger can be gripped but no longer pulled. McMillan hinted after the fight that it may be his last professional contest. It was.

'I took a couple of weeks to make the final decision. As a fighter though, you always think, "If I fought a different kind of fight, I could have beaten him." You always think that. It is always difficult to defer what you do when retired. On your way up, as a fighter, everything is geared towards fighting. Even when you're resting, you're doing it so you can start training again. In most sports you see a gradual decline where you start thinking about something else. With boxing, it can be immediate. In just one fight, it can all be over and that's why I think some fighters have problems with retirement. It can be hard to make that adjustment.'

There are numerous reasons for a retired fighter's life after boxing becoming bleak and lacking in direction. A lack of money management which gets exploited by the numerous hangers-on and 'yes men' who surround the fighter in the hope of being handsomely rewarded for their misguided loyalty is a major reason for this. Throw in to the pot also, the sinister extremes of corruption and manipulation that give the fighter short-term fame but long-term turmoil and also the basic lack of responsibility by the fighter who chooses to squander his money on fleets of cars, incessant partying and a harem of women when all that catches up with him are reams and reams of tax bills, lawsuits from embittered past acquaintances and the result of poor investment. There are, however, those who have not fallen foul of such things and were able to twig early on that feathering a nest may not be such a bad idea.

'I was quite fortunate because one of the guys who was a sponsor to me when I was fighting had a nightclub and when I retired he asked me to go down and promote a night. It was great because it was very, very similar to boxing. One night a month which you promote and it was like fighting. You're working towards the night, trying to get everything together. I did it for a few years, it helped with the transition and it kept me occupied. It gave me focus and made me some money at the same time. It was great.'

McMillan nowadays has his fingers in many pies and has so far escaped from being burnt. He emanates contentment and satisfaction in what he has achieved and what he hopes to fulfil in the future. At one point, he managed Audley Harrison after he won the gold medal at the Sydney Olympics in 2000. Many eyebrows were raised when the BBC offered Harrison a £1m contract for his first ten fights.

'I managed Audley Harrison briefly when he won the gold medal. It was another good experience for me but it was a bit of a disappointment not to see him do better which he could have done in his professional career. It was complicated, so many different issues. In retrospect you had a novice fighter who was getting the money so people were expecting him to be in genuine fights. As a fighter though, you need to be nursed along and brought along at the right pace. There were so many complications with the structure of the deal. Sometimes, he didn't help himself. He would talk a bit too much. I saw him again recently and he is so full of confidence!

'I also have an agency for fighters to give personal appearances and I have developed an academy in Redbridge to try and get the community involved in boxing. It's all non-contact but it gets them involved in fitness and also learning the basics of boxing. I also have a few properties so they keep me ticking over and I am the logistics and quality control manager for my sister's company, Devoted Ltd, which imports shoes and bags from China so I have a few different things keeping me busy!'

Charity work also plays an important part in McMillan's work. Once a year he hosts a boxing show for his amateur club, part of the proceeds going to a nominated charity. He is also a patron for the Dream Factory, a registered charity that aims to make the dreams come true for those who suffer life-threatening conditions or those who suffer extreme disability. Its work is nothing short of inspiring and life-changing for those it benefits. McMillan works alongside other patrons such as Lisa Marie Presley, Ray Winstone, Iain Duncan-Smith, Patsy Palmer and the Bishop of Chelmsford.

It is almost as if the injury suffered against Palacios, which terminally altered the route his career was destined to take, was compensated by the achievements made by McMillan since his retirement. In terms of his boxing career, there were many who doubted whether McMillan would ever be the same fighter again after that fateful September night but from May 1991 to May 1992, he was surely one of the finest fighters this country has produced. Of that, there can be little doubt.

10
Sammy Reeson

WHEN the idea for writing this book was conceived in my mind not too long ago, I had a number of ideas which I wished to convert to ink within these pages. Bringing unsung champions and contenders to the boxing public's conscience was one of the more important ones. Those fighters who plied away at their chosen trade of exchanging an array of punches with their foe while receiving limited exposure compared to those who benefitted more from higher profile promoters, more public-friendly styles or simply those that oozed the stereotypical golden boy looks that endeared them to more than just the boxing hardcore. Money talks and in boxing circles, it positively hollers from the mountain tops if certain fighters possess certain attributes. There are, however, honest, less newsworthy fighters who have scaled the heights and have, to an extent, played their part in shaping and, in a historical sense, contributing to their respective weight divisions. Sammy Reeson, the first British and first European cruiserweight champion in the division's relatively brief history, is one such fighter.

On 8 December 1979, the division's first world title fight took place in Croatia when local fighter and former European and world light-heavyweight champion Mate Parlov fought to a draw against Marvin Camel of the US. The return just over three months later in the more accustomed boxing surroundings of Las Vegas, saw Camel take a 15-round points win to become the first incumbent of a world cruiserweight title. It was not until 1985, that the division was inaugurated by the British Boxing Board of Control.

On 31 October 1985, Reeson was matched with Hartlepool's Stewart Lithgo for the vacant British title at the Latchmere Leisure

Centre in Wandsworth. While Reeson was unbeaten at the time, Lithgo was coming off three straight knockout losses. Reeson was declared the victor after a scorecard of 120-114 by referee Roland Dakin. The achievement was one which now took its rightful place in cruiserweight history. Britain had its first cruiserweight champion.

'No one can change that can they? That's there forever,' Reeson said proudly, in his mild-mannered and soft-spoken way, as he sat back in his chair at his father's home in Mitcham, south London. I let him dwell on that sense of pride for a moment. His eyes drifted off towards some shelves in the adjoining sitting room and he got up, walked over to them and returned to his seat clutching a handful of large photos, illustrating the high points of his boxing career. The champion's pose with his belts draped around him, the action images of him in his fight with Lithgo and post-fight shots of him with his father and one-time trainer, the late Tony Lavelle.

'I'll get those framed one day and put up,' he said. 'I knew Lithgo was good. He gave Bruno a hard fight. He wobbled him. I felt strong at that weight.' Both fighters put on a crowd-pleasing 12-rounder which saw both men cut but one which was ultimately decided by Reeson's effective southpaw jab.

Brought up in Battersea, Reeson didn't have a particularly hard upbringing but, as with a lot of budding fighters, he was the victim of bullying at school and was introduced to the square ring as a way of learning to look after, and defend, himself.

'I was brought up in Battersea on the Winstanley Estate. It was alright. It had a couple of good amateur clubs there. I was about ten years old. I got bullied by a 17-year-old so my dad said, "Come on, I'll take you boxing." We went to the boxing gym and I loved it. I latched on to it straight away. Dad's uncle, Doug, was the only boxer in my family. My mum never went to any of my fights. I went to Brixton when I was about 12 and then went back to Battersea when I was about 17. I turned pro when I was 20. I reached the semi-finals of the schoolboys three times. That was at 48kg, 54kg and 60kg. Errol Christie always won it in my weight. He won everything as an amateur and I always got beaten in the semi-finals. Rocky Kelly beat me.'

The transition from the amateur ranks to the professionals can be a daunting yet exciting episode in the careers of many fighters. Some have a natural style that is best suited to one or the other.

'I packed up boxing when I was 17. I went out drinking and met girls. Then, all of a sudden my mate Gary Mason turned pro and asked me to come up the gym. I used to work the door with him. I used to weigh over 17st. I went up there, lost a couple of stone and just turned pro. I had four senior fights for Battersea. Won three and lost one and then I packed up. I found it better for me being a professional with longer rounds. I started out with Tony Lavelle, Keith Bristol and Tee Jay. I used to go up the All Stars Amateur Boxing Club and spar with James Oyebola and Tee Jay.'

Reeson started his professional career with a six-round points win over Calvin Earlington on 19 May 1983. His right jab from the southpaw stance was apparent from this early stage and was highly effective in keeping his opponents at bay and not allowing them the space to get in close and rough him up. His first ten fights all went the full route and the obvious signs were there that Reeson may be lacking in the power department.

'That was how I boxed. I didn't get hit. I never got hit a lot. Yeah, the jab carried me through most of my career. I was hard to hit because of the jab and once they realised that, they lost their temper a bit. Once that happened, they'd had it. I just jabbed them off.'

His first knockout came in his 11th fight and two fights after that, he fought for, and won, his first title. The Southern Area light-heavyweight title belt was strapped around his waist after he stopped Trevor Cattouse in the sixth round of their contest in Streatham. For a fighter known for his careful jabbing and working his way in to outfight his opponents, his fight with Cattouse saw him start fast and overwhelm him with the sheer volume of punches thrown. Cuts to both eyes and a heavy onslaught, resulting in a knockdown, was enough for referee Larry O'Connell and the fight was waved off.

'Trevor Cattouse had been around years. It was the first time I ever got down to 12st 7lb. I felt strong and I had a lot of fans there. It was a good fight.' After three further fights, Reeson carved out his own niche in the division's history by beating Lithgo for the British title. With three further points wins against the respectable opposition of Ruben Williams, Roy Smith and Roy Skeldon, Reeson suffered his first loss against Cameroon southpaw Louis Pergaud in May 1986. The fight was a hard tussle from the off with Reeson appearing out of sorts and finding it hard to get to grips with his opponent's awkward style. In a messy fight with much mauling, wrestling and, fatefully, reckless headwork, Reeson was pulled out shortly after the start of the fourth with a large cut over his right eye.

'Tony Lavelle told me we'd get the British title and we did. He then said we'd get the European title but then he died. When that happened, my heart left the sport to be honest. I felt confident against the others in

Britain though. I never lost to a British fighter. You had Andy Straughn. I sparred with Tee Jay. I felt confident against any of them.'

Reeson's trainer and friend, Tony Lavelle, was tragically killed in a car crash that November and he was more determined than ever to see Lavelle's vision of him lifting the European title come into sharp focus. After a warm-up in which Reeson scored a solid points win over Roy Safford, the contest for the vacant European title took place at the Royal Albert Hall on 22 April 1987. In the opposite corner was West German veteran Manfred Jassman. Jassman had been in the ring with both of the fearsome Rocchigiani brothers and would go on to fight a number of respectable heavyweights later in his career.

In Frank Warren's first show at the venue, Reeson was after another piece of history. Like his British title win, this fight would also determine the first European cruiserweight title-holder in history. The other two title fights on the show, Tony Sibson's Commonwealth middleweight title defence against British champion Brian Anderson and Lloyd Christie's British light-welterweight title defence against Mo Hussein, had fallen through, so the spotlight became fractionally more intense and the stage was set for Reeson to impress. What transpired was a methodical showing by Reeson, who employed his advantages in the height and reach departments to good effect by outboxing the comparatively pedestrian German. Awarded a unanimous decision, Reeson's hands were raised and he was crowned the king of Europe. Afterwards, he dedicated his victory to the late Tony Lavelle. The following week's issue of *Boxing News* had a front cover which proudly announced, 'Reeson becomes first ever European cruiser champion'.

'My heart weren't in it anymore. I then went with Frank Warren after Tony Lavelle died. Gary Davidson trained me, another good trainer, and Jimmy Tibbs was there too. I was training down the Thomas A' Beckett gym. I had a stress fracture in my foot and I was having cortisone injections but I done alright. I went 12 rounds. It was good. I was sixth in the world after that fight.'

In the aftermath to this distinguished achievement, talk turned to a possible world title fight. Reeson joined Duke McKenzie and Herol Graham as Britain's only European champions and the signs were promising that various world titles could be heading to these shores. In the cruiserweight division, the world champions at this time were Ricky Parkey (IBF), Evander Holyfield (WBA) and Carlos DeLeon (WBC).

'I wouldn't have been too confident. I'd have fought Evander but no, I wouldn't have been confident. He was an exceptional fighter. He'd been around a few years and I was just sort of coming up. I could have fought Dennis Andries but they said no, it ain't worth it. Great manager, Tony was. It was after only about 18 fights and he thought I should wait.'

Reeson made one successful defence of his European title against the Belgian, Luigi Ricci. Fighting for the first time away from home, Ricci was predictably defeated, Reeson collecting a rare inside-the-distance victory in Windsor. Ricci was counted out on his feet by the referee in the seventh round and afterwards, Frank Warren sounded optimistic in getting the WBC champion, Carlos DeLeon, over to Britain to fight the new European champion.

On 9 April 1988, Carlos DeLeon faced Evander Holyfield to decide the division's first undisputed world champion since its inception in 1979. Holyfield stopped DeLeon in the eighth round and immediately announced his plans to invade the heavyweight division. In so doing, he left the undisputed title to crumble once again into three separate pieces; each piece to be fought for by the respective governing bodies' next two available contenders in line. The WBA announced that the Tunisian-born Frenchman Taoufik Belbouli would square off against the American Michael Greer, the IBF title would be contested between another Briton, Glenn McCrory, and the Swedish-based Kenyan Patrick Lumumba, and the WBC pitted Reeson against the recently deposed Puerto Rican Carlos DeLeon.

The gulf in experience was huge and while both fighters had been out of the ring for a year, the Puerto Rican was able to capitalise on this edge and reigned, for the fourth time, as WBC cruiserweight champion. The fight was terminated in the ninth round to bring the curtain down on a brave and courageous attempt by Reeson to lift world honours. The win put DeLeon in the same bracket as a man many rate as the greatest fighter ever to walk the planet. He joined 'Sugar' Ray Robinson as the only fighters to win a world title in the same weight category for a fourth time. This distinction is tenuous, to say the least, given there are more opportunities to win world titles in this age than the fiercely competitive eras of yore and the gap in ability between the two fighters about as long as the odds were of 'Sugar' Ray continuing into the 14th round against Joey Maxim in 1952. The matter of DeLeon's nickname also happening to be 'Sugar' no doubt raised an eyebrow too.

Statistics do, however, tell a tale and they put in focus the task facing Reeson on that May 1989 evening in London's famous Docklands Arena. In Reeson's favour, he started the fight well, utilising his pet southpaw jab to good effect, keeping DeLeon preoccupied and distracted like someone shielding their eyes from a blustery wind. In the end, however, experience came through.

'I went to see Bruno fight Tyson in Las Vegas. I came back and I weighed over 17 stone. I went to see Frank Warren and he told me I'd got a world title fight in six weeks. I lost three stone. That was hard. I was weak going into that fight. A good manager would have left it for about three months, not six weeks. Tony Lavelle wouldn't have done that. I should have asked him for more time but it was there and I thought "yeah". Had I been fitter, it could have been different but I done it and that's it. It's half my fault. I wasn't fit then but the left jab caught him a few times. I wasn't hurt. I was just knackered where I lost all that weight and my body weren't strong. I'd been cut and I was just tired.'

Reeson's honesty was admirable and I got the impression that any compliment I may have given would have been deflected and replaced with an all-too-harsh self-assessment. The effort he put in compared to that of DeLeon's first title challenger eight months later, Johnny Nelson, is a point in hand. Ending in a draw, the total amount of punches thrown in that entire fight would have been criticised had they been thrown in one round by one fighter in most other contests. It was no Harry Greb slugfest.

'That was a bad fight. They didn't touch each other did they? Worst fight ever I think!' Reeson said with an air of contentment knowing his performance against DeLeon had been undoubtedly more courageous.

There was never much doubt in Reeson's mind that he would retire after the world title fight. Losing Tony Lavelle two and a half years previously had a strong impact on him and retirement had been an option prior to his last fight.

'I was going to finish before that. It was just that they said I had a world title fight. I had never had the urge to come back. Once Tony Lavelle went, my heart weren't in it. He said I'd fight Jassman for the European title and I did so it all came true what he said.'

His post-retirement years saw him working in the scrap-metal industry. On noticing some scrap metal outside a house in Wimbledon one day, he asked the owner if he could take it. The owner told Reeson that he had more in his garage so when the former boxing champion but went to have a look, part of the structure collapsed and crushed his left leg, resulting in its amputation and the application of a fake limb. Reeson grew accustomed to it and, while I learnt of this while watching an interview I saw of Reeson's on the internet prior to meeting him, it is not immediately obvious in the way he moves about. If Reeson was wearing a pair of trousers instead of shorts, this mildly obtrusive disability would not be apparent.

'I was working in scrap metal and I was doing alright. Then I had the accident a couple of years ago in a £4m house in Wimbledon that collapsed. The brick lint came down and one bit was on my leg. I got an infection and I had it off. I've had this new leg now for two years. As soon as I got the leg, I went to the physio and they had me walking up and down the pool and the stairs. I was in hospital for three months. Two months after I came out I was in a wheelchair for a while then they put my leg on and I was off. It can be a burden getting in and out of the bath but it's alright.'

My mind went back to July 1990 when a fighter from the US named Craig Bodzianowski stepped into the ring with one false leg to challenge Robert Daniels for the WBA cruiserweight title. He went all 12 rounds before losing on points but the point was proved. Such a defect did not hamper Bodzianowski's opportunity to get the title shot and it hasn't been allowed to hinder Reeson's day-to-day life either.

'I've been getting around. I go out with my boys. They take me out. I don't work but I go out with them for the day and help them. I do little bits here and there but I can't pick up washing machines anymore! I have four boys and a girl aged from 27 to six. They aren't interested in boxing. They're footballers. I'd be nervous if they decided to get into boxing but I'd support them.'

Reeson is undoubtedly proud of his achievements as a fighter but one senses he feels slightly let down by the sport's lack of care for fighters after they leave the ring for the final time.

'I packed up and never heard from no one. I didn't hear from none of them. No "how you doing", none of that. I finished and that was me, you know. A lot of people, they're not working. They've been up there, go on the drink and that. I had a good life but I just moved on. So many fighters go down the pan. Look at Kirkland Laing. I'm not bitter. Life goes on. You just deal with it. I did alright though. When I fought, I was hard to hit, had a good jab and could take a punch. I used to do 12 rounds quite easy. I wouldn't be out of breath. I could have done another 12 rounds when I fought Lithgo. I did cut a few times. You can't help that though.'

For a man who shows real strength of character in dealing with what life has thrown at him, it would be easy to assume that he has no regrets. There is that one event in his fighting career that does still have an impact on him and clearly influenced the path his boxing journey took.

'My only regret is Tony Lavelle. If he was here, I'd have done better. I can't blame him. I can't grumble though. Not everyone can say they were the first British and European cruiserweight champion. That will be in the book forever won't it? Now, I just want to take life one day at a time and enjoy it. Day by day. See where it takes me. I live in Bournemouth now with my girlfriend and I love it. It's lovely there. The people are different there to London. They don't want a row. I was sitting outside a cafe with my paper the other day and a car flashed me to let me go. I wasn't even going anywhere!'

The same can't be said for him during his boxing career. With Southern Area, British and European titles to his name followed by a challenge for the world title against a highly accomplished champion, it would be safe to say that Reeson's targets had largely been met. Tony Lavelle's too. That, in itself, would appear to be the most satisfying and pleasing accomplishment of all.

11
Derek Williams

IN the mid-late-1980s, two British heavyweights dominated the domestic headlines. Frank Bruno ripped apart the former WBA heavyweight champion Gerrie Coetzee in one round at Wembley Arena in 1986 to secure his shot at the same title against America's 'Terrible' Tim Witherspoon. From that moment on, he remained in the headlines, partly because of his amenable nature and partly because he had the punching power to produce huge drawing power. Winning or losing wasn't such an important issue. Frank was the nation's adopted son and the crowds would turn out in their droves to watch him in action. Failed world title bids in the latter part of the decade against Witherspoon and, three years later, 'Iron' Mike Tyson, did little to dampen the enthusiasm.

The other heavyweight, who was deemed to be on a collision course with Bruno, was the formidable Gary Mason. Throwing punches from floor-level and detonating them on the chins of carefully-picked opponents, Mason quickly made a name for himself for being dynamic but almost overly-enthusiastic to bludgeon his opponents to defeat. If it landed, his opponent was knocked out by the punch. If he missed, his opponent was knocked over by the ensuing wind tunnel. With both fighters under the watchful eyes of Terry Lawless, Mickey Duff and Mike Barrett, a match-up seemed a certainty. The machinations involved to bring them together would be minimal and public demand was such that boxing fans were debating such a match-up at every opportunity. In 1989, Mason annexed the vacant British heavyweight title with a fourth-round knockout over the former champion, Hughroy Currie. The following month, Bruno went down gallantly in five intense rounds against Mike Tyson in the Las Vegas Hilton. He stayed out of the ring for almost two years after that. It was during this year, that another British heavyweight, again from the Lawless stable, was quietly plying his trade and started to go up in the domestic ratings as well as in people's estimations.

At the tail-end of 1988, Derek 'Sweet D' Williams had seized the Commonwealth heavyweight title with a fourth-round knockout over Tonga-born Young Haumona. Most boxing fans, however, were more occupied with the developments between Bruno and Mason than they were with the more unassuming fighter born out of Stockwell, south London. Williams always came across as a level-headed and honest professional, confident in his ability that the wins he picked up would lead to bigger and greater opportunities. He wasn't brought up among the all too common environment of gang fights and crime that infests various areas of London.

'Your name's Ben right? Not now it's not. It's BIG Ben!' the instantly recognisable former Commonwealth and European champion said with a wide grin. Any apprehensions one may have harboured upon meeting the huge frame of Derek Williams would have been blown away with such an introduction. My grin matured into a fully-blown laugh. Over the years, I've grown wholly accustomed to being likened, only by name thankfully, to the mammoth, four-faced, concrete timepiece in Westminster, but there was something highly amusing about being referred to as 'big' by someone of Derek Williams's physical presence.

'Sweet D' invited me to sit on the ring apron in an enclave to the main part of the Soho Gym in Brad Street where he tutors a number of young boxers, just around the corner from London Bridge Station. Williams starts talking. His tone is upbeat, his patter is something straight out of the Muhammad Ali book of pugilistic verse and his eyes tell you that, while he feels, to an extent, he underachieved as a professional, he is seriously focused on developing his own stable of boxers.

'When I look back on my boxing career and I compare myself to other guys, there are a lot of guys in boxing that have come up from a life of crime. I came from a stable home, a good family upbringing and a good education. I was born in Stockwell and brought up in Peckham but I stayed away from gang life. At that time, there were a lot of muggings and street crime. Cutting people's bags and if they resisted they cuffed them over the head. I never had that type of background. I was never running with gangs or attacking anyone.

'My whole thing was as an athlete and I wanted to play basketball. I had an intention to become a basketball star then I wanted to be a footballer. I was an all-round sportsman but boxing was my love. I went to my first gym when I was 16. I had no fights there but had some good training and sparring. I wanted to take it further so I joined Wandsworth Boys' Club where Gary Mason was. I turned professional while I was still at college!'

Years later when Williams became an established professional, he was labelled by the renowned trainer, Angelo Dundee, as the 'British Ali' when he worked with the legendary guru in Miami in the build-up to his fight with Lennox Lewis in 1992. Naturally, this sat well with the Peckham fighter as his inspiration in the early days was none other than the self-proclaimed 'Greatest'. 'I got into boxing because of my competitive edge and I like challenges and competition. Muhammad Ali done it to me. I loved his character, his jovial nature, his fun and his integrity. It's only now I look back and realise some of the things he said to some of the guys were hurtful but at the time when a young guy, it was fun. I loved that!'

Williams was something of a late starter in the sport and, not embarking on his amateur career until well into his teenage years, it inevitably wasn't long before he turned to the professional side of the sport. 'I didn't have my first amateur fight until I was 17. I had a short amateur career. I had a good punch though and I looked good. I had a good amateur pedigree because I trained hard. I didn't have the long amateur career of fighting championships and Commonwealth Games but I fought some hard guys. I didn't have the mapped-out route where you have the glorified amateur who turns professional and fights tomato cans.

'My amateur career was short. I was whacking these guys and I got disqualified once in 11 fights. I was training with the pros as an amateur at the Mason's Arms where there was a gym where the pros were training. I was sparring with guys like John L. Gardner. I felt seasoned and even in 1984 for the Olympics, I was sparring with the heavyweight going over there and I was punching him all around and I was thinking, "This guy isn't going to last long in LA!" At this time, I'd only had about nine fights and he couldn't touch me in sparring. We hadn't had a heavyweight champion in the last century so that was my intention.'

At this stage, Gary Mason played a big part in Williams's development and nurturing. Both fighters were eyeing up professional glory and they used their joint enthusiasm to assist each other in training. 'Gary Mason shared my intention and we would spar and sharpen each other. I wouldn't say we were good friends but we would talk and joke. We had different interests and had different friends but he was a great character.'

On 24 October 1984, Williams stepped into the ring in London's Mayfair to face Tony Tricker in his professional debut. With one win and one loss going into the fight, Tricker lasted into the sixth round before the debutant registered his first win.

'Because I had only been the distance in the amateurs twice, I didn't even know what it was like to go more than three rounds. Some amateurs would have had more fights but I had only two or three that went the distance. As a professional, I was very confident I could become the first heavyweight champion of the world from here. Mick Hill was my manager then as he was in the amateurs too. I didn't ask who or when, I was just told I was fighting Tony Tricker and I was determined to go six rounds.'

After notching up three more wins, all inside the distance, Williams went in with the comparatively experienced 18-fight pro Ron Ellis in his first scheduled eight-rounder. With just one notable opponent on his record to date, the future top-ranked heavyweight contender from South Africa, Pierre Coetzer, Ellis was not deemed too much of a risk for Williams at this stage of his development. Indeed, Williams would still believe as such after the decision went against him, handing him his first professional defeat by a margin of just half a point on referee Roland Dakin's scorecard.

'I couldn't believe I lost that fight because looking at him after five or six rounds, his face was a total mess! Because I'd already had four knockouts, I was going for a fifth so I went for him in the first round! They told me to pace myself at the end of the first round so for six rounds I was worried because I didn't want to break my knockout streak. I was bombing this guy and by the seventh round, the bombs had lost their snap but I thought that at least I won the fight if not knocking him out and the decision went against me!'

While considerably heavier by 10lb, Ellis gave away advantages in both height and reach but he showed the tenacity to overcome these shortcomings to win the decision. 'I think *Boxing News* wrote a good report on that fight but people were saying that my manager shouldn't have put me in a fight like that. I think the guy came over here to fight Frank Bruno but he ended up with me.'

Four months later, Williams returned to record a points win over the tough but limited journeyman Steve Gee. Changes in his camp were brewing and the eyes of a certain British 'cartel' zeroed in on the fighter from Peckham.

'Mike Barrett and Mickey Duff started to pay attention to me. I ended up fighting with them and Mike Barrett is an honourable guy.

They had boxing under control at that time until Frank Warren came along! I was fighting from the small hall circuit and also at the big venues. I was buzzing at the opportunity and my chance came at the Wembley Grand Hall.'

On 22 February 1987, hidden towards the bottom of the bill, Williams recorded a repeat decision win over Steve Gee. Headlining the bill was Lloyd Honeyghan's brutal annihilation of Johnny Bumphus for the world welterweight title. Also on the bill was a budding middleweight contender named Michael Watson, and Williams's heavyweight stable-mate Gary Mason. The exposure was invaluable and Williams now felt the right strings were being tugged to steer his career towards stardom.

'I was trying to bomb Steve Gee out but Dennie Mancini was working in my corner that night and he said to me, "Derek, don't try to bomb this guy out. Just box him. He's durable and takes a good punch." In my mind, I'm a puncher so I wanted to take him out. I was putting bombs on him and he was taking them. I couldn't believe how he was still standing.'

The following month, Williams appeared again, outpointing another grizzled veteran, Andrew Gerrard, on a bill headlined by Frank Bruno's comeback fight against the American cowboy James Tillis. Again, Mason appeared on the bill along with future British stars Jim McDonnell and Duke McKenzie.

In Williams's next fight, he almost came unstuck against Potters Bar's Jess Harding. Sporting a mediocre record of three wins against two losses and a draw, Harding was deemed to be a routine opponent for Williams. One of his losses came on points against Tony Tricker, Williams's debut victim. Coming in behind a range-finding jab and the occasional follow-up cross, Williams built up an early lead only to reduce the pace over the middle rounds, allowing Harding's forward offensive to narrow the gap. Harding surged forward and capitalised on his opponent's coasting. Although Williams seemed to come alive more down the home stretch, there was still an unfavourable reaction from the crowd when the referee's scorecard was read out in favour of the Peckham man. Williams has a clear explanation for this lull over the middle rounds.

'Harding was my first southpaw!' Williams exclaimed. 'People were saying, "Oh, he's a southpaw" or he's this and that. It don't matter because I'm a fighter and I make people lose! I was thinking "Whoa, how come my jab is missing him?" So after a while I was trying to adjust to the fight. If I'd had more of an amateur career I'd have known that some fighters fight like that but I didn't have that so these were still learning fights. I won that fight pretty well though with the Ali shuffle too!'

Jess Harding, when I caught up with him over the phone while at work at JBD Sports Agents where he is a partner, has a variation of what happened that night.

'God's honest truth, I thought I got robbed! I battered him from pillar to post but didn't get the decision. I just found Derek's style very easy to hit and I found him lazy and laid-back so I just jumped all over him. That fight inspired me on though. He was under the Duff/Lawless auspices at the time but I thought I beat him but didn't get it. It spurred me on though,' Harding explained. 'That crystallised in my mind what I wanted to become as a fighter. It was a pivotal fight for me. I was a full-time pro and was in great shape at the time.'

Three months later, Williams would record one of his most significant wins to date when he confronted the tough and rugged John Westgarth at the York Hall on 8 October. Westgarth inflicted the first defeat on former cruiserweight champion Glenn McCrory's record and would go on to extend the likes of Anaclet Wamba the distance, take the Norwegian Steffen Tangstad to a split decision for the vacant European title in 1986 and then stretch future heavyweight contender Donovan 'Razor' Ruddock seven rounds. Against Williams, he suffered three knockdowns in the seventh round, bringing 'Sweet D' the win and serving notice that he was ready to make a significant impact on the domestic scene.

'He was a big puncher as he showed against Glenn McCrory,' Williams said. 'McCrory had come to London and he had sparred with me and Gary [Mason] in Streatham. I'm telling you, Glenn got a pasting in sparring from us! He was a friend but he had a hard time because he was really a cruiserweight. He was too small for a heavyweight.'

'At the time I was probably in the wrong place. I had just left my manager, Frankie Deans, and was then with Gus Robinson in Hartlepool. When I was with Frankie, it was more one to one training,' Westgarth explained to me over the phone as he was travelling up to Manchester.

Having confronted other British heavyweights such as, at the time, Glenn McCrory, Jess Harding, James Oyebola and Herbie Hide, Westgarth was quick to separate 'Sweet D' from the rest of the Brit-pack.

'Oh, he was a big heavyweight! He was a BIG heavyweight! He was as tall as myself and was a stone or more heavier but with Derek, he was an athlete. An all-round ATHLETE,' Westgarth stressed, highlighting the fitness level of the Peckham boxer. 'The first time I boxed him, I punched myself out really. People were just saying, "Keep going at him, keep going at him!" I had loads of stamina and strength but I just punched myself out. He didn't half crack me with a right hand! He dropped me and I always remember going on my knees and thinking, '" think 'ic's smashed me skull!" He really hit me like. You know what I mean? Thankfully I didn't, but I fully believed him. 'For the rematch,' he added, referring to the second Williams meet a year after the first, 'I really wasn't in a good place and I did it really for the money.'

The Westgarth win was followed up with a workmanlike, if not impressive, ten-round points win over the former British and Commonwealth title contender Dave Garside, and a fourth-round knockout of American journeyman Mark Young. A rematch with Westgarth at the Royal Albert Hall in October 1988 ended five rounds sooner than their first bout and it cleared the last hurdle before making a charge towards his first title. The potential he showed was fully endorsed by his management and the programme for the first Westgarth fight was proof of Mike Barrett and Mickey Duff's confidence in him. 'He's got the size, he's got the ability and he can certainly punch,' blared the programme's introduction.

Venturing outside of the Pacific region for the first time in his career, Young Haumona squared up to Williams in November 1988 in the Royal Albert Hall for the vacant Commonwealth heavyweight title on the back of a statistically moderate record of 18 wins against five losses. He had shared a ring with no one of any legitimate note but he had shown form to last long into a fight so the prospect of Williams being extended was a genuine one. Williams need not have worried.

After four rounds, 'Sweet D' was crowned the new Commonwealth champion. Finally, his potential was being realised and he emerged on to the title scene with a bang. With the premature retirement, due to damaged retinas, of Horace Notice that same month and the pending world title challenge of Frank Bruno to Mike Tyson, the domestic scene was set to be fought over by Williams and his stable-mate Gary Mason. Williams and Mason picked up the titles vacated by Notice with their respective wins over Haumona and Hughroy Currie, whom Mason knocked out with two huge right crosses the following January for the vacant British title.

'I was buzzing. Mike Barrett told me we were fighting for the Commonwealth title. In 1988, the Commonwealth title was still a big, recognised title to have. I heard my name on TV when the fight was announced and I thought, "Whoa, that's exposure!" My whole intention was to knock him out because I was thinking this is my opportunity to make a name for myself. I'm ready for him! I threw out the left jabs in the first round and by the fourth round...BOOM! The right hand and he was out! I was saying to people, "I can be world champion!"'

With Williams's confidence rocketing, Mike Barrett didn't hang around getting him fights and it was set for the new champion to step in with the exciting crowd-pleaser Noel Quarless the following February. Quarless was coming off a solid points win over the ill-fated former WBA heavyweight champion 'Big' John Tate and a points loss to Hughroy Currie in an eliminator for the British title. Williams, however, would not be denied. A series of big right hands put paid to Quarless towards the end of the first round and Williams earned himself a few more positive headlines to enhance his reputation.

'I saw Quarless on TV knock out John L. Gardner so he could punch but because I was now a champion, I knew I could punch! We went in there and in the first round...BOOM! I hit him with the first right hand and he didn't want to know no more! He saw that I was ready for him and I told him at the weigh-in that he got no chance. I told him, "You're Quarless, not flawless!" I was just messing around, it was my Muhammad Ali character!'

In the 1982 US amateur championships in Indianapolis, a young, relentless, explosive teenager named Mike Tyson was sent reeling by a barrage of punches from his opponent, Al Evans. Suffering a knockdown in the third and last round of their match, Tyson clambered to his feet but his legs wavered and the referee's arms waved. Evans had defeated Mike Tyson by a stoppage. It was the last time Tyson would be defeated as an amateur. Evans went on to lose in the final of the championships. He turned professional in 1986 but never amounted to anything prominent. His most impressive performance was taking the future WBC heavyweight champion, Oliver 'Atomic Bull' McCall, the distance in a six-rounder in his second pro fight. By the time he stepped in with Williams, his record read a mediocre four wins and two losses. That increased to three after Williams landed more of his vaunted right crosses to bring about what many people at the time believed to be a premature stoppage by referee Dave Parris. While this may have been the case, Williams looked comfortable and relaxed in securing the win.

'Al Evans came over here to fight Frank Bruno but Mike Barrett told me he was going to put me in there with him. He was a big puncher in the amateurs but I hit him in the second round with a right hand and he staggered back. He came forward and...BANG! I hit him again and he was down and the ref stopped the fight. So I'm happy we won. Ain't no stopping us now! I'm gonna become champion for sure! Mike Tyson was gonna fight me like Muhammad Ali. That's the fight I saw! I thought it would be like Frazier against Ali. I thought this would be the fight the world would want to see!'

As the momentum increased and the Williams express lurched on towards further title glory, the wheels temporarily came off in his next outing over in America. Getting a slot on a card at New York's Felt Forum, Williams came up short against respected journeyman Mark Wills. Wills had developed a reputation as someone who would give most heavyweights on the planet a severe run for their money. Occasionally, he would produce a surprise win as he did when he defeated the former WBA heavyweight champion, and now late, Greg Page in nine rounds in 1986. He'd been caught cold twice against Tony Fuilangi, a club fighter whose résumé reads like an encyclopedia of heavyweight contenders, and the unpredictable Tim Witherspoon who happened to put in one of his better performances when faced with Wills. Williams, however, was expected to be given a good test. The test turned into a hard slog as Wills snatched a points decision over eight rounds. Caught somewhat off guard early in the third round, a right-left combination deposited Williams on the floor. He was very much in against a live opponent, one who saw this as a stepping-stone fight as much as Williams did. Williams retaliated by getting on the proverbial bike and jabbing away the follow-up from Wills. The result was a dreary, safety-first affair that went against the Commonwealth champion. The decision was greeted with discontent as it was deemed that Williams had fought back enough to at least have a share of the spoils if not be given the nod.

'They told us this guy was strong and that he'd be dangerous for the first three or four rounds. I went out and boxed him in the first, he slowed in the second but then, BOOM! He got me in the third and I'm down on my back. Never been down in my life, amateur or pro. I got back up and I was ok. I then boxed him the rest of the way and when I played it back, I heard the commentators say that Wills wasn't doing anything after the knockdown. When he got the decision they said, "oh, they've taken it from Williams!" I knew I won that fight. That wasn't right. I was disheartened but in my mind I know I won that fight. Every time I fought abroad, the decision went against me!'

While over in the States, Williams did gain valuable experience sparring with the reigning world heavyweight champion. 'We went out there and called Al Braverman, Don King's matchmaker, and he said we should go over and spar with Tyson as me and Carl Williams had similar styles and were of a similar height. Tyson thanked me for coming and said he needed all the help he could get [for his 21 July world title defence against the late Carl 'The Truth' Williams]. He came to spar a couple of days later and he looked like I'd never seen him before. He was twitching his neck and all pumped up. They had six guys in the gym and I asked them how many rounds Tyson was sparring. They said eight so I guess that was why there were so many sparring partners. They weren't lasting! That day, Greg Page went in first and I was told to go in second. He also had Oliver McCall, Warren Thompson, he'd go through anyone! Tyson and Page had a war. Tyson would walk you down from side to side and then stop and throw explosive combinations so when I went in there I started throwing jabs at him. The minute he stopped I backed away and he started looking for me. It was a real chess match with him. He'd jump in and I'd back off. Later he said to me, "Hey you a good fighter man, why don't you fight Frank Bruno? You'd kick his ass!"'

Four months later, Mark Wills was to venture over to Britain to face Gary Mason in a ten-round contest aimed at showcasing the best of Mason before moving up to test his mettle against the world's best. The crowd in attendance got their money's worth in a rousing bout which lasted the duration and saw fortunes sway one way then the other. It made compelling, if not explosive, viewing. The following night over in Las Vegas, 'Sugar' Ray Leonard battled Roberto Duran over 12 incredibly tepid rounds to leave the crowd booing. While it was this 'superfight' that grabbed the sporting headlines, it was a fight that took place in Catford the night before the Mason–Wills bout which garnered the most adulation.

Derek Williams stepped into the ring with Hughroy Currie on 5 December to battle it out for the Commonwealth and vacant European heavyweight titles. While Currie had been in his fair share of bruising encounters and was deemed to be on the wrong side of the proverbial hill, it was seen as a good test for Williams as the man on the way up, and would give him the opportunity to overcome any hurdles the more experienced Jamaican-born local fighter would no doubt pose. Williams never let Currie get started. After the Wills loss, he was aware he had something to prove and, being back on home soil, he didn't squander the chance to remind the spectators that he was very much a force to be reckoned with. Within a matter of seconds, Currie was bludgeoned with a right hand and as he staggered across the ring, was chased down and hammered against the ropes until the referee stepped in to end the onslaught.

'I made a poem about that fight beforehand, "Never before has Currie endured the power of Derek's right landing but you can be sure that if it lasts four, poor old Currie'll be panting and I'll walk through the door as the new European champion!" I felt good. I had the jab and the right hand and I knew Currie couldn't handle that. I knew he wouldn't be in top shape.'

After feasting his crosses and hooks on a surprisingly mild Currie, Williams found himself in something of a pickle in his next outing; one which took him across the Channel to face the ancient-looking carpet salesman and candy floss store owner, Jean-Maurice Chanet. Sporting a balding pate with a ring of grey hair around its edge and a bushy white moustache, the Frenchman appeared to be transported from the days in the mid-to-late-19th century when America's John L. Sullivan and Britain's Jem Mace would square up to all-comers in the booths at travelling circuses and fairs across their respective countries. He had the style to suit too. While not quite 'Two Ton' Tony Galento, Chanet possessed a severe lack of physical definition. For Williams, it was a trip abroad to pick up a successful defence of his European honours, a good paycheque and the chance to clear the final hurdle before squaring off with fellow Brit, Gary Mason, the following month in what would be a triple-title bonanza. In short, and even with the switch of his trainer from Bobby Neill to Kirkland Laing's cornerman, Joe Ryan, Williams had nothing to fear.

After an encouraging opening minute and a half, during which Williams seemed to set the pattern for the fight when he drilled the bullish Chanet with right hands, Williams suddenly slumped into a state of extreme lethargy and apparent exhaustion. He, literally, could do nothing apart from take what was thrown at him for the remainder of the fight. Round after round plodded by with Chanet gaining the upper hand and being allowed to dictate the contest. It was almost inexplicable to the viewer what was happening to the British fighter. No one would argue that on skill, technique and overall ability, Williams left Chanet light years behind. What was transpiring in the ring in St Dizier that day is how most people predicted it would go, only with Williams as the aggressor. Williams's manager claimed foul play afterwards and with Williams being assisted from the ring at the conclusion and given oxygen in the dressing room, many agreed with Barrett's accusations. Claims of Williams being drugged were proved to be groundless with subsequent tests proving negative. The feeling was that Williams had contracted a viral infection and the effects had taken hold during the fight and had, in essence, knocked him out of the contest.

'Chanet was meant to be a knockover fight for me. There was no way Chanet could last four rounds with me, right?' Williams asked me as more of a statement than a question. 'But when I sat down at the end of the first round, I didn't want to get back up again. For the rest of the fight I just wasn't there but I don't remember Chanet hurting me at all.'

Because of the bizarre circumstances surrounding the nature and outcome of the Chanet fight, a rematch was inevitable and the two combatants squared off, again in France. While home territory tends to give the local fighter a considerable edge, it is an edge that is advantageous only when an even fight is fought. It can give a lift to the home fighter and can, on most occasions, give the 'away' fighter the feeling that he is fighting several thousand as opposed to just the one. In instances such as the Williams–Chanet rematch, it wasn't regarded as a serious advantage. Williams strode to the ring with the expectation that he was going to perform in the manner he should have three months earlier. Indeed, *Boxing News* magazine had no doubts at all. 'Williams won't fail this time. He can regain his pride, and his title, with a clear points win.'

What happened in Paris on this May evening almost beggared belief. What happened inside that ring, and outside, could not be explained or described without the use of a concise dictionary to try and dig out the appropriate words. Those who were there that day were witness to an explosive punch-up where neither side were willing to capitulate. Passions were high and the intensity sliced the atmosphere in half. Unfortunately, what went on inside the ring was nowhere near as frenetic. Williams, with friend and former British and Commonwealth champion Horace Notice working with him, drastically underperformed and, again, allowed Chanet to dictate the bout to secure another points decision. Williams's performance was best summed up with *Boxing News*'s report on the WINNER's contribution, 'Chanet has no boxing ability whatsoever. It looked for all the world as if a tramp had wandered in off the Metro and had been invited up into the ring to entertain the crowd before the serious stuff got underway.' Williams was outworked, outfought and, most alarmingly, out-thought.

'Before the fight, the gypsy fortune-teller was saying how I was going to fall asleep during the fight! After the fourth round I felt like I fell asleep! But I was the champion and I had to get my belt back. The body wanted to do it but the mind just wanted to go to sleep. Towards the end of the fight, I look out and I see a big crowd fight break out. I look across and I see my brothers in the fight as well. I was no longer interested in the fight no more. I just wanted to turn to the referee and say, "Come on, my brothers are in a fight!" My sister and girlfriend were there too so I was more interested in that. By the time things calmed down, the fight was over and I had lost the chance. I was thinking, "Whoa, that's my career gone."'

Former opponent Jess Harding, who had notched up a win over Chanet in the build-up to his challenge for the British title against Gary Mason, was as surprised as anyone with the outcomes to both Chanet fights.

'I was really surprised!' Harding exclaimed when addressing the losses. 'It's always difficult fighting away from home but I still thought he had the nous to go and do a job on Chanet because the one thing about Jean Chanet was he was very hittable. With his long arms and long shots, he just piled forward! Chanet was just awkward. He wasn't particularly tall but he had immensely long arms and he'd just wing shots in and then throw himself on to you. He was very strong though. I don't know what happened to Derek, whether he froze or what, but it was a very hostile atmosphere out of there. The second time he went out there, I thought he was DEFINITELY gonna do him this time but he never did! Unfortunately for Chanet, he fought Lennox after that!'

Back-to-back losses to the underwhelming Frenchman halted Williams's career in its tracks and served as a vivid reminder of the sport's cruel twists and turns. The Wills fight aside, 1989 had been a very good year for Williams. He was climbing the ladder in earnest but in 1990 he hit the snake and slithered back down to the rebuilding stage.

'Knocking out Trevor Currie, I was the heavyweight champion of the Commonwealth and Europe. I was like a lion. I was number two in Britain. I was driving around in a fancy car, I'm pulling the ladies in the nightclubs, I'm mean and I'm "Sweet D"! The Chanet fight was just a marking-time fight for Mason. At the time, Mason was knocking everyone out, I was knocking everyone out and we had a major following. Had the fight taken off, Mason wouldn't have lasted with me. I'll tell you why. I knew Mason from the amateurs so I knew to myself I had what it took. We were about to sign the contract and I saw Mason in the West End. I have a mouth on me and I said, "Mason, man, you know you got no chance man, you know you got no chance!" He said to me, "Sweet D, we'll see on the night."'

Of course, the Mason clash never materialised. Williams headed off to New York to get his body and mind straight, decide where his career went from here and to search for reassurance and inspiration to push him into unlocking his undoubted potential.

'During that time between the second Chanet fight and the Thunder fight, I was rebuilding myself mentally and physically in New York where I was training with Tommy Gallagher at Gleason's gym. I was sparring Holmes, Cooney and other guys who weren't heard of. I sparred with a guy called T-Bone! I didn't know who he was. Big black guy. Six foot seven, six foot eight! Big wise guy and he come and said, "Yo! You Derek? You sparring with me today! Yeah baby, you gonna know about me!" He was trying to intimidate me. What he was saying to me was a challenge! He was throwing lots of bombs at me but he wasn't in shape. I went, BOOM! BOOM! He ended up knowing plenty about me!'

The determination he showed in readying himself for another assault on the heavyweight scene and the experience he picked up while training at Gleason's proved invaluable. Tucked under Brooklyn Bridge on Front Street, Gleason's epitomised everything that is characteristic with the old-style gymnasiums. As you ascend the concrete staircase from the main road, the thudding of the body-pads and the speedballs, the grunts of the boxers as their punches land and the passionate instructions yelled out by the various trainers present, rise in volume and upon opening the inner door to the training floor, hits you like an inch-perfect left hook. When I visited the gym in May 1997 to meet the then IBF light-welterweight champion Kostya Tszyu, and the future two-time WBA heavyweight champion Nicolay Valuev, it struck me how it was indeed a gym of champions. Williams benefitted hugely from this and he was about to embark on the most impressive year of his career.

His return to the ring was scheduled for 1 May 1991 under Frank Warren's promotional banner in a defence of his Commonwealth title against Samoa's Jimmy Thunder. Taking part in his 12th professional contest, Thunder, born James Peau, had suffered one defeat, a fourth-round knockout loss to fringe contender Mike Hunter. All his ten wins had come inside the distance so his punching was not to be taken lightly. The fight was, however, a clever piece of matchmaking by the Williams team and, as it panned out, the thunderstorm was blown away by the hurricane of punches which blasted through its defences. Scoring a conclusive and eye-catching stoppage in two rounds, Williams yet again raised a few eyebrows among ringsiders and insiders. In under six minutes of work, he had consigned the Chanet debacles to the history books.

'Jimmy Thunder wanted to be Mike Tyson! He annoyed me. He was knocking everyone out and he could punch. He came over to England to challenge me for my belt. We had a press conference and he said, "I'm gonna knock Williams out!" I just said, "This guy's all mouth. How is he gonna come to my country and knock me out!" I took it personal because he mentioned my name. Don't forget I'm a Peckham boy and I'm a street boy so I'm like, "You not gonna talk to me like that, man!" I stepped my training up and I planned to destroy Thunder. I was pumped up. When I was walking towards the ring, I see Thunder twitching his neck like Mike Tyson, black shorts and black boots. He was fighting me for MY title in MY country in front of MY people. I can't lose, you understand?!

'I'm in the ring, eyeballing him. I was jabbing him and he was throwing bombs at me. He was trying to knock me out but I was going to knock HIM out! At the end of the round, I went BOOM! Right hand and he's buckled. BOOM! Left hook! Second round, BOOM! BOOM!'

During Williams's hiatus from the sport for the year since the second Chanet fight, the domestic heavyweight scene had taken a shift in momentum. In October 1990, Chanet entered the ring against the 1988 Olympic super-heavyweight gold medallist Lennox Lewis to defend his European title. Systematically ripping the Frenchman's rugged face apart with an endless array of punches, Lewis then stepped in against Gary Mason two months prior to Williams's fight with Thunder. Confounding many critics, Lewis administered real damage to Mason's eyes on his way to a six-round stoppage victory. Now holding the British and European crowns, Lewis was now the aim for Williams. On 30 September, Lewis annihilated the former IBF cruiserweight champion Glenn McCrory in two rounds to defend his titles. Williams grabbed the opportunity to showcase his skills when he was scheduled to test his fists against the face of American punchbag Kimmuel Odum on the same bill. After a last-minute change of opponent, Williams instead met David Bey, the former IBF title challenger to Larry Holmes in 1985. It was a tame affair which came to an end at the end of the sixth round when Bey's corner pulled him out with injuries to his eyes.

'He fought well for the title against Holmes. I threw jabs at him with an occasional right hand and by the third round, his eye was out here,' Williams brought his hand a few inches in front of his face to illustrate the injury. 'He was strong, he was a former marine and in the first round, he tried to rough me up inside, trying to do dirty tactics. He was a hard guy. He tried to bring it to me but every time my right landed his eye got redder. It looked like a brain on the side of his head! BOOM! More right hands and they had to stop it.'

With Mason now vanquished against Lennox Lewis and Frank Bruno embarking on his latest comeback with a one-round win over the flying Dutchman John Emmen in November 1991, Derek Williams and Lennox Lewis were regarded as the two leading domestic flagship boxers. With a third-round mauling of former heavyweight title challenger Tyrell Biggs on the Evander Holyfield–Bert Cooper undercard in

Atlanta the weekend after the Bruno–Emmen farce, Williams needed to keep the wins going as he awaited the final confirmation of the triple-title showdown. This he did, against the ill-fated American, Tim 'Doc' Anderson.

Having fought largely on the Midwest circuit, Anderson fought a number of opponents who bypassed the occupational hazard of having to be licensed by assuming the names of the dearly departed and some who felt more comfortable throwing a fight than a right cross. He did, however, step into the ring with George Foreman as he embarked on his historic comeback and with Larry Holmes as he, too, threw his hat into the seniors' ring. Both times, he was hammered as he was to be by Williams. In less than a minute to be exact. It proved nothing but it kept the Lewis fight alive. Anderson's career took a far less fortunate turn. He had just three more fights. His last fight was a rematch with the former NFL player Mark Gastineau, a fighter who Parker deemed considerably more lucrative in his obsessive quest to find a marketable white heavyweight contender, in December 1992. Claiming he had been poisoned in order to lose the fight by his manager, Rick 'Elvis' Parker, Anderson fell badly ill and lost a substantial amount of weight. Holding Parker at gunpoint, Anderson begged him to disclose what he had been poisoned with so he could be treated with the antidote. Parker refused, instead telling Anderson he would pay for his threat with the safety of his family. That comment sealed his fate. Having empted a magazine of bullets into the thickly-set form of Parker, Anderson has since been serving a life sentence for murder.

In February 1992, Lewis travelled to the States to outpoint the rugged and durable journeyman Levi Billups over ten rounds to clear the last hurdle before the Williams showdown. Lewis had to ship some heavy blows in that fight and while he faced criticism for not finishing Billups off impressively, his chin withstood a severe test.

'Lewis was the golden boy. The press was there boosting Lewis up. I had come up the hard way. I'd never had no backing from no one. Everything I achieved was through me. I had no sponsors or any of that. I was training on my own. Lewis was in the papers and on TV. I was doing civil engineering at college and wasn't involved in all that gang crime so why weren't the press using me as a role model? I started getting hacked off. He was portrayed as the good guy and me as the bad guy!'

For the Lewis fight, Williams had hired some of the best help he could to assist in his preparation. Travelling over to Florida, Williams found himself under the watchful eye of a legendary trainer, a true nurturer of champions.

'I was out there with Angelo Dundee. He was an amazing psychologist. I used to do a lot of wrong things but he never told me that I was wrong. He would tell me that what I was doing was nice. He'd say he'd like the way I did this and that. By fight time, Angelo said to me, "Don't worry baby, you got this fight won. He's never fought someone as young and strong as you!" He had fought a puncher in Gary Mason but he was shorter than Lewis. I could punch and I was the same height as him! I was training for eight weeks. I had three sparring partners and they couldn't last with me. I had Egerton Marcus, Przemyslaw Saleta and others. I was doing sit-ups until my stomach was cramped. I was solid. My body felt like a rock! Lewis's camp pulled a stroke on me though. I was supposed to have a brain scan before the fight. It was only at the weigh-in that they told me! Afterwards, Lewis went back to the hotel to rest and I'm sitting down waiting for the brain scan.

'In the ring, we were eyeball to eyeball. I could see no fear in him and he could see none in me. I could see this was going to be a fight but I'm half man-half amazing!'

The fight itself was a tepid affair where both fighters seemed to be wary of each other, knowing that each had the power to cause the other problems. Williams shot out his jabs in the first two rounds with Lewis searching for the opening that he could exploit to land his thudding blows. The opening was spotted in the third round and a brace of uppercuts and a follow-up right cross were enough to make him a triple-title holder.

'Up to that point, no one had ever stopped me in a fight, amateur or pro. I thought that as he stopped me, he could become a legend. I always thought I was too strong. Lewis came and went, BOOM! BOOM! BOOM! I was on the floor and I looked at ringside and thought, "Man, how come they're at the same level as me?!" I needed to get back up again. This ain't right so I got back up but Larry O'Connell stopped the fight. He wasn't looking good up to that point. His jab wasn't working because mine WAS! The fight was even up to that point.'

The Lewis defeat was Williams's final stab at the big time. He took almost a year off before resurfacing in Atlantic City to square up against 'Smokin' Bert Cooper. Fighting passively, he allowed the former protégé of 'Smokin' Joe Frazier to run away with an easy ten-round decision. Williams still harboured respectable power as his next opponent can vouch for. Participating in the *People's Choice* One-Night Heavyweight Tournament in Bay St Louis, Mississippi, on 3 December 1993, Williams came up against the tough American of Cuban descent, Jose Ribalta. Catching up with Ribalta, he told me that Williams's power was what, ultimately, led to his own defeat in the next round of the tournament. 'How can I forget Williams?!' Ribalta told me. 'He hit me so hard with a right hand that I wish I had fought Tony Tubbs first because that way I would have beaten him. My head was hurting from the right hand Williams hit me with and it affected my performance against Tubbs.'

Williams's career continued on the slippery slope and he would lose his next four fights. The first two took place in London before he upped sticks and went to America. 'The States is a whole different ball game because they expected me to come over as a typical Brit who would fall over. I like talking a lot! I was talking trash to the American fighters so they were feeling intimidated around me!'

Winning three fights inside the distance against underwhelming opposition in 1998, he travelled to Wroclaw in Poland to lose to America's Zuri Lawrence over six rounds before retiring for good after being stopped in three rounds by fellow Brit Wayne Llewellyn in February 1999.

'You always think that you are the best. When I see other fighters now, I still believe I can see flaws in them. You see where other guys fall down and you can still do it because that's the nature of man.'

There was no doubt though, that Williams was a key figure on the British heavyweight scene in the late 1980s and early 90s. The fights with Frank Bruno, Gary Mason and Horace Notice never came to fruition but he is under little doubt as to what would have happened had they taken place.

'Horace would have been the hardest fight of the lot. He had a fighting heart. My character is this; if you have two young athletes in the ring and you think the other guy could beat you, you are in the wrong sport. You have to think you can beat them all. If someone has asked me after Lewis beat me, how I'd fair in a rematch, I'd say I would beat him. If someone beat me three times, I'd be convinced I would beat him in the fourth because I would convince him I would have learnt.'

Indeed, the British heavyweights throughout the 80s and 90s is a topic which grabs Williams's attention even now and his idea for a book on the subject is one which gets the old juices flowing.

'We had an era in boxing over here where we had Gary Mason, Frank Bruno, myself, Lennox Lewis, the Jamican-born Alex Stewart, Henry Akinwande and all these guys who had come up. Most of these heavyweights you talk about were of Jamaican parentage who came over here to have children. Something funny? Bruno's mum, my mum and Lennox Lewis's mum all come from the same place in Jamaica!'

Williams is now involved in a project called SMASH; 'Strong Minds And Strong Hearts'. 'I speak with corporate people and also go to schools. It's about telling people I'm an ordinary guy from the 'hood. Born and raised in Peckham. I was with nine brothers and sisters in a three-bedroom house. My dad never had a car so I know how hardships are. I experienced the hardships of life in the inner cities. I want to tell people that if I can do it, you can do it. It's all about discipline and self-worth.'

Reflecting on his career, Williams makes it clear that he had many strengths, few regrets and no weaknesses.

'I was an all-rounder. I could box and punch on my day. I could fight inside and out. I don't and CAN'T have weaknesses. I'm half-man, half-amazing! I wouldn't change anything about my career. If I could go back I wouldn't change a thing. Well, maybe I'd slip Lennox's uppercut but that's it!'

Williams is now the proud father to one son and one daughter and the possibility of seeing his son go into the sport he himself delved in, brings about certain reservations.

'My son came to me when he was nine and said he wanted to box! I was thinking how, when I used to train, I would be out there running in the early hours, thinking how I wanted to crush and break my opponent in the ring. I didn't want people to have that attitude towards my son but hey, my son can hit – HARD!'

Williams is now a personal trainer at the Soho Gym in Brad Street just around the corner from Waterloo train station. While I was talking with him, a number of budding students came in, ready to learn under the tutelage of the former Commonwealth and European heavyweight champion. He manages heavyweight prospect A.J. Carter and runs his own website promoting his personal training, after-dinner speaking and profiles of his fighters.

At times in his professional career, Williams fell into lapses of concentration when the quality of opponent didn't 'ignite the fire' but on his day, when the sweetness of his punches burst through the defences of fighters such as Hughroy Currie and Jimmy Thunder, he showed himself as a boxer with the potential to show supreme talent and fluid technique. As he says in his own words, 'You know what it is? I'm too slick, too quick, can't get hit, can't get hurt. I'm half-man, half-amazing. I'm too many men, I'm an ARMY!'

BOOM!

12

Jim McDonnell

A T various times between 1985 and 1989, the boxing public was enamoured with the possibility of a mouth-watering clash between two lower-weight stars to decide superiority in the featherweight division and, later, in the super-featherweight class. The boxing press in the US and in the UK were reporting on back-room developments in the hope the fight would be announced and columnists were producing opinion polls to maintain the high level of anticipation that existed across the fraternity.

In 1985, Ireland's Barry 'The Clones Cyclone' McGuigan ruled as the WBA champion and the formidable Ghanaian Azumah 'The Professor' Nelson held sway over the WBC belt. Both boxers were relentless, come-forward, pressure fighters and the public was split as to whom they thought would emerge the victor.

Boxing News printed a poll in its 15 November 1985 issue with ten of the sport's personalities. McGuigan emerged the winner with six of them. In June 1986, Nelson defeated Danilo Cabrera in ten rounds to defend his title, four rounds quicker than McGuigan had beaten the Dominican challenger four months earlier. The following night, McGuigan lost his WBA title to Steve Cruz in the sweltering Las Vegas heat.

McGuigan subsequently took almost two years off before returning at super-featherweight to record three comeback wins. Nelson, in the meantime, had also risen to the higher weight and claimed the WBC title. The momentum for the Nelson–McGuigan fight had once again picked up and created intrigue among the boxing media. The delayed superfight appeared inevitable. On 31 May 1989 at Manchester's G-MEX Centre, all McGuigan needed to do to finally get Nelson in the ring, was defeat north London's Jim McDonnell in an official eliminator for the Ghanaian's title.

Meeting Jim McDonnell at the Loughton Academy on Debden's Langston Road, I waited in the main gym as McDonnell put his European super-middleweight champion James DeGale through his paces in the ring. A huge Muhammad Ali mural adorned the far wall of the gym which had a fresh, clean, almost clinical look. As I took in the surroundings, I noticed a couple of men approach the ring, McDonnell get out to shake the hand of one and then step back as the man climbed in the ring to spar with the champion.

McDonnell, who still looks in prime fighting condition with just a few greying specks of hair as proof that time has moved on and still sporting the lean physique that allowed him to snap out that whipping jab while maintaining that tight defence that caused so many past opponents untold frustration, informed me the man who stepped up to spar with DeGale was George Gracie, a member of the well known Brazilian fighting family and a cousin to the famous Royce Gracie, the former mixed martial arts, Ultimate Fighting Championships and ju-jitsu participant.

'We were put into a home waiting to be re-housed,' he said, discussing his childhood, as he ushered me into the gym's office and flicked the kettle switch. 'We eventually got a house in Packington Street in King's Cross. I was only a kid and went to primary school there. Then we got a place off the council in Somerstown where I really remember growing up. I met all my best friends and my wife in Camden. I was Camden's adopted son and was called the "Camden Caretaker" when I used to box!'

Like many inner-city youths, it wasn't boxing that grabbed the future champion's attention at first. Kicking a ball around instead of swinging a pair of leather gloves at an opponent was the preferred choice. Having had trials with Watford FC, football was McDonnell's initial choice.

'My first love was football. All I ever wanted to be was a footballer but everything went against me. I thought I wasn't big enough. One of my heroes was Alan Ball because he was five foot nothing! I became an outstanding footballer and thought I could realise my dream. I was with players who went on to play at the highest level. On talkSPORT recently, they had a school friend of mine who went on to do well and boxing came into the conversation. My name came up and he said, "Jimmy was boxing mad but he was such a good footballer. The best footballer in our district!" He said I was the best footballer he'd ever seen who didn't play professionally! I've got a guy who comes up here from Stevenage and he went, "I didn't know you played football in this and that tournament. I was talking with someone who played for AC Milan and he said you were the best player he had ever played with!" I asked him who that was and he said Luther Blissett! I picked up some injuries when I played a couple of charity games after years of not playing though. To get fit, I got into boxing.'

Ultimately it was the noble art that took its hold and with the help of his friend and future Commonwealth light-middleweight champion Mickey Hughes, McDonnell's passion for the sport grew.

'I was always fascinated by Mickey Hughes because he was at my school and he was boxing and I was playing football. I just felt like I could fight. I was game and wanted to be the best fighter in the school. I went to St Pancras and think I actually left there three times because they wanted to make me a southpaw. When I went back the fourth time, Pat Newman gave me another chance. I only had eight junior fights. I won the Junior ABA London title and the schoolboy championships. My dream was always to be a world champion.'

Participating in an England vs. Young America amateur tournament at London's Lancaster hotel, McDonnell would register a win over Andy Minsker. Minsker gained an element of fame in the 1984 Olympic box-offs when he defeated Meldrick Taylor, who would go on to win the featherweight gold medal and become a two-time world champion in the professional ranks. 'I beat Minsker and his record was phenomenal. He had loads of fights but I was one of his few losses. We got hammered that night though!'

In 1979, McDonnell won the London ABA finals by defeating St George's southpaw fighter Tony Taylor. Using his superior ability, McDonnell took the last round by boxing at long range to grab the title. This paved the way for his participation in the bantamweight division in the national ABAs the following month. Beating Scotland's Joe Park in a foul-ridden semi-final scrap, he stepped in with the St Vincent-born but London-based Renard Ashton in the final. In what went down as the tournament's fight of the night, the two fighters waged war for three rounds with Ashton grabbing a close decision. Working as a painter and decorator for Camden Council, McDonnell did not lose heart and was straight back in the mix the following year. Still competing at bantamweight, McDonnell easily overwhelmed Edinburgh's Willie Amos, stopping him in the second round, to advance to his second consecutive ABA final. In the opposite corner stood St Helens's Ray Gilbody. Taking counts in the first and second rounds against the future British bantamweight champion, McDonnell was rescued by the referee in the second stanza to give Gilbody the win and make it a family double as Ray's brother George picked up the lightweight title.

In 1982, McDonnell proved there is substance in the old adage 'third time lucky'. Entering the ABAs, this time as a lightweight, he lifted the trophy when defeating Keighley ABC's southpaw, Gary Felvus, by a unanimous decision. McDonnell fought brilliantly without allowing Felvus the room to either set his punches or plant his feet. McDonnell's trainer Ron Smith and the St Pancras club could boast their own champion. Along with their featherweight, Herman Henry, they had a celebratory double to pop the corks over.

'Felvus hadn't lost in years and I battered him! I jumped two weights from bantamweight to lightweight. I don't think anyone has ever done that, jumping two weights to win an ABA title. People asked how I did that but I just had this strong mental attitude.'

In October of that same year, McDonnell narrowly missed out on the lightweight gold medal in the Commonwealth Games, held in Brisbane, Australia. In the finals he lost a 3-2 decision to the Kenyan Hussein Khalili. A year in which the St Pancras youngster scooped the lightweight ABA title and took the silver medal at Brisbane proved his final in the amateurs. The time seemed right for McDonnell to throw his hat into the professional ring.

'Going from amateur to pro was like going from a sprinter to a marathon runner. One was a sport and one was a business. When I started in the pros, I had George Francis in my corner and he said to me, "Listen, it's all about the 'W'. Don't matter how you get it. It's all about the 'W'. You got to think about your family. It's a business, not a sport. You're in a ruthless business now." I had this mentality from day one. George knew me 'cos I sparred his world champion, Cornelius Boza-Edwards, in his gym. He knew what I was like. I have superb memories of George. He was a great coach.'

On 22 March 1983, McDonnell's professional journey commenced when he scored a commanding six-round points win over fellow-debutant Phil Duke. With impressive combination punching, it appeared as if McDonnell had carried his slick technique forward from his accomplished amateur days. Two weeks later, he shared a bill at the Royal Albert Hall with amateur nemesis Ray Gilbody and stopped Willie Wilson in three rounds. His education continued and his opponents gradually increased in quality and experience. While his opponents tended to have losing records, he was fighting known 'stayers' and those fights which went the distance did nothing to harm his profile. They built the foundations for the tests ahead that his supporters felt would show McDonnell up to be the genuine article they believed he was from the amateur days. Among these learning fights were two stoppage wins over Central Area featherweight champion Steve Pollard and solid points wins over durable journeymen Alec Irvine, Gerry Beard and Keith Foreman.

On the same bill at Wembley for McDonnell's tenth fight, an eight-round points win over Rory Burke, Frank Bruno suffered his first loss to James 'Bonecrusher' Smith and Mark Kaylor lost to 'Buster' Drayton. McDonnell remembers vividly the atmosphere in the camp that night. 'Terry Lawless walks in to the dressing room, chucks his jacket down and says he's leaving boxing. Kaylor and Bruno are stretched out and I'm just shadow-boxing.'

In his 12th fight, McDonnell squared off with fellow prospect Pat Doherty. The winner would take one significant step nearer to a British title fight, a championship held at that point by a certain Irishman called Barry McGuigan. Many favoured his Croydon opponent to come out on top but in a convincing show of skill and class, McDonnell took a clearly deserved points win.

'Doherty was a big step as well. He was a puncher and had stopped quite a few. I boxed brilliant. He couldn't get near me because of my angles, my movement. It was a big win beating him. I never lost a round. Once I beat him, I'd arrived on the scene. They were talking about him fighting for the British title and all of a sudden I got in the mix. Even some of my own people were surprised at how easily I beat him. I watched it the next day on *Grandstand* and was really proud of it. I went clubbing with my mates after that fight. I was buzzing!'

His win was rewarded two fights later with a clash for the Southern Area featherweight title against champion Clyde Ruan. Ruan had already been defeated by McGuigan in four rounds in a European and British title defence three months before facing McDonnell and this is no doubt what led *Boxing News* to suggest, 'One doubts if Barry McGuigan will be losing any sleep over it.'

Stepping into the ring at Wembley on the undercard of a show which featured Britain's heavyweight prospect Frank Bruno, and Barry McGuigan, McDonnell turned in a stellar performance, utilising his superior reach and speed to nullify Ruan's forward offence. McDonnell rightly took a comfortable decision on referee Harry Gibbs's scorecard.

'A lot of people thought I was going in too early with Ruan. He was up there with the top boys, just boxed McGuigan, and was a top amateur. I was getting stepped up quick! I wanted to fight all the top boys and Ruan was in that group. If you have a look at all my good performances, it was when the challenge was there. I could go down a level if I fought somebody who weren't as good but when there was a challenge I'd get excited about it. I was like that for Ruan. I wanted to get up there and fight McGuigan. I was always after McGuigan.'

This attitude of McDonnell's rubbed off on his camp-mates, earned him their respect and got him known as someone who would consistently fight with the same level of dedication, therefore marking him out as a genuine crowd-pleaser. 'Frank Bruno and people on the England squad used to say, "I love being on bills with Jim McDonnell, he's buzzing and so positive." I used PMA, "Positive Mental Attitude". In the changing rooms for England before we boxed the Yanks, I boxed at the Lancaster and after that fight, I got an offer to box two days later in Coventry because someone had pulled out of a fight. I said, "Yeah, I'll have it!" I got down there and boom!'

With his first title in the bag, McDonnell registered a workmanlike points win over New York-based Guyanese journeyman Troy Roberts, before being chosen to contest the European featherweight championship, recently vacated by McGuigan, against the Spaniard Jose Luis Vicho on Bonfire Night of 1985. Vicho had fought a high level of opposition leading up to the fight at Wembley but his form was poor and McDonnell was expected to join compatriots Terry Marsh and Charlie Magri as the country's other European champions. It was a cautious performance at first as McDonnell bided his time, fathoming out Vicho's awkward style and fleeting movements. With a hard left to the body in the fourth round, Vicho fizzled out and McDonnell claimed his second title in just his 16th fight. 'I fought Vicho soon after turning pro. I wanted McGuigan. I was so impatient to get to him. He was the big cheese!'

As the new European champion, McDonnell had to wait patiently to see who his first title challenger would be. Not one to remain idle, he squared up against Colombia's future WBO featherweight champion Ruben Dario Palacios. Palacios was coming off a points loss to South Korea's Ji-Won Kim in an IBF super-bantamweight title challenge and a points loss to former European featherweight king Valerio Nati. Of tough Colombian stock and the owner of a solid punch, McDonnell was aware of the potential dangers but he got himself an impressive seventh-round win over a fighter of extreme quality. It was also a steep learning curve when it came to enduring various infringements and being able to carry on without being knocked out of his game-plan.

'He was a typically tough Colombian,' McDonnell stated. 'I got a good, tough education that night. I was in deep and learnt the hard knocks of pro boxing. He banged me with both gloves around the ears at the same time and used his elbows. In the corner, Jimmy Tibbs put his head through the ropes and screamed at me, "Listen, you gotta man up! You wanna pull out? MAN UP!" I knew that night I was to be world champion.'

Two months later, McDonnell was back in the ring to defend his European title on the undercard to Frank Bruno's WBA heavyweight title challenge to 'Terrible' Tim Witherspoon at Wembley. In the other corner stood Italian champion Salvatore Bottiglieri. On an unbeaten run of eight fights, the Italian's last loss was to the champion McDonnell disposed of to win the title. There was speculation that McDonnell, if victorious against Bottiglieri, could face the new WBA featherweight champion Steve Cruz, who had beaten Barry McGuigan the previous month over 15 absorbing and punishing rounds in Las Vegas.

'I would've jumped at the chance to fight Cruz. He weren't no Brian Mitchell or Azumah Nelson but he was a very good fighter indeed. A pure boxer but I believe no one at that time could outbox me. I never lost many rounds at all in any fight! I fought Palacios but would have definitely preferred a clean-cut boxer like Cruz instead. Palacios went on to win the WBO title so excuse the pun but in comparison, Cruz would have been a cruise!'

Showing polished skills, impressive in-and-out movement and good accuracy, McDonnell grabbed a unanimous points win over the Italian. The scoring reflected the bravery and courage of Bottiglieri where a number of rounds were scored even, acknowledging the Italian's willingness to trade punches and ability to take the fast pace McDonnell set.

'Again, some people thought I may be going in a little too early but they didn't realise the level I was at. I was calling out the big fights soon after I turned pro. I honestly believed I could beat all of them. Because I was sparring with people like Boza-Edwards and being with world champions every day in the gym, my mindset was there. I once asked Emanuel Steward what the single most important ingredient is for a boxer to succeed. He said, "When you get better competition in the gym than on the night." I sparred with Eusebio Pedroza when he was preparing to fight McGuigan and I sparred with Edwin Rosario too. Rosario was a gentleman. He seemed to go easy on me!'

McDonnell's career path was now destined to lead him into a world title fight. He had bagged the European title and made one defence in impressive fashion. He had defeated a high calibre of national and international opponents and didn't shirk any challenge; whether that be in the ring or in the gym. That alone garnered respect and this attitude would ultimately pay dividends with some good purses and good opportunities. The British title was one of the belts McDonnell was never able to strap around his waist though. McDonnell has his own reason for not fighting for it. 'I did regret not winning it but I was head and shoulders above all the others around,' he said. Though this statement could be interpreted as arrogance, it struck me during our chat that it was more the impenetrable self-belief he had in his own ability.

In the next two years, McDonnell built up his case for world title honours with six victories over a range of international competition. In November, he outpointed tough American Troy Davis in a near whitewash at Wembley, in March 1987 he returned to the same venue and punched Louisiana's Ricky Clements into retirement with a fifth-round win, in May he travelled to Switzerland to beat near-novice Sammy O'Neill in one round and in February 1988 he appeared at York Hall to outpoint Mexico's Rafael Gandarilla. While Gandarilla sported a losing record, he had scored a stoppage win over the formidable Ruben Olivares although the result came at the tail-end of the great Mexican's career. Two more wins followed in the spring of 1988, one of which came against Mexican Angel Hernandez, who hurt McDonnell in the second round only to be beaten decisively on points. The time had arrived for McDonnell to step into the ring to challenge for his first world title.

Over those last six contests, McDonnell's weight had been gradually increasing whereby he was now finding new comfort in the super-featherweight division so it came about that on 2 November that year, South Africa's brilliant WBA super-featherweight champion Brian Mitchell squared up with McDonnell at the Elephant and Castle Leisure Centre to defend his title for the sixth time. After 12 tactical rounds of excellent boxing, Mitchell kept his championship with a unanimous points win. Mitchell's greater experience paid off but there were many rounds during which the defending champion seemed to ease off the pressure, allowing McDonnell to score with eye-catching blows. Indeed, after six completed rounds, commentator Harry Carpenter remarked how he couldn't split them. It was simply down to how you interpreted the fight. McDonnell's jab-and-move style won the fight through some spectators' eyes while the more methodical beat-down approach of Mitchell won it for others. The judges sided with Mitchell who fought with an air of confidence; nothing less than you would expect from a proven veteran of the ring.

'I thought I was unbeatable!' McDonnell exclaimed. 'Terry Lawless once said to me that the best technical fighter he had ever seen was Brian

Mitchell. There was nothing in the Mitchell fight though. It was like a chess match but because the rounds were close, they probably edged towards him. I learnt that night that you can't nick a title. You have to rip it from a defending champion and when I learnt that lesson against Mitchell, I boxed a different fight when I later fought Nelson.'

Taking heart from such a performance against such an opponent, McDonnell's self-esteem was not damaged now that his record's loss column had endured its first blemish. It was a loss in statistic alone. He had proven his world class capability against Mitchell and with Barry McGuigan settled into his comeback, also at super-featherweight, the potential fights available to McDonnell were enticing.

To mark time, McDonnell scored a points win over America's Benji Marquez at Brentwood on 10 March 1989. It was announced a short time later that McDonnell was chosen to fight in an eliminator for Azumah Nelson's WBC super-featherweight title against the one man he had wanted to fight from his early days in the sport – Barry McGuigan. McGuigan had now notched up three wins on his comeback trail and he too was eager to get on with the eliminator as his eagerly anticipated fight with Azumah Nelson was finally inching nearer to being signed and sealed. 'Barry Hearn called me at one o'clock in the morning and told me he had offered Barry McGuigan's lawyer £250,000 for the fight! He fainted then got up and accepted the fight! That was one o'clock! I put my tracksuit on and went out running for 1 hour and 45 minutes. Ten weeks to the fight and I was on it! There was no way I was coming second in this fight. I had always wanted this.'

McDonnell's sense of conviction goes undoubted. It was a fight he had wanted for years, was convinced he could win at any given time and had no doubt that his adversary's style was tailor-made for him. Years before the showdown took place, McDonnell had the full support of his family when it came to assessing his chances against the Irish 'Cyclone'. His father proved to be the most ardent fan of all. 'My dad passed in 1986 and that fight took place in 1989. My dad was a typical paddy and he was in pubs telling everyone that his son would win against McGuigan. They were all singing McGuigan's praises and they would say to him, "Mark, stop being such an eejit! Barry McGuigan would knock your son into next week!"' McDonnell said, adopting an impressive Irish accent.

'He seemed to think that his name was going to scare me but I won the mental battle. Barry Hearn will tell you that I made that fight. I kept telling him, "If you can't get me Mitchell, get me McGuigan." I always wanted that fight. Speaking to people, I heard he didn't want Mitchell, he didn't want Nelson and I also heard that he wasn't too keen on fighting me. Credit to him, he just thought I was too much risk for too little gain. So he was going to fight Tony Lopez for £150,000. He got £250,000 to fight me! When he weighed it up, he realised it was fight me or go to Sacramento to fight Lopez. He thought it was less risk to fight me than fight Lopez in Sacramento. It was more money here so he thought he'd build himself into the Lopez fight that way. That was when Barry Hearn called me to say he'd made McGuigan's lawyer faint with the offer! That is how the fight came about.'

One of McDonnell's concerns about the fight was the lack of discipline he believed McGuigan to have with regard to the Queensberry rulebook. He wanted to ensure the contest was tightened up and the chosen third man would have his eyes focused for any infringements.

'The referee for the fight was Larry O'Connell. I put a steward's inquiry in on the ref. The reason was, he had done one of Barry's fights before and he let him hit low, let him use the elbow and leaned towards him. When Mickey Vann came on board as the new ref, he did the pre-fight talk in the changing room. At the end he asked if we had any questions. I said, "Yeah, I have one. Do you know why you're the referee?" He looked quite shocked. I said, "You're the referee because of me. There is a lot of grudge here, a big build-up and 16,000 people out there but if it is fought by the Queensberry rules there is only one winner. I've watched every fight McGuigan ever had and when he gets in close he smashes the elbow into your face. Not once, but EVERY time. He will also step to the left to throw a left to the body on the blind side of the referee. As long as you take care of that, there'll be only one winner!"'

It was a definite crossroads fight for both fighters. The winner would go on to a world title shot against one of a number of world champions. For the loser, the chances of being able to mount another climb to the top of the tree would be considerably harder. The options would be either trying to rebuild from the domestic level or, to be brutal, retirement. McGuigan had taken five months off since his last appearance when, ominously, he had suffered cuts to both eyes when seeming to labour before putting the Argentinean Julio Miranda away in the eighth round.

While Barry Hearn had won the purse bids from McGuigan's promoter Frank Warren, there was more a sting in the tail than a twist when McDonnell's former trainer Jimmy Tibbs appeared in McGuigan's corner. Tibbs had switched teams to Warren a couple of years earlier. Ultimately, what it would come down to was the style of each fighter and which would prove more commanding on the night.

When the fighters left their dressing rooms to start their walks to the ring, the atmosphere bristled with tension and the electricity pricked the hairs on the backs of the thousands of necks present. 'When we got in the ring, the atmosphere was outstanding. We had a police escort into the ring. A real grudge fight. I could see the ref was nervous because we'd really built it up massive. McGuigan had said to me at the press conference two days before the fight, "I just hope you're there." I just looked at him. I didn't say nothing. I knew I had to use that. So many people asked me what I'd said. You can see I'm talking to him in the ring when the ref asked us forward. I went right up to him and said, "I'm here you little c**t!" I stared at him and said it. He turned to the ref and when we went back to our corners, I knew I'd got him. I knew then, I'd got him!'

The first round set the pattern for the fight. McDonnell kept the contest at long range with a stabbing left jab mixed with follow-up lefts to the body of the Irishman. McGuigan bobbed and weaved, trying to find a way in under McDonnell's left. His sharp movements allowed occasional success but the left of McDonnell scored enough to McGuigan's face to take the round.

The fight's duration was numbered from the second round. After landing a long, hard right hand to McDonnell's body, McGuigan paid for such impertinence when a long slashing left hand scraped passed his left brow and opened a cut over the eye. Blood immediately leaked down his face and McGuigan seemed to realise the severity of the injury when he increased the pressure on his opponent. This brought some success as he appeared to stun McDonnell on a couple of occasions with head shots. With the fight firmly in his favour, McDonnell was warned by Mickey Vann for pulling McGuigan's head down.

'I battered him, absolutely battered him! I'd destroyed McGuigan at his own game. I was rough. I elbowed him, hit him low and thumbed him in the eye. He got roughed up and he turned to the ref and said, "Ref!" There were no excuses. He was 28 years old and I was 30. We were both at our primes.'

With McGuigan's cutman Ernie Fossey working frantically on the eye, he came out for the third round but found himself on the end of McDonnell's left hand again. McDonnell now had a specific target to aim for and the injury got gradually worse and the end of the fight seemed clearly in sight. The start of the fourth round was delayed for a short while to allow excessive Vaseline to be wiped off from McGuigan's brow. Upon resuming, McGuigan went straight on to the offensive, knowing he had to unload everything to try and salvage the fight. McDonnell was too controlled and saw through the storm to settle down and chip away at the injury. With blood seeping out of his wound and leaking down his face, McGuigan was ushered away by Mickey Vann who took a long look and waved the fight, and the Irishman's career, over. There were no complaints from McGuigan. He had fought with his usual intensity and pressure but the coolness of McDonnell was enough to pacify the 'Cyclone'.

While taking those two years out undoubtedly produced some ring-rust, the case that McDonnell simply had the right style to combat McGuigan at any stage of his career could have given any jury cause for serious deliberation. 'George Francis was at my fight with McGuigan and as I got out of the ring, he came running up to me and said, "You done a f*****g good job in there!" He'd seen it all and he taught me!

'I honestly believe McGuigan and I could have boxed ten times and I'd have won ten times. I would beat him every time. He was strong, had long arms and could hit but listen, I could move, I could box, my fitness and skills and my great defence. You could hit me once but you couldn't hit me twice!' His moment of jubilation, however, was very much a moment of deep poignancy too. McDonnell's most ardent fan, the one who had supported him from the very early days and told all those who would listen that McDonnell was the man to defuse the 'Cyclone' was there in spirit only. 'One of my biggest regrets in my life was that my dad weren't there when I beat Barry McGuigan. He really believed in me. He thought I was the best. My mum never used to watch me box. When the fight was on telly, I knew she wouldn't be watching it. She goes into the kitchen! When Jim Rosenthal was interviewing me after the fight I said, "Can I just say one thing. Mum, I've won, come out the kitchen!" I got letters from people about that and mums contacting me saying how moving that was!'

After the fight, the possibilities were plentiful. An official eliminator for the awesome Azumah Nelson's WBC title, McDonnell's win held him in pole position for such a dubious honour. Also on the horizon were challenges to the IBF title held by Tony 'The Tiger' Lopez in the intimidating atmosphere of the Californian's home territory of Sacramento, the WBA title which was still held by Brian Mitchell or the recently inaugurated WBO title held by John-John Molina. 'When I won the McGuigan fight, Barry Hearn said to me, "What we're going to do is make a lot of money. We'll do this deal and you'll fight for the WBO title. Leave it to me!"'

It wasn't long before the next step in McDonnell's career was announced, even if it proved premature. McDonnell's promoter, Barry Hearn, reportedly went on to say a challenge for the Tiger's IBF title had been made for Sacramento on 7 October with McDonnell receiving a £150,000 purse and naming the time the fight would be screened live back to Britain. Lopez's recent form was impressive and his eight-round annihilation of Tyrone 'Harlem Butcher' Jackson in his most recent defence suggested McDonnell would be up against it. McDonnell remained unfazed by such circumstances and simply replied to the situation by saying, 'A ring is a ring wherever it is in the world. I studied him in great detail with those tiger-skin shorts! A good boxer with a good variety of shots. He was really well supported. A great fighter.'

It didn't take long, however, for this speculation to be reduced to fabrication. Negotiations had taken place between the two camps but ultimately, nothing had been finalised and the plans fell through. Hearn remained stoic in his belief that the fight had been made and described the turn of events as 'quite strange'.

As it turned out, McDonnell may have found himself in the right place at the right time had that fight taken place. Lopez went on to fight the WBO titleist John-John Molina in a rematch and was beaten in ten rounds. McDonnell's feeling of dejection didn't last long. In September, it was announced that he would fight Azumah Nelson for the Ghanaian's WBC title at the Royal Albert Hall on 5 November in a fight which was sure to produce a cracker and a bang along the way. With the number of governing bodies increasing at a pace of what seemed to be one every few months, the onus was strictly on 'the man who beat the man who beat the man etc' to be the real world champion.

Fast forward to 2014 and you have numerous levels of 'world' titles per governing body. Back in 1989, it was bad enough with four bodies. In his biography, former world middleweight champion Alan Minter openly criticised the existence of just two bodies back in the late 1970s and early 80s, saying the situation had become 'a joke'. McDonnell's challenge to Nelson, however, gave him the opportunity to beat a champion who would have slotted in nicely in any era. Arguably Ghana's greatest ever fighter, there could be no mistaking or doubting the authenticity of the contest. McDonnell, as expected, was supremely confident and stated in *Boxing News* that fighting in front of his fans at the Royal Albert Hall 'will be like having a three-round start'.

The former WBC featherweight champion Nelson rose in weight to the super-featherweight division in 1988 and claimed the vacant WBC title. He recorded three inside-the-distance defences before walking to the ring in Kensington to face off against his British challenger. Nelson was an intense come-forward fighter who would throw fast combinations with substantial power to wear his opponents down. He was a formidable warrior. His sole loss to date had been a somewhat premature challenge for the WBC featherweight title against the Mexican great Salvador Sanchez in 1982. Sanchez had cleaned out the division and was in his 46th and, tragically, last contest. Ironically, his hardest defence came with a split decision win over Britain's Pat Cowdell, who would go on to be sent to sleep with one monumental left uppercut by Nelson in 1985.

Against Sanchez, Nelson had just 13 fights behind him but he still managed to last into the 15th and final round before succumbing to the Mexican's superiority. Nelson's class and ability had been proven and over the ensuing seven years, he grew into one of the world's finest boxers. He'd travelled across the globe to take on all-comers and having boxed in Britain before, against Cowdell, the McDonnell contest held no fears for him. McDonnell 'had it all to do' and was therefore put in a 'no-lose' situation. The consensus in the press was that he would go out a typically gallant and courageous loser after taking his beating like a true warrior. Hardly anyone gave him a chance of making a dent in the African, let alone the scorned-upon notion that he would actually win.

If McDonnell proved himself in the McGuigan fight, he defined himself in the Nelson fight. Combating Nelson's forward advance with crisply delivered left jabs and follow-up one-two combinations, McDonnell used his foot movement and boxing brains to move away from Nelson's vaunted left hand. Nelson was able to soak up the jabs and combinations thrown his way without appearing visibly hurt but he was kept off his stride and for large parts of the fight, was unable to set himself to unload his lethal volleys. McDonnell kept him moving and off-balance with point-scoring blows. The first sign of real trouble appeared in the fifth when a left-hand counter over the top landed flush on McDonnell's chin and sent him crashing sideways to the canvas. It was a big punch which connected perfectly. McDonnell rose and responded in a way that gave Nelson all the evidence he needed that he was going to have to earn his wage the hard way. McDonnell stormed back in to take the sting out of the Ghanaian's offence and made the champion back up in a corner with a prolonged tirade of punches. 'The Professor' adopted the look of one such teacher whose theory had been proven wrong by the young, pretentious student. Try as he might, Nelson couldn't retaliate to such audacity. The bell sounded and one held the belief that, while McDonnell would take the minute to refresh and rejuvenate after the heavy knockdown, Nelson would scramble through the knowledge in his head to search for the solution to this Camden-based enigma.

What was apparent and becoming more noticeable was how Nelson's energy levels never appeared to diminish. His forward surge continued and as McDonnell's appetite for victory increased with each passing round of his highly effective jab-and-move strategy, his endurance was being stretched to its limit and his resilience was put through the most stringent of tests at not seeing any change in his opponent's charge. The rounds went by with McDonnell heroically flailing away but his energy was being sapped and the harder shots were landing from the champion. McDonnell's challenge effectively ended in the 11th round when his right eye completely shut, blocking out any view of Nelson's thunderous left hand. Even with this injury, McDonnell still boxed well and commentator Jim Watt was heard to say, 'I've never seen Azumah Nelson looking so ragged and it's Jim McDonnell making him that way.' What happened, or didn't happen, during the interval prior to the last round led the press to heavily criticise the actions taken by all those who had the authority to do the noble thing and pull McDonnell out. Instead, McDonnell was sent out to face his adversary in that 12th round. To all but McDonnell himself, going out for that last round was like the first slave in line to walk out into the Roman Coliseum and into the path of an iron-clad, mace-wielding Roman gladiator. There was the strong sense of inevitability about the next three minutes. While Darkie Smith and the rest of McDonnell's cornermen made a commendable effort during the break, managing to prise the severely puffed-up eyelids apart so that a limited amount of vision could seep through the swollen shelves of flesh, it was not enough.

After slipping to the canvas, McDonnell went toe-to-toe with the champion. Nelson's superior strength and bigger reserves of fuel shone through. A volley put the challenger down by the ropes. Up at the count of nine, American referee Joe Cortez waved the champion back in, who waded through the last shreds of McDonnell's resistance to put him flat on his back. Through his one good eye, McDonnell stared up to see Cortez's arms waving the fight over.

To confirm McDonnell's admirable showing, Swiss judge Franz Marti had him in the lead by two points. The other two judges had Nelson ahead and with the one-sided final round, McDonnell would have lost a unanimous decision had the fight reached the final bell. This is merely statistical fact. What is more important is the manner in which McDonnell handled an opponent who was expected, in many quarters, to fly back home unscathed and with a destructive win within the first half of the fight under his belt. It was, ultimately, 'mission accomplished' but not without being kept at bay with frequent retaliatory assaults.

'I fought the best that came out of Africa. I was asked after the fight what I thought of Nelson. I said, "What can I say about Nelson? He is who he is. The greatest fighter to come out of Africa,"' McDonnell said, showing no shortage of respect to his conqueror, 'but after rounds six and seven, he was finding the pace hard. He was really looking to slow the pace down but I weren't having it. I'd have beaten Nelson if my nutrition had been right. I know 100 per cent that if my nutrition and the day before weigh-ins were in place, it would have made no difference if I'd fought Nelson, McGuigan or Lopez. People forget I shed five pounds on the morning of the Nelson fight and I was still up on one of the cards at the end! Getting through the ropes for Azumah at 9st 6lb and 10st for Barry! THAT is the reason I lost there, not the opponent! Training hard with good rest and good nutrition, it wouldn't have made any difference if I was fighting King Kong! In a boxing marathon like when I fought Nelson, bad nutrition means dehydration. You hit the wall, simple as that!

'The day before the fight, the scales had been taken from the hotel for the weigh-in. What I didn't realise is that they had been re-calibrated. These people knew we were going to have these scales because it was implemented into the contract. I checked my weight 24 hours before the fight so this was all done. Nelson had been standing on these scales every day because he was worried about his weight and the scales were weighing light so he thought he was near his weight. You know what? I think it cost me a world title. On the morning of the fight, my brother came to the hotel with my own scales. When I weighed on them, I knew I was five pounds over. I told Barry Hearn that the scales the day before were light. The morning of the fight, I'd had a light breakfast which I never do! Nelson didn't beat me because he was a better fighter than me. He beat me because he had better nutrition. I spoke to Brian Mitchell's people years later when they came to my gym with Harry Simon. They told me when Mitchell got in the ring with me, he'd put 11lb on. ELEVEN POUNDS! If it was down to pure ability alone, I could school anyone at boxing; anyone! If I got that last 24 hours before the Nelson fight right, I'd have beaten him. I know it!'

McDonnell's fight with McGuigan was a genuine 50-50 affair with spectators either swayed by McGuigan's more pressured style or McDonnell having the right tools to defeat a slightly over-the-hill McGuigan. The Nelson fight was one which McDonnell was expected to lose. This he did, but not before causing severe headaches for the African. In Nelson's next fight the following May, he stepped up to lightweight and was comprehensively outboxed over 12 rounds by world champion Pernell 'Sweet Pea' Whitaker.

McDonnell took ten months out after the Nelson loss. It was a time of reflection and his thoughts were dominated by a whole variety of 'what-ifs' that went round inside his head, teasing him and telling him that he could have been the one lifting the WBC belt against Nelson if a few preparatory issues had been refined in the immediate build-up to the fight. 'I was devastated,' McDonnell expressed with no lack of sincerity. 'That nutrition in the last 24 hours before the contest cost me the belt. In my head, to this day, I know 100 per cent, if I got my weight spot on and hydrated properly, I would have been the champion. To this day, I know that. Damn!'

Leaving on such a note, coming agonisingly close to winning the world title, was never going to be easy. Retirement for McDonnell after this would be about as smooth and placid as a Nigel Benn fight. The return was inevitable. With a fight lined up with the WBO lightweight champion, Mauricio Aceves, later substituted with a challenge for the WBC international super-featherweight title against Pedro Gutierrez, sidelined by a wrist injury, McDonnell had to wait until 22 September 1990, when he returned to the scene of the Nelson fight and fought Louisiana's respectable journeyman Kenny Vice. Vice was, however, a last-minute substitute for McDonnell's original opponent, Santos Moreno of Mexico. Vice, a light-welterweight, was coming off three losses in his last four outings but the calibre of his opponents was hard to surpass. While it is a journeyman's unwritten prerogative to be pitted in against some of the world's best to prevent them from developing ring rust, Vice went in against the new WBC light-welterweight champion and arguably the greatest boxer ever to emerge from Mexico's back streets, Julio Cesar Chavez.

Chavez took him apart in three rounds but two fights later, Vice challenged for the vacant NABF light-welterweight title against the fearsome former world lightweight champion Livingstone Bramble. Defeated in six rounds, Vice lost once more before stepping in with McDonnell.

Floored at the end of the first round, McDonnell was knocked unconscious in the fourth round after his neck whipped against the bottom rope. With Vice visibly distressed in the ring, McDonnell remained on the canvas for several minutes before being taken back to his dressing room and, later, to Charing Cross Hospital where he was later discharged upon making a good recovery. McDonnell appeared out of sorts as the contest got going. Vice was able to get his jab going and while McDonnell landed the occasional combination, it was ominous to see how Vice simply walked through them, undeterred from his game-plan. The end, courtesy of a big left hook in the fourth, was as convincing a finish as one could witness.

'That fight was the biggest regret of my career. I shouldn't have took the fight. I found out he was my opponent at the weigh-in. I spoke with Terry Lawless through my brother and he said, "What is your brother doing fighting Kenny Vice?" I had fallen out with Freddie King who was the coach. I had pulled out of a fight a few months earlier and didn't want to do it again. I was due to fight the Mexican, Santos Moreno, instead of Vice. It was to be a safe match after fighting Nelson. He was a non-puncher and about 9st 7lb. We got to the weigh-in and Barry Hearn said there had been a change of opponent. "You're fighting a kid called Vice. Don't worry…" I should've smelt a rat. I told Barry Hearn to his face that I was stitched up. I was fuming. Vice was a big lightweight. I was a super-featherweight!'

While McDonnell had lost his comeback fight, it was around this time that he had gained his trainer's licence. His foray into the training side of the sport would lead him into the paths of, aside from Lennox Lewis and David Haye, two of Britain's most accomplished heavyweights of the last 20 years. Herbie Hide was a youngster when McDonnell first got to know him in the Matchroom stable and the relationship between the two grew.

'The frustrating thing with Herbie is that I was his hero because when I was in the Matchroom gym he was a 17-year-old kid and I was number one in the world. He looked up to me and watched me train. I then went on to train him and was with him for ten weeks up to the Michael Bentt fight. Even though I wasn't in the corner for that fight, which goes back to politics, if you spoke to Herbie now on the phone and asked him who trained him for that fight, he'd say me. I trained him twice a day every day and he was sparring with Freddie King. I got his mind right and trained him to become the world heavyweight champion.'

The frustration came in when negotiations started for Hide to defend his WBO title against the formidable Riddick Bowe. It was to be Hide's first defence of the title and with the calibre of his challenger such as it was, team Hide were naturally out to cash in and get the best possible deal for the champion.

'Herbie hadn't boxed for a year. Hearn got him this fight with Bowe and was offering him stupid money. Frank Warren offered him a lot more money. He wanted me to come to this meeting with Warren which I wish I hadn't went to but I went. I heard the amount of £3m to fight Bowe. Frank Warren gave me a cheque for £300,000. He asked me to get Herbie to sign which I didn't do but I could have and should have. Herbie asked me to go downstairs for a coffee. Frank Warren looked at me and that cup of coffee cost me £300,000! We went back upstairs and Herbie is kicking me under the table. "Jimmy, what do you think I should do?" I told him he had to make his own decisions. I said to him, "It's a business. It's the same fight in the same place. It's not rocket science but it's your call."

'Anyway, he didn't sign with Frank that day. He wanted time to think about it! Frank said he didn't have time. He had Don King on the phone. Warren tried to force me as I had a post-dated cheque. I didn't fall for it. I went back to Norwich the next day and Barry Hearn was round his house and his money went from over £1m to whatever he got; just under £3m. Herbie had obviously told Hearn that I'd taken him to Warren. Barry Hearn called me and asked how much I wanted for training Herbie for eight weeks. I told him I was entitled to ten per cent. Hearn said, "Herbie's told me he'll pay you £1,500 a week and £20,000 for the fight. You want to take it or leave it?" I told Hearn he needed three months to get ready as he hadn't fought for a year. He may even have needed a couple of warm-up fights. "Well," Barry said, "he's in the big league now!" I thought, well, that's it. That was my fall-out with him and Hide.

'I read an article by Bowe that said the fastest he ever boxed was Hide. If Hide had trained properly for that fight, he'd have beaten Bowe. He was exceptional. A bit erratic but was SO fast. He just didn't have the discipline.'

As it transpired, Hide didn't possess the power to stem Bowe's charge and the fight was stopped after six rounds with Hide having visited the floor on several occasions.

The bug to entice him back into the ring was still strong inside McDonnell and seeing the success he'd had in training top level fighters such as Hide only added fuel to that fire. 'I never wanted to go out on a loss. I thought that my whole life and I would never let that happen. I spoke to every promoter in town to give me that opportunity. No one came across, probably for my own safety and my own good. I just thought I'd been out all them years and I'd never missed a day's training. I was going to fight again whether that be in Timbuktu or on the moon! I had to go out on my own shield. I was always a winner. The late, great John Robinson sorted it out for me.

'I boxed a guy called Peter Feher in Slovakia. I got a guy in my corner who don't speak a word of English and I dropped the bloke in the second round with a shot to the body. I'm not saying I was the fighter I was but the kid was not in my class. He had nine wins before we fought? I don't know how. He was pony! This geezer wasn't good enough to be my sparring partner! After I decked him, he got up and the bell rung about a minute into the round. It was a joke! The judges were cheering for him! At the end of it, he won it! It weren't even close. I just thought if I can't fight at home then what's the point? My genuine feeling looking back? I had two losses. Nelson and Mitchell. The Feher fight was a farce and the Vice fight shouldn't have happened.'

Steve Holdsworth, the Eurosport commentator, remembered that fight and described it as 'an absolute travesty'. Indeed, if the 'loss' to McDonnell was a genuine result, one could go through the sport's history and have a legitimate case in reversing enough points decisions to send the likes of Nat Fleischer, Bert Randolph Sugar, Reg Gutteridge and Gilbert Odd spinning in their graves at the futility of their chosen professions.

Along with Herbie Hide, McDonnell was also the driving force behind Danny 'The Brixton Bomber' Williams's career-best victory over a shop-worn and over-the-hill Mike Tyson in July 2004 in Louisville, Kentucky. It had been two years since Lennox Lewis's right hand had brought the final curtain down on any hopes Tyson had of regaining a morsel of the world title. With a self-proclaimed broken back, Tyson had come back in 2003 with a ridiculously easy one-round win over the 'Black Rhino', Clifford Etienne. The Williams fight was to be his chance to see what shreds of his former self he still possessed. Ever since James 'Buster' Douglas's monumental upset of Tyson in Tokyo in 1990, everyone who was anyone in boxing gave their verdict of what Tyson had left in terms of percentages. A one-sided win or a particularly devastating showing in training would get rumours circulating that he was '90 per cent' of what he was. It was more in hope than in genuine expectation. People continued to yearn for the return of the fighter who tore the heavyweight division apart during his potent best of 1986–1988. Against Williams, Tyson still had his aura about him and his vocal entourage were on hand to glare at people with unnecessary scowls, scream out to anyone within earshot what their man was going to do in the ring and generally feed the former heavyweight champion with as many 'yesses' as they could when in reality he should have been hearing 'no' far more often.

The fight? Tyson's last hurrah came in the very first round when a blizzard of punches tore through Williams's guard, leaving the 'Brixton Bomber' swaying from side to side like an old fishing boat through the rough sea. The combination of an unexpectedly good chin and a total stripping of Tyson's confidence upon seeing the Brixton fighter still standing, led to Tyson falling apart and unable to take Williams's onslaught three rounds later. Tyson collapsed by the ropes and was counted out. As McDonnell will tell you, the win was in the bag before the fighters even stepped into the ring.

'That was phenomenal! Tyson was staying in the same hotel as us. The first day we come down in the lift, the doors open and there are six guys there standing in tracksuits. Tyson was one of them! Danny said, "Jim, Jim let the doors shut." I said, "Dan, get out the lift." "Jim, it's Tyson!" he said. "Dan, GET OUT THE LIFT!" I told him. We got out the lift and Danny ducked his head and walked past. I looked back and they're all looking over at us. I went, 'Morning gentlemen!' We went for our run and I said, "Dan, you just won the fight. You just WON the fight! If you'd gone back in that lift, it was over."'

McDonnell and Williams had confronted the bullying mob-mentality of the Tyson camp and had exploited the former champion's weakness in failing to intimidate an opponent. The inclusion of the wailing Steve 'Crocodile' Fitch, boxing's answer to the NFL's pom-pom cheerleaders, only not quite as attractive, wasn't enough to deter the British camp. This, however, didn't put off team Tyson from attempting to unsettle their opponent at a press conference later that day.

'They got up and said, "Danny Williams went out for a run this morning and has greatly underestimated the great Mike Tyson. He was only out for 15 minutes." They said Mike was out for longer. Tyson tries to intimidate at the press conference and Danny bites. Tyson knows me and he addressed me. He calls me Jimmy Mac! He got up and was saying all these good things about me!' McDonnell impersonates Tyson's soft tones to an impressive degree and carries it through to when Tyson turns on Williams and tells the press and media what fate awaits the Brit.

'"Man," McDonnell mimics, '"Danny Williams man, in one or two rounds, I'm gonna get to him and bust his ass, bust his body and bust his head! Danny got up and made a real weak thing! Mike Tyson's a great fighter, I've come here to win and this is the opportunity of a lifetime."' Freddie Roach then got up and said how Tyson was in great shape, working all the angles and they done a great job. I knew Tyson had got bigger in the press conference. It was rammed. I got up and said, "First of all ladies and gentlemen, the great Mike Tyson, Freddie Roach and everyone else in the room, I'd like to say hello. Now I'll say what I've got on here to say. Danny Williams is the future of heavyweight boxing! Come tomorrow night, let me tell you all something. There will be a new king in town and it's this young man sitting next to me from Brixton in London called Danny Williams. He KNOWS he is gonna knock Tyson out. He's told me he's gonna knock him out!" You could feel the electricity in that room. I had to get inside Williams's head.'

Ironically, it was Tyson's last opponent, Clifford Etienne, who, unwittingly, played an instrumental role in preparing Williams for this inevitable assault. 'I hired Etienne as our sparring partner. He came over here and I said to him, "Clifford, you'll be well looked after but I don't want you to talk to Danny Williams. When you come in the gym, it's business. You're only sparring two rounds. You don't talk to him, you have nothing to do with him, you keep your distance from him." I had a bag with thousands and thousands of dollars in and I said to him, "If you knock Williams out, and I will even count over him, you will take this money home. You just knock him the f**k out!" He came in the gym and it was packed! News got out about this sparring. Danny turned to me and said, "Jimmy, I don't like this guy!" I said to him, "Dan, I found something out about him. Someone told me he's racist! He don't like Muslims, that's why he don't talk to you!" The anger was incredible! Danny Williams was coming out and giving it! One thought he was getting $20,000, the other thought he didn't like Muslims! The gym was RAMMED! I wanted Danny to deal with the pressure and the intensity to get him ready. Like I said to Clifford, after two rounds it was over but Danny was saying, "Jim, leave him in. I want to knock him out!" That training drill with Etienne was what made Danny Williams knock Mike Tyson out!'

At the end of the first round, McDonnell turned to Williams in the corner and told him how Tyson was blowing hard already and how Williams needed to get his jab going. At the end of the second, McDonnell told Williams the fight was as good as won. Tyson struggled to continue his earlier pace in the third and became disheartened by the sight of Williams still standing in front of him. In the fourth, Williams let rip with a blazing salvo of punches which floored the former world heavyweight champion by the ropes. The look of dejection and surrender spread across Tyson's face as the referee reached the count of ten.

Williams's prize was a challenge for Vitali Klitschko's WBC heavyweight title that December. It was an uphill struggle from the start. Klitschko dominated and eventually took Williams apart conclusively in the eighth round. 'He got hurt early in that fight and Klitschko just never let Danny in,' McDonnell said. 'Danny was really shocked by his power. He jumped on Danny early and just never let him in.'

At present, McDonnell trains James DeGale, the 2008 Olympic middleweight gold medallist and the former British and European super-middleweight champion. It is during this relationship that McDonnell noticed the differences in contemporary training techniques and support available for a fighter compared to his heyday in the 1980s. Such realisations enhance McDonnell's view that, had he been the beneficiary of such support, he would have achieved more and would have more than held his own among today's elite fighters.

'I watch James and he has people around like a nutritionist telling him what he needs. I was living off one meal a day and drying out for two or three. That was old school. People laugh when I say I could have beaten Floyd Mayweather but I genuinely believe I could have beaten anyone. I fancy myself against Floyd Mayweather at nine stone four. I've watched him. I went out to America and trained with him. He's a brilliant boxer but I tell you who would have given him problems from Britain; Pat Cowdell. Massive problems. Have a look at Cowdell's fight with Salvador Sanchez, a great fighter. Mayweather is brilliant at what he does but he don't do a lot. The way to beat Mayweather is to throw at least 40 jabs a round.'

McDonnell is an accomplished fighter, an accomplished trainer and seems at peace with himself after a career which saw him fall just short of two challenges for genuine world titles; titles which would sit atop the mountain of existing world titles around today. 'I could hold my own with anyone around today. People say to me, "What did you win?" I tell them I won the European title and they tell me that so-and-so is a three-weight world champion. You have guys walking around today calling themselves a world champion when they wouldn't have been in my league.'

That four-fight span from 1988–1989, during which Jimmy Mac fought Brian Mitchell, Barry McGuigan and Azumah Nelson, is strong evidence to suggest that, not only were world titles in past times harder to acquire and therefore more treasured, but also that this particular fighter could indeed have held his own against many around today.

13

Horace Notice

THE quest to become the first British heavyweight to claim the richest prize in sport since the Cornish-born, red-haired 'Ruby' Bob Fitzsimmons lifted the world heavyweight championship by launching his now famous solar plexus hammer blow deep into the midriff of defending champion James Corbett in 1897, was an achievement attempted by many but left unfulfilled by all those that tried. Gunner Moir against Tommy Burns, Tommy Farr against Joe Louis, Don Cockell against Rocky Marciano and Henry Cooper, Brian London and Joe Bugner against Muhammad Ali. All these Brits tried but fell short.

One fighter, however, who was showing genuine promise as a future world title contender and who would win the British and Commonwealth heavyweight titles was West Bromwich-born Horace Notice. Notice won the British heavyweight title seven months before Mike Tyson destroyed Trevor Berbick for the WBC title in November 1986 to become the youngest ever heavyweight champion. He had his final fight, before his enforced retirement on medical grounds, a couple of weeks before Tyson knocked out Tony Tubbs in March 1988 in Japan. Tyson was therefore the champion whom Notice may well have confronted within the next couple of years, had he not been struck down by circumstances beyond his control.

'Yeah well, you never know!' Notice said amid a bustling coffee shop in the Glades shopping mall in Bromley, south-east London. While I ordered the drinks, Notice picked up my bag and walked off to an altogether quieter, and more sensible, place to sit. Still looking trim at the age of 55, Notice relayed his impression of the champion he seemed destined to meet. 'He was a good fighter. I respected him as a fighter.

I know because of his upbringing he had negative parts and the press saw this but he didn't do anything to correct that part of his life. He was hanging around with the same type of people. Not that you got to put them aside but you must know how to communicate with them. He went to prison and I remember reading an article about those guys who he bought Rolex watches for. Where are they now? He comes back out of prison and he goes and does the same thing all over again.'

Notice's early years involved much travelling as was characteristic of families back in the 1960s and 70s originating from the Caribbean, in order to look for the places best suited to bringing up a family and find work. Unlike many families of the time, Notice started his life in the UK and then moved to Jamaica.

'I was born in West Bromwich. My mother took me to Jamaica when I was four and a half years old and I came back in 1978. I lived in Birmingham for about four years then I came to London in 1983. I had relatives living in London so from time to time I used to visit so the move was quite comfortable. I wanted to get into boxing in Jamaica but it is a small island and it is not as big as over here. When I came over here, I was working as a panel beater and one day I was talking to a work-mate and he recommended me to Nechells Green Amateur Boxing Club. I went there and started. That was in 1980 and at first I wasn't that dedicated. Later that year I was made redundant so I decided to go back and take it more seriously. I told myself that if I was to do it, I'd do it not just as an amateur but with the intention of turning pro.'

This notion that boxing was something he wanted to commit himself to and strive hard to hit the dizzy heights in, was not something shared by his mother. 'My mother wasn't too keen but she accepted it because at that time I was 23. She always said that boxing and being in the police she would not want me to do. In Jamaica, sometimes cops get shot. It's not like over here where things are different. In boxing there is too much blood she said and in Jamaica, because you're a cop you're hated. If they have a gun and they have a chance, they will shoot you!'

With no past generations in his family having participated in the sport that Notice could think of, he had started a fresh trend within his family history and his development was quick. In 1982, he reached the final of the heavyweight ABAs after defeating future professional opponent Dave Garside in the semi-final. In the final, he met and lost to Harold Hylton.

'I was disappointed. From the quarter-finals, we saw each other box in Gloucester and then the semi-finals in Preston we had another look at each other. I'm saying, "This guy can't beat me." I get to Wembley and he put me down with a left hook in the first round. Maybe through inexperience, I got up instead of taking a count. I said, "This guy can't do it again!" He put me down a second time! I got up and I think there was some water in the ring and as he throw a punch, I slipped. His back was towards the referee and he thought I got caught and counted me out. I went down three times but I wasn't hurt. I was gutted. I remember about a week later and this guy saw me. He said, "Hi, do you do boxing?" I felt so ashamed because I know he saw me get beat. I wanted to say no but I didn't want him to think I was lying!'

When I mentioned the following year's ABA tournament, Notice sat back in his seat, put his head back and laughed loudly as the images of him holding aloft his trophy re-entered his memory. The win also involved gaining revenge over Hylton for the previous year's loss, one which would prove to be the only loss Notice would suffer in both the amateur and professional ranks. 'Yes, yes, yes! I couldn't feel any better. It was like winning the lottery. I was confident of beating him because when he came back from the Commonwealth Games in Australia, I wanted to fight him that December but they said he wasn't training. I knew they didn't want him to fight me!'

Harold Hylton went on to win the heavyweight ABAs again in 1985 and reached the finals once more in 1988 but lost out to future Commonwealth, European and WBO heavyweight champion Henry Akinwande. Having reached the summit of the amateur boxing mountain, the natural progression was to move into the professional side of the sport. Attempting to retain his ABA title the following year was never a consideration and the emphasis was on making shockwaves through the paid ranks. 'It was time. I started at the age of 23. I won the title when I was 24 so there was no time for me to make the decision or think about it. I knew it was time for me to turn pro as quick as possible. I had Jimmy Tibbs and Frank Black behind me when I turned pro so I was ready.'

For his professional debut on 24 October 1983, Notice was served up the tough Welshman Andy Gerrard to exhibit his skills against. In his previous contest a month earlier, Gerrard had picked up a comfortable points win over Notice's former amateur opponent Dave Garside. With a useful record of five wins, four losses with two draws, Gerrard went the six-round distance, giving Notice his first win.

'I had the advantage of sparring with Frank Bruno and also Adrian Elliott for that fight and they were good fighters. We didn't just spar before a fight. We sparred as part of our training. Whether we were fighting or not, we were sparring. I think by that time I had got used to handling the pressure. When I had my first amateur fight, I saw him and I was so nervous. I said to myself, "Is this how I'm going to feel every time I have a fight?!" I had to learn to overcome those feelings.'

Notice closed out 1983 by taking on a 37-fight veteran for his second opponent in Theo Josephs. Josephs had a first-round knockout victory over Liverpool's Noel Quarless to his credit but while his bout with Notice ended in the same round, Josephs found himself with an extra loss to his name. A return with Andy Gerrard was next up and Notice improved on his previous performance with a second-round stoppage win at Wolverhampton's Civic Hall. After a six-month gap, he returned and fought Paddy Finn. While Finn had only five fights to his name, he proved too hot for Hughroy Currie and defeated Noel Quarless in two rounds. Having also been in with an unbeaten Anders Eklund, the future two-time European heavyweight champion, his record looked particularly impressive. With a third-round win, however, Notice marched on.

'Because I turned pro late, in every fight I was in, I go in not to lose. I always remember when Joe Bugner made his comeback fight over here, he said, "Because of my age I cannot afford to lose." I always take that attitude. I was always dedicated to my training. I would be out running and I'd ask myself, "Why am I doing this?" I'd then tell myself that I was giving this the best I can. I didn't want to say, "What if?"'

He was back again the following month to face the durable American veteran Winston Allen. Boasting a first-round knockout over a former Muhammad Ali world title challenger, Jean-Pierre Coopman, and with opponents such as Alfredo Evangelista, Joe Bugner, Frank Bruno, Anaclet Wamba and Steffen Tangstad on his record, it was no real surprise that Notice had to venture the full course of the fight over six rounds to collect his win.

'To me, he was just another opponent. Even though I didn't have a lot of fights at the time, I learnt a lot in the gym and I was dedicated. My sparring with Frank and, at the time, Gary Mason, was harder than the fight itself. I was up for sparring with good guys. When I moved to London, I used to spar with Hughroy Currie a lot at the Old Kent Road. We met before I started boxing and we sparred and became good friends.'

On the undercard to Barry McGuigan's successful European featherweight title defence against the Frenchman Farid Gallouze in March 1985, Notice picked up a quick second-round win over Croydon's Bob Young.

With this successful start to his professional career, the British title appeared over the horizon and Team Notice commenced their charge towards this goal by signing up to an eliminator against the rugged 22-year-old, Noel Quarless. 'That was my hardest pro fight. They stripped David Pearce of the title and they were gonna have Rudi Pika and someone else fight for the vacant title. Terry Lawless rung up the board of control and said how come Rudi Pika is fighting for the vacant title when he is not even fighting at the moment because he was semi-retired? That was how I got the opportunity to fight the eliminator against Quarless. Funso Banjo and Hughroy Currie was gonna fight for the vacant title.'

Quarless was a temperamental fighter to say the least. He became the first man to defeat Anders Eklund after scoring three heavy knockdowns for a clinical first-round stoppage, followed this up with a second-round stoppage of the former British, Commonwealth and European champion John L. Gardner and recorded a workmanlike win over ten rounds against former WBA heavyweight champion, 'Big' John Tate. On the flip side, he suffered seven quick knockout losses over the course of his career but had been up against the likes of Funso Banjo, Derek Williams and Lennox Lewis.

'I felt good in that fight. I'd only had six fights and had only been six rounds. I'm now going into a fight and I have to go 12 rounds. I trained really hard for that fight. I think I may have trained myself too much. I fought on the Friday and Frank Bruno fought on the Wednesday [winning the European title with a fourth-round knockout of Anders Eklund]. The Monday was my last training day so the last few days before the fight, I just lay in bed to keep my energy. The fight was in his hometown. Sometimes when he throws some punch at me he would go wild but I was determined and I stopped him. Believe me, he was the hardest puncher I fought.'

The fight started at a frenetic pace with hard shots being thrown and landed from both sides. By the fifth round the pace had mellowed and Notice began to take charge. Each time Quarless went to mount a big rally, Notice fought back to keep the upper hand. In the seventh round a barrage from Notice drove the Liverpudlian to the ropes where a final right and left dumped him for the full count.

Now unbeaten in seven fights, Notice was faced with his first undefeated opponent just 13 days after the Quarless eliminator. Over from France came Anaclet Wamba who boasted an unblemished record of 13 wins. He'd been taken the distance against Notice victims Winston Allen and Andy Gerrard. While not regarded as a heavy puncher, Wamba was a skilful fighter with a good defence and it was a genuine contest between two unbeaten European contenders. 'He was good.

Every time I hurt him, he wouldn't stand still for me to catch him. He'd move away. Yes, he was a very good boxer.'

As time would tell, a very good boxer indeed. This was one of those results which, when looked back on in hindsight, will surely raise eyebrows in admiration. Anaclet Wamba went on to remain unbeaten for another five years when he was disqualified in the 12th round after having five points deducted from his score against the Italian Massimiliano Duran in a challenge for the WBC cruiserweight title. During this time he had annexed the European title and in a rematch with Duran, he won the WBC crown with an 11th-round stoppage. With a repeat result in their third fight, Wamba went on to make another six defences of his world title before retiring undefeated as champion. Notice's win early in the Frenchman's career is suddenly brought into focus and provides a solid measuring stick as to how far his career could have gone.

The path was now clear for a shot at Hughroy Currie, the British champion. After a particularly easy warm-up against the five-fight German-based American novice Curtis Jones on the undercard to Frank Bruno's world title eliminator against the South African Gerrie Coetzee, the Currie fight was set for the Isle of Man a month later. Also on the line was to be the vacant Commonwealth title.

'I felt confident going into the fight. I know Currie was a good fighter but sometimes I think he wasn't a dedicated fighter. Sometimes he allowed himself to go up but I could tell he really trained hard for that fight. I could see he had lost a lot of weight unlike when he fought Funso Banjo. We were friends so when you fight someone you meet every day on the streets, you try for your own pride. That was the only fight where I watched the fighter on tape before we fought. I watched his fight with Kilimanjaro and Funso Banjo.'

Notice was crowned the British and Commonwealth heavyweight champion after the fight was stopped in the sixth round. While Notice was forced to take a count after a flash knockdown, he stormed back to force the stoppage.

There was no resting on his laurels as Notice signed to fight respectable American journeyman Mike Jameson a little over three weeks after his title-winning effort. Jameson was coming off a sixth-round stoppage loss to a lightning-quick powerhouse, smashing his way to the top of the heavyweight division, called Mike Tyson. Jameson was something of a known quantity to British fans as Frank Bruno had travelled to Chicago in the summer of 1983 to stiffen him with a left hook before flattening him with a monstrous right uppercut halfway through the second round. While Notice was unable to repeat this feat, what he gained was valuable experience from a fighter who knew his way around a ring and would, subsequently, go on to fight some of the division's top fighters before retiring in 1992. 'I think I was over-cautious because having just won the British title, I didn't want to suddenly get beat. I look at it as a boring fight because I know deep down I could have done better. I didn't go in with that hunger in me like I had when I fought for the British title. It gave me ten good rounds though.'

The fight went the full ten rounds with Notice's hand hoisted at the Royal Albert hall. A frustrating time awaited Notice as his next fight, a Commonwealth defence against Zimbabwe's African Boxing Union champion Proud Kilimanjaro, had to be put back from the following November to March the following year when it was discovered Notice broke a couple of ribs in sparring. The injury happened during a sparring session with the future British heavyweight champion, Gary Mason, a short while after the Jameson fight. In a ringside interview held during the Notice–Kilimanjaro dust-up with the inimitable Harry Carpenter, Gary Mason explained what occurred.

'That was an old injury that happened in June before the Bruno fight in Wembley [Bruno's WBA title challenge to Tim Witherspoon]. He should have fought on that bill. It happened then and it re-occurred just before November last year. A lot of things happen in sparring within the gym and I don't think a lot of us are fond of each other in there!'

Kilimanjaro was deemed to be a stern test for the champion as he held advantages in reach, weight and height. As it happened, the fight was an easy night's work against a surprisingly withdrawn and non-committed challenger. The official result was an eighth-round stoppage win for Notice but in all fairness, the fight had been punched out of the challenger from round four. By this stage, nothing was coming back from Notice's non-stop barrages, it was obvious there was going to be just one winner and the remainder of the 'contest' saw a painfully one-sided drubbing that seemed wholly avoidable and unnecessary. While it was surely a fight which dented Proud's pride, he can say he finished the fight on his feet long after many would have stepped in to end it. 'That was another boring fight for me,' Notice says. 'Sometimes when your opponent doesn't come to fight, it can be a boring fight. I was supposed to fight on the bill when Frank Bruno fought Tim Witherspoon but I got an injury with a cracked rib and I didn't fight for about ten months so maybe a little ring-rust.'

In a re-acquaintance of the 1982 ABA semi-final, Dave Garside was next to try and block the path that Notice was treading to seek bigger and better rewards. Having earned his chance for a shot at the title by stopping future IBF cruiserweight champion Glenn McCrory on a cut eye in the seventh round and defeating John Westgarth in nine rounds in an official eliminator, Garside entered the ring at Wembley Arena confident of revenge. His confidence had received a huge boost too when, in December 1985, he had travelled the Channel to France to take on the Moroccan-born 50-fight veteran and former European heavyweight champion, Lucien Rodriguez. Rodriguez was coming off a one-round loss to Frank Bruno but he was expected to use Garside as a way to ease back into the frame. Garside turned the tables with an emphatic eight-round points win. However, Garside's record also showed losses to Hughroy Currie, Anaclet Wamba and Andy Gerrard, three fighters who Notice had handled with comfort. As Notice said, though, his performance had improved much since their meeting in the amateur days.

'Oh yeah, definitely. He improved but with every opponent I have only one intention. That is to win. What you have to realise is that Frank was in front of me, I was in the middle and Gary was behind and I am older than both of them so I have to treat each fight as a crossroad fight. It's all or nothing because I wasn't getting enough fights. I didn't fight as often as I should so every fight I go into I want to make I sure I won that fight.'

History beckoned in Notice's next appearance when he defended his British and Commonwealth heavyweight titles against Newcastle's Northern Area champion, Paul Lister. His sole loss had come in his third pro fight to Dave Garside on points over eight rounds but with his win over Stewart Lithgo for the Northern Area title, his big opportunity against the formidable British champion had presented itself. The Lithgo result was just the second inside-the-distance win on Lister's record so whether he had the power to get the champion's respect was open to debate. He did however have home support with the fight taking place on Tyneside. The fight proved itself to be a clubbing show of power from the champion, recording a convincing third-round knockout. Lister's comments after the fight, stating he felt able to go on, seemed little more than a man trying to convince himself that there was a glimmer of hope in the face of a brutal bombardment of heavy artillery. Notice picked up the win and more importantly, picked up the Lonsdale belt, an image proudly displayed on the front cover of *Boxing News* with the sub-headline 'Horace bridges gap of 18 years'. Bridging that gap moved him into the same elite class as 'Bombardier' Billy Wells, Joe Beckett, Frank Goddard, Jack Petersen and Henry Cooper as the only British champions in the division's 77-year history to receive the prestigious belt. 'I was very proud. After Henry Cooper, no one had won the Lonsdale belt. I still have it but it's put away!'

Notice was seemingly carving out a niche for himself. With Frank Bruno very much the country's number one heavyweight and the one most likely to cause ripples on the world scene (despite his unsuccessful challenge to Tim Witherspoon), Notice was plugging away and his combination of hand speed and power was making him a fighter for others to be aware of. Aside from the points wins over foreign fighters, Anaclet Wamba and Mike Jameson, he was stopping all challengers to his domestic supremacy and the next natural progression was to move into the wider picture. However, with Australian Dean Waters as the next challenger for the Commonwealth title and Hughroy Currie earning the right for a challenge to his old title with a points win over Noel Quarless, Notice had his domestic obligations to see to first. His achievements were slowly moving him out of Bruno's shadow and into the boxing spotlight.

Dean Waters left his home country for the only time in his career to challenge Notice for his Commonwealth title in December 1987. With just five wins and two losses to date his credentials were open to debate. He was coming off a loss a month earlier to American journeyman Eddie Richardson, who in turn had lost nine of his previous 12 contests and whose head was often used as a shock absorber for the division's elite. Unable to get past this type of contest did not bode well.

Promoted jointly by Mickey Duff and Mike Barrett, the fight proving to be a painful experience for the Australian, the evening's shenanigans proved a frustrating chapter in Notice's development. Being the headlining fight of the show at Wembley's Grand Hall, he capitalised on the occasion by pummelling Waters into a fourth-round stoppage defeat. Topping a bill that featured the emerging force of Nigel Benn and the European flyweight champion Duke McKenzie in a non-title fight, Notice's opportunity for media exposure was overshadowed by another fighter on the undercard.

Cruiserweight Bobby Frankham lost his three-fight unbeaten streak to London's Billy Sim via a first-round stoppage. Taking umbrage with the referee Richie Davies's decision, he verbally abused Davies and landed a couple of right-hand punches to his head. Sparking a reaction from Frankham's supporters, the referee was rushed from the scene amid chaotic scenes. Bobby Frankham never fought again.

In contrast to these regrettable scenes instigated by Frankham, the Waters fight showed the professional approach from Notice that the fight game had come to expect. 'To me, when I have an opponent I don't really put them up on a pedestal. It's between you and I. Imagine we meet in a dark alley fighting. I treat it that way. I've got to go and fight to win. From the moment you saw your opponent up there, you can't really see them as if they are nothing. That's when things can go wrong.'

With his Commonwealth obligations fulfilled, Notice just had Hughroy Currie to deal with to satisfy the board's requirements before he could press on to the European and, ultimately, the world stage. With a second-round knockout over Glenn McCrory (which resulted in McCrory abandoning his hopes in the heavyweight division to drop down to cruiserweight) his biggest win since the first Notice fight, Currie was out for revenge against a fighter who had advanced at a better pace and had shown more signs of improvement since their initial meeting. As well as defeating McCrory, Currie had come up short against the American Melvin Epps, a fighter aspiring heavyweights should be getting past, if only on points, but not losing against. *Boxing News*'s Tim Mo predicted it would be a repeat result in a tougher fight but may have to go a few rounds longer before the champion got the win. The duration predicted by the weekly magazine was accurate and the fight given by Currie was tougher than in their first encounter, though this is not agreed on by the defending champion.

'I know that fight shouldn't have lasted that long but my mind and my body was not co-ordinating together. It wasn't my preparation. I already beat him and when you beat your opponent once, you have that little bit more confidence. I've already beat you so I'm confident you know? I had my instructions but I just couldn't get it together. I had an off night that night. Towards the end, I was thinking this fight is going on too long and then I felt a difference like someone switched something on like a switch and I stopped him. I think he fought better in the first fight. When you're champion you can have confidence without having a fight because the confidence is there already. When you're challenging for a fight, you know you don't have anything to lose. When you're champion and you're defending, you know you have more to lose so you're more nervous. At the same time, I try not to get careless. Some guys who are champions get careless and relax. You NEVER relax.'

In a gruelling affair, both fighters took it in turns to gain the initiative but it quickly became a fight of wills and the question was who could simply outlast the other. Notice held the edge in stamina and simply broke Currie down towards the end which came in the tenth round with the Catford challenger still upright but taking too much punishment before referee Adrian Morgan made the stoppage. Both boxers had performed admirably.

Currie would carry on for almost another two years, taking part in four more fights. He travelled to Brazil to be stopped in eight rounds by developing South American contender Adilson Rodrigues. After a repeat points win over Noel Quarless, he got knocked out in four rounds courtesy of two sledgehammer right hands from Gary Mason in January 1989 for the vacant British title and that December, in his farewell fight, got stopped in 55 seconds by Derek 'Sweet D' Williams for the Commonwealth title and the vacant European title. In a cruel twist, what no one expected was that the Currie rematch was to be Horace Notice's final fight. There were rumours and much speculation that Notice's next fight would be a challenge for the European title held by the unbeaten Italian, Francesco Damiani.

'Deep down I think that guy tried to avoid me because, as a business, he would take the world title shot instead. The fight was demanded by other countries and I was pleased to finally get my opportunity but that's when I got my injury.'

The fateful problems with Notice's eyes came to light some time before he faced enforced retirement from the sport he was making waves in. 'I had a cataract in my left eye a year before I retired. I noticed sometimes in sunlight my vision was not that good in my left eye but I didn't take much notice at first. I know I hadn't sparred for about six weeks before I found out I had the cataract from the operation. When I told the doctor that maybe I had done it in training, he said I could have gone blind by the time I'd had the operation. They said the retina was like a damp, worn paper that was slowly peeling.'

Facing up to the reality that one's career in the ring is over can be one of the hardest things for a boxer to come to terms with and get accustomed to. With most, it is the only thing which they have ever been able to do and the only thing which can give them a sense of fulfilment and pride. To have this ripped away from you in a doctor's surgery over the course of a few words after the realisation of a dreaded test result can leave the fighter faced with an uncertain future and the immediate task of finding something to fill the gaping void left by the shattering news.

'It was over. The doctor tested my left eye and I had a detached retina and when he tested my right eye, I had one there as well. He said to me, "Close your left eye." When I closed it he put his finger up but I couldn't see it. So I knew it was all over at that time. I was gutted. I had just fought that fight and I was feeling good but when I look back I say to myself, "Well, I didn't get beat. I did the training well and I took the retirement because of injury." I look at the Chris Eubank–Michael Watson fight and I say I'm lucky. I may not see as good as I used to because I need glasses for driving. I still am in good health.'

What would have happened in Notice's career after this, had he not been hit with such news, is anybody's guess. What is beyond doubt in boxing is that it is a business and money tends to be heard loudest over all else. While Frank Bruno and Gary Mason both fought out of the same stable as Horace Notice, it wouldn't have been beyond the realms of reason, certainly not for boxing, for these men to have shared a ring between them. 'In the back of my mind, I could see a fight with Gary over a fight with me and Frank. After the Damiani fight, maybe I'd have given up the British title for Gary to fight for and then we could have fought anyway so I had this feeling that Gary and I would have fought over Frank. We were good friends though.'

In his post-boxing years, Notice went into coaching and offered tuition to the likes of Derek Williams and Kid Milo. Williams was the Commonwealth champion and later acquired the European title with the blast-out of Currie but it was Williams's next fight among a gypsy community in France against Jean-Maurice Chanet, a balding, fair-haired, bushy-moustachioed brawler that temporarily derailed his career. Confounding the critics, Chanet upset the odds and won a 12-round decision over a surprisingly morose Williams. The rematch three months later led to a stack of adverse press that gets Notice most animated. Williams was expected to win as he pleased, pack his bags and return to England after leaving the pudgy Frenchman a gory mess. The fighting spread to outside the ring and what transpired was a scene from the proverbial western saloon. Anything that wasn't nailed down was launched into the air, either with someone else as its target or simply as a means of a ringsider letting off some steam. Everyone seemed to be caught up in the frenzy, including Notice. He laughs loudly as soon as I mention the contest.

'I got hit over the head with a chair but I was lucky as it could have got caught in my eye. I think what started it was that Williams brothers were there. Maybe, they stood up in front of the gypsy fans and a punch was thrown and all hell broke loose. We couldn't understand what they were saying but we knew they were angry. It had nothing to do with us in the ring but they were throwing chairs at us! It was a strange night though. In the first round he almost stopped him but then from the second round he was looking at us saying, "This isn't me." I was in his corner for that fight as an assistant. I knew it wasn't him in that ring. I trained Kid Milo for a bit. He was a good fighter but he wasn't dedicated. I trained him for the Nigel Benn fight [in July 1991] but we had a little dispute and I didn't go to the fight. I used to help out but we had a dispute.'

Horace Notice comes across as an amenable individual who appeared to come to terms with his stroke of bad luck just as his career appeared to be rocketing. Because of what happened to him, he could have been racked with bitterness and the negative feeling of believing the sport owed him something as it had no doubt been contributory towards his eyes' condition. He appears relaxed, content and pleased with his many ring achievements. It will come as no surprise then that he will tell you he wasn't hard to manage or deal with during his boxing career.

'I was maybe TOO easy to deal with I think!' he says with another deep chuckle. 'Before the British title, I didn't talk. I just went and did what they says. After this, I tried to give a bit more pressure to get fights. I would say Lawless was more like a father or mentor than Mickey Duff. If you're not fighting, he won't put you in if you're not ready for the fight.'

Since his input with Derek Williams and Kid Milo, Notice's wife, Jacqui Gordon-Lawrence, has appeared in *EastEnders*, playing the role of Etta Tavernier from 1990 to 1992 and briefly again in 1994. 'Even though I wasn't earning much as a trainer, because she was working, it helped me to stay a bit longer. When she got written out, I had a mortgage to pay so I'd better do something now. I went back to college and did plastering. While working as a plasterer, I had a mate who became a London cabbie and he said I should do it. I started it in 2000 and had an accident in 2002. I was riding in the evening to do the runs for The Knowledge. I was living in Welling and this car that was stationary decided to do a three-point turn and I went into the side of it. I needed a hip replacement and I shattered my pelvis. I didn't do the runs for about two years but I now have my green badge and got it last June just before the Olympics!'

For proof that the former British and Commonwealth heavyweight champion is at peace with himself, one just needs to hear him when describing how he feels these days. 'I just want to carry on doing what I'm doing. Boxing is behind me now. It is not what it used to be.'

What Horace Notice used to be was a trailblazing heavyweight, piling up a series of impressive wins against mostly worthy challengers. Winning the European title was well within his capabilities and the big surge towards the world title would then have begun in earnest. What would have transpired will always be a big 'IF'. What was a real possibility, however, was that many of the world's leading heavyweights in the mid-1980s were sitting up and taking notice of Horace before the curtain came down.

14

Mark Prince

'I'M not here to pop out and just disappear by getting beaten out the blue,' Mark Prince said to me when addressing the reasons behind his decision to resume his boxing career after 14 years away. Still showing the solid and chiselled physique he sported in his first incarnation as a professional between 1993 and 1999, he appeared relaxed and upbeat as I waited for him at Don Charles's gym just off Finchley Road. He shadow-boxed, looked light on his toes, showed fluid movement and lent his time to other aspiring fighters who wanted to bend his ear about various techniques and moves. This was a fighter in demand. He was in his comfort zone surrounded by others who wanted to hear what he had to say and listen to an individual who had been through enough in real life to make your average Hollywood director raise an eyebrow in intrigue. When we walked around the corner to his favourite cafe, he assumed the same air of friendliness and warmth as he took me through the remarkable story of his life to date. A story riddled with promise, tragedy, inner strength and hope. A story yet to see out its final chapter.

The story starts in Wood Green. Unlike the reflections and memories of many other fighters, Prince speaks highly of his formative years and is quick to portray this period as a happy time and a stage of his life which was relatively comfortable and trouble-free.

'It was as normal as anybody else's. It wasn't dangerous, threatening or anything like that. It was very different to how it is now. When I was growing up around Wood Green and Bounds Green, I didn't see many black people down there. The skinheads used to be a bit of a problem. They'd used to meet in this hut. We'd be weary and we had to run past them. The police were more blatantly racist then. What was I doing with a bag of sugar for my mum from the shop? They'd come up and say, "What you got there? You nickin' something?" I'm telling you, I'd be scared! "Let's have a look in your bag. Where d'you get that from?" We had to put up with that on our travels even as a little kid. At the same time, there was a really nice copper! We had one of these neighbourhood police. I still remember his two daughters and he was just genuinely a really nice guy. Let's look at it from both sides. It's all too easy to look at the negative sides being in a neighbourhood but let's look at the positive side. I believe in the same way there are kids who are in gangs as there are kids that aren't. Same with the police who could be racist and pick on you for no reason, there were ones who wouldn't dream of doing that.'

Prince had a strict upbringing with his father administering stern discipline when and where required. It was during this time that he got introduced to the sport.

'My inspiration was to change my life around. My dad taught me how to fight and how to look after myself. He made us train when we got back from school and do press-ups and sit-ups every morning. I sparred with my dad and my older brother. My dad was the light-heavyweight champion of Guyana. He had nine fights unbeaten. Ernie Fossey once told me, "I remember your dad. Bloody great fighter he was. You've got nothing on your dad!" My dad said to me once, "I knocked a guy down in every round and they still gave it to my opponent!" He said he went to his dressing room and cried. He did some sparring with Brian London too.'

Prince's father, Clarence, was indeed a capable boxer. Between 1961 and 1971, he built up a professional record of ten wins with 12 losses. While this may look mediocre on paper, it is worth noting that his last victory came against Freddie Cross, who was able to boast a stoppage win over Paddington's former world middleweight champion Terry Downes. All of Clarence Prince's victories came by knockout so it was clear where his son's vaunted punching power came from. While Prince is adamant that his upbringing wasn't as hard as others from similar backgrounds, it wasn't without the odd obstacle. One that was set high was the issue of skin colour. Even then, the comments that Prince was subjected to were more to do with inquisitiveness than malice. He enjoyed being part of his school and participating in its sporting activities and he puts the jibes down to misunderstanding and cultural ignorance.

'I loved school. I loved the sport, it was great. Dad was such a strict disciplinarian, I had to get away from home. In my opinion, he went too far. Going to school was freedom. At home I wasn't allowed out. At school though, white people at the time didn't really understand

black people or black culture. There were times when they'd be racist
and they wouldn't even know it. They'd rub your hair and say, "Ah
look at you and your hair. You don't even have to comb it!" I'd say,
"What? Everyone has to comb their hair." School was like that, teachers
were like that. School had a few blacks, a few Indians but hardly any
different ethnics. Now it's completely different. You have the whole
world at your school!'

Prince's father may have been strict when dealing with his children
and passionate about them learning to look after themselves but his
mother, like a lot of boxers' mums, was the opposite. The thought of
her son swapping punches with another man was not something she
could endear herself to.

'My mum never came to a fight, never watched it and never went to
sleep until I got home and said, "Mum, I won and everything's all right."
She'd praise God and then go to sleep.'

Prince had a very short amateur career before deciding to turn
professional. In this short span, he defeated the future Commonwealth
cruiserweight champion Chris Okoh on a second-round stoppage to win
the 1992 London ABAs.

'I only went in as an amateur to see how I'd fare against the best
young fighters in the country. I actually didn't want to be an amateur
as I never got paid! I wasn't interested in training and not being paid.
I decided to fight because I wanted to come out of the lifestyle I was in
which was criminally-minded. I wanted to make something of myself
before the kids got big. I was trying to change my life around.'

One of the fondest memories Prince harbours is that of his first
sparring session. While still only an amateur, he donned the headgear
and faced a future three-time world title challenger. What transpired
prompted praise from both his sparring partner and his sparring
partner's trainer. 'My first sparring partner was Michael Watson. His
trainer, Eric Secombe, said to me, "You're going to be a champion one
day." The sparring was absolutely brilliant. One lesson I learnt was not
to mess with the pros. I was boxing the socks off Mike for two rounds.
He came and told me after how good I was. What happened was he
started hitting me to the body. I never knew about stuff like this. All of
a sudden I couldn't move as quick. I couldn't do anything as good. He
was taking the energy out of me and I was against the ropes. By the time
we finished he was having his way. He came up to me and said, "When
I beat Eubank [in reference to the now infamous rematch], I'm gonna
manage you." Eric Secombe used to take me out to the cafe after training
and used to make me feel like someone. Those were the days when the

pros used to mix with the amateurs. Apart from being with my dad, this was the first bit of sparring I had in my whole life.'

Prince's amateur days wound down after the win over Chris Okoh. It was during the build-up to this fight that Prince first encountered the man who would guide him through the professional ranks.

'As I was getting ready to fight Chris Okoh, this guy walks in and says, "My name's Carlie Carew. I've been watching you. You know those guys out there? You've got them all shooked! Go out there and knock the guy out." I don't know what he done to me but I went out there and put it on Chris Okoh!'

Prince kicked off his professional career in exciting fashion. He also presented the paying public with a performance that would come to epitomise his crowd-pleasing style. On 4 April 1993, he stepped into the ring in Brockley to face Bobby Mack, a four-fight novice but who, two fights after the Prince contest, would go on to take the future WBC light-heavyweight champion Montell Griffin the distance. In a frantic display of punching from both sides, Prince's pro debut resulted in a second-round stoppage win.

'I was swept off my feet against Mack. I was anxious to show my family I wasn't hurt but my legs said otherwise. I endured some worrying moments as Mack attacked! Nobby Nobbs had loads of journeymen. They were good. Better than the class of journeymen you're getting now. They beat a lot of the prospects coming up. They teared the script up. All they needed was the investment and the opportunity. When Ernie Fossey, Frank Warren's right-hand man, used to say to me, "Mark, I got you a fight," I'd go, "What's he like?" He would say, "Ah don't worry, you'll knock him out!" As soon as Ernie said that I was like, "Ah man, this guy's bloody dangerous!" I could swear he gave me a cruiserweight 'cos when I hit him I thought, "Fudgin' hell, I hurt my hand!"'

With his professional career underway and off to winning ways, Prince returned the following month to face the toughened 36-fight veteran John Kaighin. I clearly remember watching Kaighin fight the future European light-heavyweight champion and IBF light-heavyweight title challenger Ole Klemetsen in the Norwegian's fourth pro fight in January 1993. His tactics were rough and at times borderline and in conflict with the Queensberry rules. He gave the Scandinavian all he could handle and he achieved the same with Prince four fights later.

While Kaighin lost in the third round, he gave a good account of himself and provided Prince with a good learning fight. Coming out strong in the first round, he was pounded in the subsequent two sessions and the referee waved it off with the Welsh fighter taking punishment against the ropes.

'He was a hard bastard!' Prince said of Kaighin. 'All these guys were. I have so much respect for them. It's like life and death with me though. I don't know why it's different at fight time 'cos in sparring I don't have that. I'm always aware in sparring if you hit me, what if that was a real fight? How would I have taken that in a real fight?'

Two more victories closed out 1993 for Prince. In June he knocked out Art Stacey in two rounds and in August he outpointed Simon McDougall over six rounds to get some experience under his belt. The winning continued into 1994 with a couple of wins over Zak Chelli in the first round and a third-round win over the experienced John Foreman. Foreman had proven his mettle in earlier, albeit losing, fights with the likes of Anthony Hembrick, Eddy Smulders, Fabrice Tiozzo and Crawford Ashley.

'As a young guy, I just wanted to knock these guys out. Even though you say this and that to the cameras, I didn't realise what it was I was actually doing! I only realised what I'd done when my career was over. I look back and think, "Fudgin' hell, did you do that?!" I didn't feel that way when I was actually doing it. Wow, I was beating these guys. That's amazing! I really started to appreciate who I was and what I'd done.'

On 21 July 1994, Prince stepped in with experienced campaigner Tony Booth. Winning on a third-round stoppage, they had a return three fights later and Prince improved on his performance with a win in the second. Between the two Booth fights, Prince recorded wins over Kofi Quaye and Steve Osborne, both by stoppage.

'What do those fights with Booth tell you? I was a student learning. The relationship I had with Carlie, he was like a dad and I was like a good son. After my fight with Kofi Quaye, I got myself noticed so Frank Warren thought, "I want him on my shows." That changed my whole life.'

Tony Booth would go on to provide future world cruiserweight and heavyweight champion David Haye with his first professional fight and Steve Osborne had competed with other British stars in Carl Thompson and Herbie Hide.

Prince's next outing got him a wider audience and the chance for a new fanbase. In Pairc Ui Chaoimh, Cork, he faced the American Scott Lindecker on the undercard of the Steve Collins–Chris Eubank rematch. Collins recorded a split decision win over the Brighton man. Prince had a far easier time with the Iowan. A crushing win in the second round gave Prince his 11th victory.

'That was one of my best fights. I didn't care where I fought. Stick me anywhere. I didn't see it as pressure. I'm what you call a real street fighter. That's where my skills were honed. Pick someone from the streets, I'm your guy. I don't have time to think about where I am. I'll fight anywhere.'

Returning closer to home for his next fight, he fought his first fringe contender. The American Lenzie Morgan had an impressive track record. While most fighters' records have the occasional big name hidden in there, if you looked very carefully through Lenzie Morgan's list of opponents, you may find the odd unknown had gatecrashed a party for better-known, higher-profile guests. His record was liberally showered with former and future world champions, top contenders and European champions. He would travel anywhere in the world to test the latest prospect. Failing to hear the final bell in just seven of his 33 losses is testament to the calibre of opponent he faced and also the appeal he held with boxing managers around the globe. He could be relied upon to provide a steep learning curve to anyone he faced. He fought some of the best middleweights out there and then, post-Prince, proceeded to step into the ring with some of the toughest light-heavyweights before curtailing his career in the heavyweight division. Not surprisingly, it was one of these distance fights that Prince benefitted from. After eight hard rounds, Prince impressed with his tenacity and patience in fighting someone who wouldn't fold as easily as he had been used to seeing in his opponents. Prince did manage to score a solid knockdown with a stiff left jab. It reminded me of Michael Watson's jab that finished off Nigel Benn in their 1989 superfight. The difference here was that Morgan was more than equipped to continue.

'Even now,' Prince began, 'I can watch that fight and appreciate it. How many fighters do you know who put people down with a jab? It doesn't happen a lot so credit where credit's due. It was a sharp night's work.'

After an unnecessarily close shave against Newcastle's John Pierre next time out the following March, in which he narrowly snatched the decision by one point, Prince stepped into the ring against the former British light-heavyweight champion Maurice Core on the undercard of the first Steve Collins–Nigel Benn clash at Manchester's Nynex Arena on 6 July 1996. Core had tasted defeat just once previously, in a challenge to Fabrice Tiozzo for the European title. Tiozzo would go on to win a segment of the world light-heavyweight championship twice along with a portion of the cruiserweight world crown so form suggested that Core could handle himself against anyone not at the highest level. Prince was a fighter on the upward curve but this almost boomeranged for him as he suffered a cut to his left eye in the sixth round. Prince was, by this stage, appearing to take command of the bout after feeling his way in during the opening couple of rounds. Upon being cut, Prince released the heavy artillery to terminate matters in the seventh round. It would be Core's final fight before hanging up his gloves and announcing his retirement.

There were now whispers of Prince taking long strides towards a challenge to the European title held at this stage by Holland's Eddy Smulders. Indeed, Maurice Core was being touted as a possible challenger to WBO light-heavyweight champion Dariusz Michalczewski so the significance of Prince's win didn't go unnoticed.

Prince's next step towards the title throne added another dimension to his repertoire and in the process provided viewers with a candidate for the domestic dust-up of the year. Fighting the Central Area light-heavyweight champion Michael Gale for the WBO's spurious intercontinental title, Prince was expected to notch up a solid victory in convincing fashion. The memories of seeing that first belt stick in his memory like a vivid dream.

'The excitement was ridiculous, man! I saw this belt in Frank Warren's office and I thought, "That's mine that is!" I just wanted to hold it up!'

While the ending could not have been more convincing had Prince's gloves been wrapped around machine guns, the course of that incredible sixth round followed a script that would have made Rocky Balboa and Apollo Creed revise their lines. Gale took an early lead, capitalising on Prince's leaky defence, but faded as the fifth opened. Prince started connecting with some heavy blows but there was no hint as to what was in store in the next and, ultimately, final round. Taking it in turns to drill the other with wild punches, most of which landed with sickening accuracy, referee Paul Thomas appeared to go from one to the other to decide who should be saved from further punishment. Just as one was on the verge of being flattened, so the other would suddenly soak up more hellish blows. Prince was the first to flounder around the ring, desperately struggling to defend himself against Gale's whirlwind of blows. The old adage that one's offence is the best form of defence was highlighted as fists were hurled with malicious venom to stem the other's onslaught. One of Prince's howitzer-like blows struck Gale with particular intensity and floored him heavily. Rising with a deep cut over his right eye, the referee allowed the brawl to continue only for Gale to walk on to a left hook that deposited him onto the canvas with a loud thud. The look on the victor's face when Thomas waved the fight off illustrated just how savage the encounter had been.

'Oh man,' Prince sighed as if he could still feel Gale's punches hitting home over 16 years later. The sigh turned to laughter as he reflected on the contest. 'In that third round I had a thought in my head that I'm not feeling that good. I dropped weight and I didn't prepare well. They told me it was an eliminator and it was the first time I had ever made 12st 7lbs on the dot. For me, 12st 9lbs was a struggle but 12st 7lbs? That hurt but I had stuff going on in my life at the time. I wasn't really ready for this fight and I knew I shouldn't be going through with it. I said to God, "If anything happens please take me through this." If you look at the end of the fight, I went straight to my knees. I wasn't my normal self.'

The talk now turned to Prince squaring up against Crawford Ashley who picked up the vacant European title a few weeks after Prince's terrific win.

'I wasn't that smart [to admit he wasn't ready]. I thought Crawford Ashley was a really good boxer. I'd seen him down the gym. We knew of each other but there was no love lost. I wanted it. Looking back, I probably wasn't at that stage yet for a title fight. Like I said, I was a young guy so I didn't really know what I was doing anyway. I was asking for that fight. That would have gone down as one of the classic British title fights. He was taller than me, had a good reach and a great punch. I had the resistance and the determination.' Prince laughed loudly as he proudly proclaimed, 'I would have won!'

Unfortunately for the British fan, while it was a fight that was discussed and pondered by both camps, it never came off. Ashley made a quick defence two months after winning it before being obliterated by the aforementioned blonde-haired, pony-tailed Norwegian Ole Klemetsen in two rounds in the October.

Prince moved on to defend his WBO intercontinental title against the American Bruce Rumbolz. Fighting for the first time outside North America's Midwest, Rumbolz ventured across the Atlantic to swap blows with the Tottenham puncher. Coming off such a vicious brawl with Michael Gale, Prince could be forgiven for facing an opponent who could be used to pad out his record. Aside from a jab that was more of an annoyance than a genuine obstacle for Prince to overcome, Rumbolz was despatched with relative ease in three rounds.

Like the previously mooted match with Crawford Ashley, speculation gathered pace about a prospective fight with the former WBO middleweight and super-middleweight champion and Britain's most famous punching enigma, Chris Eubank. Eubank was keeping himself busy with a couple of fights over in Egypt and Dubai while awaiting another crack at the world title. Indeed, it was a match with Wales's Joe Calzaghe for the vacant WBO super-middleweight title that Eubank ultimately went for when the Prince fight fell through. As Prince says, it was more to do with a disagreement over money than anything.

'I was gutted that I didn't get the Eubank fight. I watched Calzaghe take him. It was hard because that should've been me. It fell through because Frank offered me money that I thought, "Are you having a laugh? Come on Frank, look at what money's on the table. Chris is a name. I don't ask for a lot but gimme some money where I don't feel like a bitch." Carlie gave me some advice which I wouldn't take again. He said, "Every fight you have, take it on that merit. Don't let no one make you promises about what they're gonna give you for another fight 'cos every fight may be your last." I thought it was a fair point but then afterwards when I missed the opportunity I realised I wanted people to sit down and remember me as the guy that knocked out Eubank. I can handle losing and I can handle winning. It's what happens in the fight that concerns me more.'

To soothe the blow of missing out on the Eubank fight, Prince did as he pleased in dismantling Wayne Hankins in the third round with a heavy right hand. In retaining his WBO intercontinental belt, he added the IBF's version to his collection. What he wanted to obtain, however, was the real thing and as he was now installed as the number one contender for Dariusz Michalczewski's WBO title, his chance was imminent. In facing another American in Bristol on 31 May 1998, whose name could be mistaken for a question put to Prince to establish whether or not he could hit with respectable force, Prince was taken the full 12 rounds by one Kenny Whack. Suffering a bout of near exhaustion in the middle rounds, Prince fought through and prevailed on all three judges' cards. After the contest, there was already talk of Prince travelling to Germany on 19 September to challenge the formidable German-based Polish champion who had to date racked up 12 successful defences of his title. Ominously, after the Whack fight, Prince had stated how he wouldn't have minded if the fight had taken place a little later than rumoured as he had more 'homework' to do. Reiterating his comments from before about 'not knowing what he was doing' until after he left the sport through injury, Prince made no excuses for the poor preparation he had leading up to the biggest boxing fight of his life which was after all confirmed for the speculated date.

'You know what done me? I went to LA! What the hell was I doing there?! I had no preparation stuff in LA. I didn't get caught up in all the nightlife stuff but my stability for the fight was all wrong. Carlie was having problems in his life and I could tell he wasn't focused on me like he would normally be. I was into all the big training and the big spas but I hadn't made it yet. I was trying to run before I could walk. When we went to LA we didn't have no money so we contacted Frank and he said he'd send some money over. The money wasn't coming over and we couldn't eat so we took the little we had and had these little Chinese meals. You don't prepare for a world title fight on cheap Chinese meals. At the end of the training I was weighing 175lb and I was still four weeks away from the fight! I've never weighed that. Every time I train I weigh half a stone over the 12st 7lb limit and I slowly, bit by bit, take it off. I stick around 12st 9lb and then in the last week I take it off. I'm always so tight at the weight I make sure I come in bang on. I don't sit on the weight for too long though. For this fight, it was all wrong.'

In his first fight outside the United Kingdom, Prince knew little of what to expect and while he stated that locations didn't matter and showed willingness to fight anyone and anywhere, the reaction he received when landing in Germany needled him.

'It was like the twilight zone. I got off the plane and it was cameras in your face straight away. I just wanted them to leave me alone and go home. I was treated well but I had no sparring. I got there about seven days before the fight but it was all wrong.'

While Michalczewski had twice as many fights as Prince going into the fight and having faced tougher opposition, Prince was the first unbeaten opponent the champion had faced. Michalczewski was generally regarded as the only worthy opponent left for the uniquely-talented and brilliant Roy Jones. With both fighters being strictly home fighters (Jones fought just three times outside the USA at the tail-end of his career while Michalczewski fought just once outside Germany and that was in Poland, his country of origin), neither was willing to give ground for the match to be facilitated. As Don King once confessed, 'The only colour that matters is green.' This proved the problem here as the German and the American each demanded hefty wads of cash to be deposited in their accounts for the fight to be arranged.

'Roy Jones wanted nothing to do with him,' Prince said with animated gusto. 'No one wanted to fight him. Eubank said he'd refuse to fight Dariusz. "You're mad!" he'd say. He was a tough fighter. I'm in Dariusz's biography apparently. He says I'm one of his toughest fights! At the post-fight press conference, they were saying they were stuck with me. They had to work me out. They couldn't settle and never dreamt they'd knock me out. I looked in his eyes. He'd hit me with some of the best right hands he'd thrown. Ones that had put Nicky Piper down. I punched him straight back. I watched the fight back and was almost kicking myself.'

In the end, it was the champion's abundant supply of energy that wore Prince down. Michalczewski controlled the ring centre from the off and consistently pumped out his piston-like jab which landed with increasing accuracy. In Prince's credit, he stuck to the task at hand and landed a commendable amount of blows himself. Unfortunately, aside from being tactically superior, the champion's strength and resilience was such that they were taken with minimal fuss. Prince was keeping up his efforts but was finding himself more and more on the retreat until the end came in the eighth when a final left hook from the champion landed flush, spun the challenger around and floored him to bring about the end. Prince was nothing short of gracious in defeat, labelling his conqueror as, 'Just simply a great champion.'

'I wanted one more fight before the end of the year. I kept asking but Frank wouldn't give me a fight. I got married in that time but it didn't help me. What I needed was to get back in the ring because the Michalczewski fight actually made me better. I nicked Dariusz's jab off him. He had a jab that baffled me and I'm a jab specialist. I found his jab hard to read throughout the fight. He'd throw his jab with his whole body and you'd feel the weight of his punch. I was surprised by his power but Carlie said, "This guy is massive compared to you." He was doing things which I wanted to add to my repertoire.'

It was to be over a year before Prince set foot back in the ring. Without Carlie Carew in his corner anymore, Prince had risen in weight to enter the cruiserweight division. He stepped in against Brockley's Kevin Mitchell and destroyed him in just 43 seconds of the first round. A solid return to the ring was hampered a short while later by an incident that would have lasting effects on his boxing journey.

'I was working in security at a concert up at Wembley. I ended up getting into an incident where I took someone down. As I went down, my knee stayed in the same place while my body moved. I heard my knee rip when I felt the pain. It was really painful but as I was dealing with someone I had to pretend I was alright. I finished him and my knee off at the same time! I was helped into an ambulance and had a plaster cast put on. The muscle had separated and the doctors said it was one of the worst knee injuries they had seen because the ligaments had all gone. They told me they'd have to put a screw in and get someone else's tendons to keep it all together. They also told me I couldn't box on.'

Aside from death or suffering a life-changing injury in the ring, for a fighter to be told that his career is over is arguably the harshest hand that fate could deal. Boxing is a means of receiving an income and providing for the next generation so that they needn't fight to survive. It's this very element that makes the sport a metaphor for life. Numerous times have I had long conversations with fellow boxing nuts about how to categorise the sport. The mutual decision is always the same. You play other sports. You never PLAY boxing. In boxing, you FIGHT. Even for those hundreds of thousands of boxers around the world who fulfil the roles of 'journeyman', 'bum', 'perennial loser', 'tomato can' and the ever-present 'Mexican cab driver', they have still fought for a genuine reason. There is little else they can do. The thought of having this outlet snatched away is what makes them want to fight harder for maximum success in a short space of time. The term 'Mexican cab driver' simply illustrates both sides of many fighters' places in the sport and what drives them. While it exists to condescend many low-level fighters and to pad out others fighters' records, it also serves to highlight the spirit of the man on the street in underprivileged corners of the world.

While Prince was not necessarily void of direction or hope, the decision was devastating and a rethink was required to decide where his life would take him from that moment on.

'I was in bits. It takes a while. They're telling you it's over and you're sitting at home not able to do nothing when you're used to going out training. I was broken.'

His interaction with youths, something which would become such a dominant feature in Prince's life a number of years later, was what gave him a sense of direction and purpose in the aftermath of his boxing career hitting the almost insurmountable obstacle of enforced retirement. He filled this void through his sister, who held a position with the local authority.

'My sister worked for the council so I did this course to be a youth worker. I wondered if I could give back to these kids what I had to go through on the streets. I seemed to get on really well with my studies and I realised I had something really valuable. Slowly and surely I was getting better at my new trade. I also felt my knee getting better. I had my youth sessions and a lot of these kids just wanted to train with me. They wanted me to teach them how to box. I was finding my feet.'

While he was indulging in this new venture, what took a while for Prince to realise was that he was getting himself back into shape and edging closer to being in a position where he could contemplate a ring return.

'I was doing all these squats and exercises but it hadn't dawned on me yet that I may be able to come back. It was like that part of me just shut down. I was a youth worker and I never gave myself space to think about anything else.'

His new work continued to be a success and joining a friend of his in the gold-plating business was a sign that he was getting himself established in a new career. Life had taken a definite turn for the better.

'I had a mate who was gold-plating so I did some on the side. We gold-plated mobile phones and they went like hot cakes. We even considered *Dragons' Den*. We could gold-plate anything that had a metal base. There was a Nokia phone coming out at the time, around 2005 to 2006, and we were killing that. They were going for £500 to £1,000 per phone. I was in my mate's house all day gold-plating. So there I was, working with kids and doing this other work. I think I'm getting back up again. Then the phone rings. It's one of my boys. "Dad, Kiyan's been stabbed." Life changes.'

On 18 May 2006, Prince's 15-year-old son Kiyan was walking out of his school at the London Academy in Edgware. Upon seeing another boy being bullied, he intervened to help the harassed youngster. The perpetrator, believing Kiyan was showing him insufficient respect, inflicted a single stab wound to the heart. Kiyan passed away a short while later while receiving emergency treatment at Whitechapel's Royal London Hospital. This short, violent incident tore his family's life apart.

Having to deal with such a tragedy as this would be enough to eradicate any hopes and plans most bereaving parents would have for the future. Once the initial outpourings of rage and helplessness subsided, Prince was left with a feeling of responsibility and duty to others who had either been put through the same or who were finding more comfort and solace in the menaces of street crime and gang culture. A self-defined mission to rescue those who were being drawn into a degenerate lifestyle that would ultimately convince its followers of its own rectitude. A way of life that seems to draw in ignorant youngsters who lack the support, warmth and discipline of a stable family home and develop them into violent, feral criminals. These youths would see it as a way of forming their own identity, building self-esteem and earning respect from others around them.

'For a long period, your world stops. Your son's been killed but you go out and everyone's going about their own business. I couldn't leave Kiyan's room. I put his clothes on. I could smell him.'

Kiyan was a budding star with Queens Park Rangers Football Club. The club spotted his talent and had signed him up to their academy.

Shortly prior to his untimely death, Kiyan's contract was extended and plans were afoot to sign him on as a professional player.

'People would say, "You watch Kiyan playing football and you know you're watching something special." The club called us for a private meeting to tell us that at 15, Kiyan's outgrown the under-16 team. They wanted him in the over-18 side. He continued to develop. He was big, strong and fast. They have his face in the tunnel so when they come out, they see him.'

Kiyan's 16-year-old killer was later arrested, charged and, after two retrials, found guilty of murder in July 2007 at the Old Bailey. Finding it in one's heart to forgive a person for such a callous, horrific deed is something most parents would understandably and justifiably find too painful to do.

In May 2007, Mark established the Kiyan Prince Foundation. A non-profit-making organisation, its primary role is to reach out to secondary school children and show them how to combat knife crime and other forms of youth violence. To show them alternative ways of channelling their energies and becoming more responsible in planning their futures instead of slipping down the slope towards a life of crime and antisocial behaviour. One of Prince's initial aims? 'To get my son's murderer to come and work for the foundation,' Prince says without a hint of bitterness. The man's resolve is almost tangible.

Such a statement takes a hefty amount of inner strength and while Prince inhabits a strong affinity with God, the true Christian trait of forgiveness is one which he expresses with ease and sincerity.

'I wanted forgiveness in action. I didn't want to just say, "I forgive." I wanted to see something. We hear all this nice talk from Christians but how about seeing it in reality. The effect of that is much more powerful. Me going out and seeing other kids who have stabbed kids and wrecked other families' lives who have been torn apart. THAT'S action. I'm showing true love, passion and patience. It's easy to say, "They're no good. How could they do such a thing?" I'm saying, "Look, let's take time and see what's going on. What's the damage? What are the reasons? How can we help? How were they brought up? Were they brought up by parents who let them down? Everyone's got potential but they need guidance and help. Let's find out if you've had that opportunity or not. Let's treat you as an individual instead of painting you all with the same brush."'

The foundation has produced remarkable results and the effect this has had on Prince is obvious.

'We do a lot of work with schools. We will go anywhere. I've seen the changes in people and it's really beautiful hearing them talking about it.

Sometimes I get really choked up because I didn't realise how much this really meant to them. People say it's like a family. I like to be humorous and muck about so we have a good laugh too.'

The parallels between what Prince has been through and what carried him through his boxing career, is something which has clearly occupied a generous part of his time. The attributes required to survive the pain of losing a loved one and to succeed in the boxing ring are comparable, in terms of what is needed to overcome an obstacle. What that obstacle is, shouldn't necessarily matter. As Prince states, the strength needed comes from within.

'I've thought about that loads,' Prince says, looking off to the side to ponder his response. His head bows slightly towards the table as his train of thought drifts off into deep rumination. His attention is momentarily brought back to the present as the cafe assistant delivers a plate heaped with a champion-sized omelette to his place. After playfully admonishing the waiter for adding a hefty portion of chips to his order, he returns his attention to the subject at hand. 'I've realised that there is an element of it being your personality and character because from a very young age I saw determination in me. I saw strength in me even when I used to go running with my dad at ten years old. My intent was to keep up with him and not to let him run off ahead. It was what came to me naturally. I was always setting goals for myself. The real key to this is realising that there is a serious power in having a relationship with God. I didn't feel as if I knew what was going on. I didn't feel I had control and how I could handle things. It was the only belief I felt I could hold on to, that was going to keep me going. There were things that I said to God that I'd seen played out. Look, I wanted to kill this guy so badly throughout the court case. That's how I felt. I felt this weight as if I was carrying someone on my back. I didn't feel as if I was going to get closure from the court case. It came to a point where I was such a broken man.'

The strength which he had stated had come from his personality, was coming through heavily in the way he was talking. The confidence, which oozed from his demeanour while talking to me about his son, was almost disconcerting. His belief seemed unshakeable. He spoke with a calm and self-assured tone and left me in no doubt whatsoever that he was a man firmly at peace with his own feelings and in full control of where his life was heading.

'I cried out to God, "Take this from me. I can't take this. I'm gonna trust you. You show me what to do." After I said those words, it was like someone had lifted this table off me. Before I'd actually finished those words, I actually felt lighter. In the Bible it says, "Let vengeance be mine." I said, "I'm gonna do that. I'll let it be yours." For me, my journey began then.'

It was at this time that the idea of the Kiyan Prince Foundation was conceiv d and soon Mark was finding himself in demand.

'I g ɔt an invitation to go to a school with parents. Kids and parents alike saw what I was trying to do. I came with warmth and love. I didn't hold anything back. They saw my pain. I realised that this is not something I planned. It was what God planned. He wanted me to do this, to follow my feelings. The calls started coming in. More schools, more kids and more media campaigns. It blew up!'

In 2010, Prince confronted one of his fears. Marking the fourth anniversary of his son's passing, Prince travelled to Kent's Headcorn parachute club. Climbing two miles up and flying at a speed of over 120mph, Prince leapt out of a plane in tandem with an instructor. The relief at hitting the ground was written all over his face but it was mixed with elation at having conquered a fear of his and bringing him closer to his son.

'It was a fundraiser for the foundation. What I realised is that fear is a great part of everyone's life. We all have things we have to overcome. To have anything happen to any of my children was a fear of mine. I had to deal with what happened through no choice of my own. If I could deal with that I thought I could deal with any fear. I was scared of heights since I could remember being around. Doing that jump, I was never scared so much in my life. You could see the fear in my face.'

Indeed, you could. While waiting in the body of the plane as it cruised at the level needed to jump, Prince looked on as the exit door was released and the jumper immediately in front of him was shuffled to the edge by the instructor. Prince's face was tense as the enormity of the task hit home. A nervous grin spread across his face as he took up position with his feet hanging over the edge. The soles of his feet were parallel to the Kent countryside a couple of miles below. Then he dropped.

'After my feet hit the ground, they were calling me. "Mark, Mark!" I was like, "I can't move! I can't move!" They thought I was joking but I couldn't move. I remember the freefall. It was insane! I remember shouting out Kiyan's name in the sky. I was shouting out to God as well. Brilliant experience!'

With everything the north Londoner has been through to date, his personality has had to mature, develop and grow hardened to an extraordinary sequence of events. The mark he made in the sport, the tragedy of dealing with a loved one's untimely passing, his relationship with God, the sense of achievement the foundation has produced and the challenge of what lies ahead have all shaped Prince into an articulate, matter-of-fact and inspirational person. A far cry, he will tell you, from the younger Mark Prince who blasted a path towards light-heavyweight title contention. Like the Michalczewski loss matured him as a boxer, the twists and turns of his life outside the square ring have shaped him as a person.

'The Mark Prince of years ago would look up to, and respect, the Mark Prince of now but he would still think he would know everything! He would have something to say about this and that. He's a lot more humble now. He understands people more now and is a lot more patient with people's shortcomings. That is all part of my journey. Telling people they can choose who they want to be. They have choices. That's what I used to tell Kiyan. Life is a blank page. Fill it in. What do you want to have? Whatever you want people to say about you after you die is who you need to be now. What you do now shapes what you do in the future. The Bible says, "Foolishness is wrapped up in the youth."'

In June 2013, Mark received the green light and had his boxing licence reinstated under the Maltese Boxing Commission. Having been out of the ring for 14 years, he feels the time is now right to step back in and get back to what he did best all those years ago.

'It's not a comeback because I never retired,' Prince says firmly. 'I think me going back in the ring and boxing is going to kick everything off. I've been preserved since I last fought. My knee has come through everything I've put it through. It's a personal test for me.'

The big question for him is the shape his comeback will take. The most recent example of a failed comeback in the media spotlight was that of Ricky Hatton, the former world light-welterweight and welterweight champion. After a devastating loss to Manny Pacquiao in 2009, he returned in November 2012 to face the former WBA welterweight champion Vyacheslav Senchenko. After a promising start, Hatton suffered a cruel ninth-round stoppage to send him packing into retirement once more. The sort of return to the ring that Prince can relate to is that of former world heavyweight champion George Foreman. Starting again with four-round bouts, Foreman built up the sort of ledger akin to someone starting their professional career for the first time.

'That's what it's going to be like; almost starting your journey over again. I'll be having a talk with the guys. They need to have that same understanding that I have. I feel like this is the second part. People forget I had only nine amateur fights. I turned pro without any real experience. I've always been in the deep end. I've swam in the deep end, I've lived in the deep end. Sparring is different to fighting. You can spar and look good but when it comes to the fight, there are different things that you need. Mentally, I'm very prepared. Physically, because I've been to the top level, I want that intenseness and one-on-one with my trainer and I haven't developed that relationship yet. I have enough in me though to go out and fight. I'm that mentally strong. There is something about me that produces everything it takes to be a winner. I'm a champion inside the ring and outside. Even as a human being, my fears of, "am I good enough", I say, "No Mark, you're an individual so why don't you finish this story and let it play out for itself because when you started this journey you wanted to win a title and be a champion." I have faith and I will come out on top.'

While putting the finishing touches to this piece, Labi Siffre's soul hit 'So Strong' drifted from the stereo speakers. The final verse reverberated around my head as it struck me how accurately it summed up Mark Prince's vision for the future and his steely determination to assist others while empowered by his son's memory.

'MY LIGHT WILL SHINE SO BRIGHTLY IT WILL BLIND YOU BECAUSE THERE'S SOMETHING INSIDE SO STRONG.'

Regardless of whether or not Mark Prince's boxing resurgence is a success, it would take a brave man to bet against his light shining brightly for a long time yet.